New Materialisms and Embodied Encounters in Education

Radical Politics and Education
Series editors: Derek R. Ford and Tyson E. Lewis

With movements against oppression and exploitation heightening across the globe, radical activists and researchers are increasingly turning to educational theory to understand the pedagogical aspects of struggle. The Radical Politics and Education series opens a space at this critical juncture, one that pushes past standard expositions of critical education and critical pedagogy. Recognizing the need to push political and educational formulations into new theoretical and practical terrains, the series is an opportunity for activists, political thinkers, and educational philosophers to cross disciplinary divides and meet in common. This kind of dialogue is crucially needed as political struggles are increasingly concerned with questions of how to educate themselves and others, and as educational philosophy attempts to redefine itself beyond academic norms and disciplinary values. This series serves to facilitate new conversations at and beyond these borders.

Advisory Board:
Jodi Dean *(Hobart and William Smith Colleges, USA)*
Margret Grebowicz *(University of Silesia, Poland)*
Davide Panagia *(University of California, Los Angeles, USA)*
Patti Lather *(Ohio State University, USA)*
Nathan Snaza *(University of Richmond, USA)*
Stefano Harney *(Singapore Management University, Singapore)*

Also available in the series:
Against Sex Education: Pedagogy, Sex Work, and State Violence, Caitlin Howlett
A History of Education for the Many: From Colonization and Slavery to the Decline of US Imperialism, Curry Malott
Experiments in Decolonizing the University: Towards an Ecology of Study, Hans Schildermans
Rethinking Philosophy for Children: Agamben and Education as Pure Means, Tyson E. Lewis and Igor Jasinski
Althusser and Education: Reassessing Critical Education, David I. Backer
A Voice for Maria Favela: An Adventure in Creative Literacy, Antonio Leal
Rancière and Emancipatory Art Pedagogies: The Politics of Childhood Art, Hayon Park

Forthcoming in the series:
Queers Teach This!: Queer and Trans Pleasures, Politics, and Pedagogues, Adam J. Greteman

New Materialisms and Embodied Encounters in Education

Curiosity's Vital Potential

Cala Coats

BLOOMSBURY ACADEMIC
LONDON • NEW YORK • OXFORD • NEW DELHI • SYDNEY

BLOOMSBURY ACADEMIC

Bloomsbury Publishing Plc, 50 Bedford Square, London, WC1B 3DP, UK
Bloomsbury Publishing Inc, 1385 Broadway, New York, NY 10018, USA
Bloomsbury Publishing Ireland, 29 Earlsfort Terrace, Dublin 2, D02 AY28, Ireland

BLOOMSBURY, BLOOMSBURY ACADEMIC and the Diana logo are trademarks of
Bloomsbury Publishing Plc

First published in Great Britain 2024
This paperback edition published in 2025

Copyright © Cala Coats, 2024

Cala Coats has asserted her right under the Copyright, Designs and Patents Act, 1988,
to be identified as Author of this work.

For legal purposes the Acknowledgments on p. ix constitute an extension
of this copyright page.

Series Design: Adriana Brioso
Cover image © bortonia/iStock

This work is published open access subject to a Creative Commons Attribution-
NonCommercial-NoDerivatives 4.0 International licence (CC BY-NC-ND 4.0, https://
creativecommons.org/licenses/by-nc-nd/4.0/). You may re-use, distribute, and reproduce
this work in any medium for non-commercial purposes, provided you give attribution to the
copyright holder and the publisher and provide a link to the Creative Commons licence.

Bloomsbury Publishing Plc does not have any control over, or responsibility for, any third-
party websites referred to or in this book. All internet addresses given in this book were
correct at the time of going to press. The author and publisher regret any inconvenience
caused if addresses have changed or sites have ceased to exist, but can accept no
responsibility for any such changes.

A catalogue record for this book is available from the British Library.

A catalog record for this book is available from the Library of Congress.

ISBN: HB: 978-1-3502-7874-5
PB: 978-1-3502-7878-3
ePDF: 978-1-3502-7875-2
eBook: 978-1-3502-7876-9

Series: Radical Politics and Education

Typeset by Deanta Global Publishing Services, Chennai, India

For product safety related questions contact productsafety@bloomsbury.com.

To find out more about our authors and books visit www.bloomsbury.com and
sign up for our newsletters.

To my fellow travelers, attracted to life's strange intensity, affected by curious contagion, and collectively attuned to the world's indiscernible expressions.

Contents

List of Figures   viii
Acknowledgments   ix

Prelude: Ghostly Palimpsests and Locust Transformations   1
Introduction: Vital Curiosity's Disruptive, Connective, and Collective Force   13

Part I Disruptive Curiosity: Unsettling Education's Neoliberal Monoculture

1 What Can GMOs Teach Us about Curriculum Reform? Coding Pedagogical Vitality through Neoliberal Logics   35
2 What Did the Cafeteria Just Become? Educational Fundraising's Affective Intensity   49
3 What Can a Body Earn? School Fundraising as Immaterial Labor and Affective Currency   58

Part II Connective Curiosity: Permeating Thresholds through Transcorporeal Movement

4 What if We Dig It Ourselves? Mapping a Transcorporeal Inquiry across the Composition of Clay Bodies   73
5 What Else Could We Create by Suspending Our Reality? Traveling Isolation's Intensity as Frictions of Potential   89
6 Is This Land Just Layers of Bodies? Mapping Spectral Flows across Skeletal Forms   104

Part III Collective Curiosity: Affirming Our Ethico-Aesthetic Potential

7 What Can a Body Express? Nesting as Collective Sociality   119
8 How Might We Live as Pollinators? The Joyful, Strange, and Vital Uncertainty of a Pedagogical Life   128
9 What if We Learn This Together? Composing Collective Ecologies through Curiosity's Radical Interconnectedness   143

Notes   159
References   162
Index   173

Figures

4.1	Digging by the shed	76
4.2	Walking along the pipeline clearing	78
4.3	Buckets with clay	79
4.4	Single clay figure	80
4.5	Overlapping images with GIS map	82
6.1	Close-up of cholla cactus	105
6.2	Peering inside saguaro	106
6.3	Cactus skeleton on the ground	106
6.4	Saguaro on a mountain	108
6.5	Saguaro with an encroaching suburban community	108
6.6	Overgrown grasses along the trail	111

Acknowledgments

I have a lifetime of family, friends, teachers, students, and passers-by to thank for inspiring this book. Most importantly, I want to thank Bill, Ben, and Rose—my clan, who listened and encouraged me everyday. Tyson Lewis, I want to share my sincere gratitude for your valuable feedback throughout, and Derek Ford as well, for seeing the potential of my eclectic set of stories in the Radical Politics and Education Series. Jennifer Quincey, I cannot thank you enough for your insight and craft, your feedback encouraged me to continue seeing the work with fresh eyes. I also want to thank friends and mentors, who provided advice, motivation, and feedback throughout this process, as well as those who inspired or participated in the stories: Denise Clyne, Ken Nelson, Stacey Moran, Adam Nocek, Erin Manning, Melissa Button, Forrest Solis, Jason Wallin, Brent Hirak, Terry Barrett, Brooke Hofsess, and Mindi Rhoades. I also want to thank the Herberger Institute for Design and the Arts at Arizona State University for your support. Finally, I owe so much of this to my Mother, whose sense of humor and attunement to the uncanny shaped my curiosity from the beginning.

Prelude

Ghostly Palimpsests and Locust Transformations

In an attempt to spark your curiosity prior to providing an intellectual and academic context of the book, I start with a story to which I have returned many times over the last decade (Coats 2014, 2015). It acts as a warm-up and a guide to engaging with this book. In the coming chapters, I use a range of techniques to activate attention, such as bolded words that point to affective intensities, expressive attractions or shifts, and strange stimuli that reappear at different moments. Some chapters incorporate dialogue written more like a novel or screenplay, than academic interviews, and other chapters incorporate images to evoke a sense of place and curiosity about the movements described, rather than mere illustration. Some chapters include "curious paths" that embrace the tangential movement curiosity often creates when following uncertainty down unexpected or seemingly senseless directions. Stylistically, the book attempts to take up Lewis's (2020) call for an educational philosophy that embodies curiosity through "a form of writing that wanders, that yields to the features of curiosity that ensure it remains curious" (104). This opening story provides a sense of how to begin to pay attention to the expressiveness of the world, as well as the layering of time through a folding, spiraling, and eternal returns throughout the book.

This story begins ten years ago, when I was regularly driving around North Texas documenting food trucks for a research project. I would stop in different neighborhoods to write down my field notes, and I began to notice that many backyards had underground shelters, recognizable by their characteristic **rusted vents sticking out above cement slabs**. I found myself curiously looking for them all the time. Sometimes, I would get out of my car and snoop around people's fences to photograph them, wondering what the structures looked like below ground. Were these bomb shelters, like in old movies? I didn't think they still existed. I asked friends who had grown up in the region if they knew why this was so common. Some reminded me that they might be storm shelters because of all of the tornadoes in North Texas, but then I learned that there was an old missile base about 5 miles north of the town square, just off of **Locust Street**.

The base was built in 1960. It originally housed live missiles, which explained the unusual amount of residential fallout shelters. I decided I would drive out to see it firsthand, hoping it might become a new series of photographs. I hadn't gone that far up Locust Street before, so I didn't know what to expect. I envisioned the base as a shiny metal structure, like something out of a science fiction movie. I headed out alone. As soon as I passed the highway that looped around town, the street quickly narrowed to two lanes surrounded by open fields. I passed what looked like an abandoned elementary school on my left. There was a chain-link fence around the property with a number of **Keep Out** signs, so I kept driving. I had gone more than 5 miles before turning back to check out the school structure. The gate was open; I decided to ignore the "Keep Out" signs, rationalizing that they were probably decades old. Pulling into the driveway, I passed an empty guard stand filled with old construction materials. As I ascended a hill, I realized there was actually a series of buildings—all **cement** structures, overgrown with tall **grasses** and few **doors** or **windows** remaining. A newer-model **white car** was parked in the distance. I quickly turned around and headed back out.

Curious Path . . . The Community Fallout Program

Starting in 1944, the US military constructed 241 Nike missile bases across the United States. Many of these sites were near urban residential areas, resulting in an increased demand for private and community fallout shelters. Interest also grew in the popular imagination that swarmed around the potential for nuclear war and a future dependent on these types of structures. As I looked into this history, I was intrigued by how intensely anxious the cultural and political climate of the United States must have been in the 1950s and 1960s to generate this kind of demand for backyard bunkers. In 1961, the federal government started the Community Fallout Shelter program, identifying sites that could serve as community shelters throughout the country. Entire schools were built underground. Life Magazine from September 15, 1961, featured a photographic essay on fallout shelters, with the cover exclaiming: "How can you survive fallout: 97 out of 100 people can be saved. . . . . Detailed plans for building a shelter." Shelters were promoted as patriotic; as a DIY, family-survival initiative; and even as an extra recreational space for hobbies and crafts. An entire industry sprang up seemingly overnight, and the **Fallout Shelter sign** became almost emblematic of that period of American popular culture (Bishop 2019). The craze was short-lived, though, as skepticism grew over what many residents felt was fearmongering by aggressive shelter salesmen. Some viewed the initiative as the commercialization of civil defense:

> "Why the hell would I want to buy a tomb for the wife and kid?"
>
> —Tom Baulk, Letter to the Office of Civil Defense (November 1961)
> (in Bishop 2019, 117)

Still, the intrigue of the fallout shelter remained; they even appeared in episodes of the Twilight Zone *and other science fiction shows. In May 1972, the United States and the Soviet Union signed the Anti-Ballistic Missile Treaty, which regulated the production of nuclear weapons for both countries, and the US government ended the deployment of the Nike missile bases in 1974. The sites were turned over to local municipalities and school districts rather than demolishing them.*

Curiously Trespassing across Intensive Thresholds

The old missile base rode on my mind for several months after my first visit, but I was afraid to **return** alone. I asked my friend Brent, a photographer, to come with me. I sold him on the idea that he might get some good photographs out of it. As we approached the long chain-link fence, I noticed the gate was open again.

Feigning enthusiastic confidence, I exclaimed, "Come on, let's see what it is—isn't it creepy? There are not even any windows on the buildings. . . . It feels like a post-apocalyptic elementary school."

We drove in, passing the guard stand, which was still full of old building materials. As we parked in front of the first building, I noticed the white car was there again. We got out and walked slowly up a broken cement pathway to the next building. It had no windows or doors. There were **old, brightly colored plastic school chairs** clustered outside of its entrance. Once we reached the top of the steps, I noticed colorful Tibetan prayer flags and Christmas lights hanging inside.

Brent and I looked at each other—"What is this place?"

Crossing the **threshold** of the open entryway, I saw pieces of old linoleum tile remaining among the **cracks** in the cement floor. A chipped, waist-high brick wall divided the large room lengthwise, and there were more plastic chairs scattered inside. On the left, two plastic, life-size human **skeletons** were seated next to each other on a steel countertop that flanked an inset space with a large sink. I began to step inside, when a **voice growled** behind us.

"Can I help you?"

We turned with a **jolt**. A tall blond man stood holding **a screen door** open to a building we had passed. I hadn't noticed until that moment that it was the only building with windows. The white car was parked in front of it. How had I missed the windows and the screen door when we pulled in? Two medium-size dogs, one black and the other orange, ran toward us. The man yelled for them to stop. They paced near us as he approached.

I nervously uttered, "Um, oh well, yeah, hi. We were curious what this place is. I—I'm a teacher and he's a photographer. We just wanted to look around."

"What do you need?" the man asked.

Brent responded, "Well, I had heard something about a missile base. Is this it?"

We walked quickly down the steps to return to what felt like safer territory near the car. The man slowly approached us, blank-faced and stern. As he drew closer, I realized he was much taller than either of us.

"It was. What are you looking for?," he responded. His **expression** remained **unchanged**.

Again, to lighten the mood, Brent chimed in, "Oh, so do you live here now?"

"I might." The dogs continued to slowly circle around us.

"Oh, I'm sorry we . . ." I tried to find a way to explain.

"**Did you not see the signs**?" the man asked. We had driven past three "Keep Out" signs entering the property.

I responded, "well, yeah, I did. I just thought maybe they were old. I was just really interested in . . ."

Again, Brent tried to **break the tension**. "Wow, so this was a missile base? When would that have been built? We are students at the university."

"Come this way," the man said, as he looked up the hill toward another large open building that looked like a garage. I looked at my friend. **Our eyes said**, "Should we?"

I shrugged, and we turned to follow him. I walked a little distance behind. The man was strange and intriguing. He was clearly suspicious of us. The ground was **parched** from a **drought** that had extended over a number of summers. There was no shade from the sun, and long, brown grasses impeded the broken sidewalks. Large, **pale-green grasshoppers** leaped through the air, passing in front of my face. I could **hear their wings** buzz as they soared past. No one spoke as we moved up the hill. Through the hum of cicadas, I heard a car pass behind us on the highway **outside of the chain-link fence**. It was a reminder that the rest of the world didn't know we were here and of the **haunting magnetism** of the land barely separated by the open metal fence.

The Ghostly Spatial Palimpsest

The man, who I learned was named Ken, walked us through the buildings that had once been the barracks, mess hall, and missile control center. He didn't smile. He answered questions directly, with few words, and it was obvious when one of us asked a stupid one. He was frank, but not rude. He shared very little about his personal background—his **relationship to the land** was the story. It was all about the buildings, but every once in a while a **clue** would sneak out about how he got there and that his alterations were intended for a community. I sensed that he was **flattered** by our interest in his property. Each time I thought the tour was about to end, he would say, "**Follow me** over here. Have you ever seen a . . . ?" Each new direction generated a burst of excitement and nervousness. Ken bore some kind of **residue**, like the **land** itself, but I couldn't place it yet.

During the mid-1970s, the base had passed to the local school district after the Army National Guard moved out. Ken bought the missile control side of the base for $50,000 in 1995, which included ten acres of land with the administrative buildings and the Integrated Fire Control (IFC) area. He told us he spent three years cleaning out the old school furniture that had been stored there. He saw the buildings and surrounding land as a **readymade community gathering** place. It was secluded but close enough to town to afford easy access for his friends. He thought the open interior spaces and solid cement structures that had been designed to house a hundred soldiers would be ideal for a community of artists and musicians. After buying the missile base, he and his friends **collectively** repaired many of the utilities by **bartering time, knowledge, skill, and other goods** rather than relying on capitalist forms of **currency and exchange**. Artists have used the site since the 1990s for making large-scale work.

Many of the buildings on the land have no windows and still bear the signs of the original military installation. **No Smoking** spray-painted on the wall of the empty barracks hall **intensified the void** where rows of beds would have existed, men strewn along them with Lucky Strikes in hand. I have never witnessed an active barracks firsthand, and my image of this scene is derived entirely from popular culture. It's a scene of **masculine camaraderie**, where men's bodies relax closely and confidently together. I wondered how the **testosterone flowing** through this space would have felt. Did their **bodies link up** after a while in the ways that women's **menstrual cycles** seem to?

Shifting Intensities

We followed Ken further up the hill, where he had constructed sitting areas out of cinder blocks among rows of planted oak trees. From that height, the adjacent towns could be seen in all directions. Ken kept goats and sheep to manage the tall grasses, but it was the middle of summer, and the **overgrown** brown **blades** of grass **rustled** in the wind. The **grasshoppers** moved with us, **zigzagging** through the air to perch on walls and vacant windowsills as we passed them. The **repetitive cracks and snaps** of their wings intensified the **atmospheric pressure**. They covered the surfaces of the decaying complex of buildings, forming a **comfortable band of new occupants**.

My wariness of Ken and the base had waned, and I was now following closer behind him. We approached a set of stairs, where he was about two steps ahead of me. I noticed him gently cupping his hand around a grasshopper **perched** on the handrail. Suddenly, he shifted his arm backward and tossed the grasshopper toward me. I jumped back a little and gasped, barely dodging its wings. I looked up at Ken, perplexed. His **posture** had **shifted**, and his body seemed more relaxed now. He looked back at my face with a **boyish grin**. I could see his straight white **teeth** and the vitality in his **eyes** that had not **registered** until that moment. His **peculiarity transformed** into a familiar warmth, like a cousin with whom you share a distant past. A **flow** of compassion **surged**, forming as a kind of **stickiness** between us.

Ken's body had become **discernible** at that moment. His arm was **shaking** uncontrollably. It had been in his pocket most of the day, but he took it out to reach for the grasshopper on the handrail. I confess that this difference might have made him feel even more unknown to me just an hour earlier, but now it just seemed to be another texture in his story. The intensity of the land shifted as well, as the **porous** buildings, with their **empty** spaces and missing windows, became **connective openings**, layered on the **magnetic field** of its military history.

Curious Path ... Locust Transformation

*The **atmospheric volatility** of the grasshopper landscape resonated differently, as my **relationship** with Ken crossed a **threshold**. The previous summer had brought* *the culmination of one of the worst droughts in Texas history. Livestock across the state had died from malnourishment because the costs of water and hay had increased dramatically. North Texas was deeply **affected**. Grasshoppers, which are typically solitary insects that remain in one general geographic region for the extent of their lives, began to **swarm** across the state. Atop that hill, the **shrill chirping** of their **stridulating bodies** echoed through the wind as the rubbing of their hind legs against their wings screeched like an out-of-tune violin. Grasshoppers do this when **courting** and **mating**. Other grasshoppers detect the sounds by **listening** through **organs** in their abdomen. This **transmission** of sonic **desire** is **internalized in the gut**. Both male and female grasshoppers can chirp, though it's primarily males that do so.*

*The potential for a locust transformation seemed increasingly **imminent**. Only a few species of grasshopper can transform from their typical **solitary** phase to enter the **gregarious**, locust phase. It is a **phenotypic plasticity** that gives them the ability to dramatically **mutate in response to environmental conditions** that trigger **pheromones**—serotonin, specifically—as a result of a **tipping point** in their population density. For locusts, **serotonin acts** as "an **evolutionarily** conserved **mediator** of neuronal plasticity" (Anstey et al. 2009, n.p.). The neurochemical mechanism **links interactions** between individuals to large-scale changes in population structure and the onset of mass migration.*

*In humans, serotonin is the primary hormone affecting **mood** and regulating feelings of well-being, happiness, and anxiety. Too little serotonin can cause **depression**, while too much can likewise decrease human **arousal**. It also acts as a medium for brain–nervous system communication. **Normal** serotonin levels create the **ability** to focus and stabilize **gastrointestinal** conditions. Serotonin is the primary chemical regulated in antidepressants, to either increase or **block reception**. Like humans, the regulation of serotonin responses is a point of **experimentation** for locust species. Serotonin blockers are added to some **agricultural pesticides** to diminish their capacity to shift to a gregarious phase (Guo, Ma, and Kang 2013).*

—

Wait. A flood of questions emerged after reading about locust transformations. If the chemical process to eliminate social formations in grasshoppers is based on their potentially devastating agricultural effects once in the gregarious phase, I wondered: Might a similar concern be lodged in human pests when an overwhelming emotion or distracting socialization gets in the way of production?

Did my exchange with Ken cross an affective threshold that echoes the swarming effect by activating flows of serotonin through a compassionate, collective intensity? The change emerged from our proximity, expressed through nonverbal signaling, revealing a similar neuronal plasticity, as our isolating suspicions dissipated, and a curious energy flowed between us.

—

The next day, I sat on my porch and looked out at the field in the direction of Locust Street, and a flow of images ran through my mind as emotions flooded my body. I thought about all that happened there. Tears welled up in my eyes, but I had no idea why. Ken's mischievous gesture and the expression on his face kept coming back to me. The simple playfulness made the property seem magical in all of its eccentricity.

He later told me that the shaking in his arm started as a result of using a jackhammer so frequently. Over the following months, I would realize that he had become obsessed with the idea that underground tunnels connected the missile base to other bases across the country. Maps of the surrounding area covered the tables and shelves of his living room as he doggedly pursued this curiosity. He began using a jackhammer to dig holes throughout the property to aid his search for tunnels.

I wondered if the affective residue of a suspicious generation, who felt the need to construct these bases and the fallout shelters that followed, was somehow sedimented in the architecture and the land. Had Ken's body reached a kind of neurochemical tipping point, mutating in response to his environmental conditions?

Unpacking the Missile Base Story

From the outset, my inquiry process was driven by material objects that activated my curiosity. The vents and doors of the underground shelters created questions about the history of fallout shelters and the cultural conditions of the 1950s that drove suburban homeowners to desire underground barracks. The barracks' appearance, with the majority of the structure hidden underground, was haunting and strange and activated my imagination, but mostly left me to base any familiarity on images from popular culture. This curiosity led me to Ken's property with a combined desire to witness this historical relic and possibly capture some residues of its history in photographs. The first section of the story progressed through material expressions in the form of rusty vents, "Keep Out" signs, and pop culture representations. I had taken an interest in a history of fear materialized in domestic spaces, but strange coincidences emerged immediately, such as the base's location on Locust Street. I did not realize the potential of this spectral connection until returning to the story ten years later. The concept of the "return" operates on a range of levels, from my return to the base, to a new community returning to the site after the military abandoned it, to Ken's repeated return to the land to dig for suspected tunnels. In each return, a new potential resonated from the land that drew us back in.

Curiously Trespassing across Intensive Thresholds

The second section of the story resonates through bodily intensities expressed through verbal and nonverbal communication, gestures, and proximity. The dogs approaching, grasshoppers flying, and wind rustling the dried grass, along with an awareness of being in a remote place closed in by a gate, all affected my way of coming to know the site. More broadly, it is triggered by the ways we are positioned culturally in relation to gender norms, racial perceptions, physical abilities, and other forces. As Ken surprised us by emerging from the building, I became aware of my gender in relation to both him and Brent and conscious of my appearance, my nervousness, and the physicality of the research site. Affective transmissions (Brennan 2004) flowed between Brent and me in our nervous gesturing, through the dogs swarming around us, and in Ken's evolving affection. At the same time, the theme of porosity emerged in the open gate, the cracked floors, the missing doors and windows, and in the mutual transformation of our acceptance of each other.

Another haunting coincidence appeared in the skeletons in the old mess hall. On the one hand, they echoed the generation of men who would have occupied the base fifty years older, but they also foreshadow the theme of skeletons in Chapter 6. What began as a deeply humanist endeavor to understand how subjectivity was produced (an epistemological study) became a more-than-human ontological investigation embedded in thought, force, movement, and expression, realizing the significance of becoming with the research process that could not be coded, as the research exceeded the qualitative methods that initially constituted it.

The Spatial Palimpsest and the Grasshopper Landscape

As we toured the site, the physicality of the buildings' past vibrated in the present absence of the beds in the barracks and the ghostly reminder in the words "No Smoking," painted in red on the wall. We could feel the land, but our curiosity was connecting us to that history and to each other. Our mutual care and closeness increased as we moved together across the spaces.

On the day of the visit, I remember the grasshoppers flying around us, but it was more of an atmospheric background to our relational intensity with Ken. When I return to the day in my memory, the grasshoppers take on a different significance. I can still see them in my mind, flying through the air in front of me, against the bold, mid-afternoon sunbeams and the parched land. The long, brown grass blades that blew in the hot air rustled in concert with the grasshopper wings, compounding the eeriness and atmospheric intensity. The sounds reinforced the feeling of isolation from our everyday lives, creating a sense that we were miles from home.

The Locust Transformation

The impact of the moment Ken flung the grasshopper at me is beyond words. Deleuze's (1990a) description of his relationship with Foucault—"It's easier to remember a gesture or a laugh than a date" (83)—was never more resonant for me than in the moment on the steps. The image of his grin still gives me goose bumps and a strange feeling in my stomach. My initial curiosity about 1950s culture had turned into a fascination with this strange man, which transformed into an overwhelming sense of connection and compassion. At that moment, the heat, grasshoppers, abandoned buildings, and Ken's stoic disposition all transformed as his joy revealed a very different person.

Now, upon returning to this story for the third time (after Coats 2014 and 2015), a different connection has emerged. I had always wanted to think more about the impact of the playful grasshopper story, and, out of respect, I had always been reluctant to mention Ken's arm. But both lingered with me. In the process of recounting the experience, but foregrounding its physical intensity, I realized the atmospheric elements told a different story. The sun, grass, cracks, and grasshoppers had territorialized the space, creating a presence that infused its degraded physicality with a new vibrancy. The drought had parched the land, making their physicality stand out against the barren landscape.

I started to think about locusts when describing the sounds that the grasshoppers were making, and followed that curious attraction to the **shocking** discovery that locusts *are* grasshoppers. I could not believe that their phenotypic plasticity allows them to physically transform as a response to environmental conditions. Even more fascinating is that it turns them from solitary to gregarious.

As I learned more about how the transformation occurs in response to drought but also to the proximity, movement, and sound of other locusts, I kept thinking about the sounds and movements between their bodies and mine that day. What else could we learn from this mutative capacity? As I continued following this trail, I came upon a study that mentioned serotonin. I didn't know a lot about serotonin, except for some connection to antidepressants. My mind was racing, wondering if there could be some connection between locust formation and human experiences of depression. What would this mean? And how did Ken's playful gesture, and the change in our bodies and relationships from isolated to connected, relate to a possible locust formation? The questions posed after the curious aside are still new paths I hope to pursue:

> How do our chemical responses hold potential for new social formations?
> What is a comparable gregarious phase, where humans are treated as pests?
> And what are the cultural fears of overwhelming emotion or distracting socialization?
> When do those responses have potentially dangerous effects?
> Did the exchange between Ken and me create a swarming effect?
> Could our collective flows of serotonin reveal similar neuronal plasticity?

Perhaps the locust transformation reveals a different potential for vital curiosity.

Introduction

Vital Curiosity's Disruptive, Connective, and Collective Force

This book is about the life of curiosity. Through a series of spiraling narratives, I develop a concept of *vital curiosity* that animates learning with affective intensity, aesthetic intuition, and collective emergence. We travel with curiosity's energy and vitality, following strange attractions across territorial boundaries and institutional bodies, weaving a residual web that illuminates life's complex interconnectedness. Fleshed out through everyday experiences that form an ecology of interrelated inquiries, the book explores curiosity as an onto-epistemological subject, an affective capacity, and relational process, drawn to the strangeness of the everyday, and attuning to the invisible, uncanny, silenced, and buried.

Vital curiosity creates flows of desire through and between moments, where the world transmits signals realized through embodied encounters, aesthetic attentiveness, intensive attraction, and a durational drive toward complexity. At the same time, I introduce curiosity as a multifaceted and complex emotion, disposition, and capacity that emerges from a range of intentions and creates a spectrum of effects. Curiosity enlivens relationships to question the ethical complexity of embodied engagements (Sedgwick 2003). Thinking with human and nonhuman bodies, a spectrum of curious intensities emerge that press against established boundaries to trace their conditions of emergence, while becoming an index of their pliability, porosity, and rigidity.

Throughout the book, stories of curious learning encounters explore entanglements between human and nonhuman forces, where bodies of land, physical structures, and physical objects express a vitality that generates new questions, unsettles habituated understandings, and creates new relationships. "Curiosity is something that is done, expressed in behaviors, habits, architectures, and movements across physical, conceptual, and social space" (Zurn and Shankar 2020, xiii) through active engagements that resist the desire to define what the world *is*, asking instead what it can *do*.

I invite readers to embrace curiosity's world-building capacity as a vital force in education. Chapters follow critical hunches and emergent questions down lines of inquiry that are less about a need to resolve uncertainty than a passionate attraction to travel with it; imaginatively rethinking common learning environments, experiences, and procedures to create transdisciplinary and collective energy. Each experience activates questions about established sociocultural, physical, and institutionalized practices. Tracing curious encounters across institutional, private, and public spaces, each chapter dilates porous boundaries between pedagogical milieus, disciplinary bodies, curricular structures, and institutional ontologies. While this book is rooted in schooling and education, it serves as a proposition to realize curiosity's disruptive, connective, collective, and residual force in any context. Together, the plurality of experiences forms a cartography of shifting environments as a "processual assemblage" (O'Sullivan 2010a, 256) that illuminates the profound beauty of life's durational interdependence through curiosity's critical and creative force for thought, where:

> The activity of thinking cannot and must not be reduced to reactive ("sedentary") critique, but must also involve significant doses of creativity. Thinking can be critical, if by critical we mean the active, assertive process of inventing new images of thought. Thinking is life lived at the highest possible power, both creative and critical, enfleshed, erotic, and pleasure driven. (Braidotti 2012, 84)

Curiosity's Dynamic Multiplicity

Curiosity has garnered renewed attention in transdisciplinary inquiry, particularly among those asking how to approach research and pedagogy differently through methods that play with established processes to question disciplinary boundaries (Lewis 2012, 2020; Loveless 2019; Manning 2020; Massumi 2002; Tsing 2015; Zurn 2021; Zurn and Shankar 2020). As research and education are being rethought globally to address contemporary ecological and humanitarian crises, Anna Tsing (2015) argues that "curiosity . . . [is] the first requirement of collaborative survival in precarious times" (2). I take inspiration from Tsing's collective sentiment, recognizing our interdependence in the face of existential uncertainty, to explore curiosity's potential in educational inquiry that, as Jason Wallin (2011a) argues, "must become *more than critical*. It must itself begin to survey and mobilize creative practices of a different kind—

practices adequate to an ethical challenge that purports *we do not yet [know] how a life might go*" (111, emphasis original).

Curiosity is generally defined as a strong desire to know or learn something, but this tepid description underestimates curiosity's emotional and intellectual force of attraction. It is often assigned embodied and affective traits of love, appetite, and thirst—an "insatiable hunger, irresistible attraction toward enfolding each other [as] the vital motor of living and dying on earth" (Haraway 2016, 58). Curiosity acts as a capacity for attentiveness and desire; at other times, it relates to an affective strangeness of the world. In this sense, curiosity becomes an embodied attraction and affection, a mode of engaging the world through ecologically oriented, transdisciplinary, and transversal inquiry that links to and flows with the world through vital currents of affect and commitment.

Historically, perceptions of curiosity range from a desirable ability to wander, connect, imagine, and innovate, to the pesky busybody, with irritating distraction or superficiality. As to its etymology, curiosity's root, *curiosus (Latin)* means "careful" or "inquisitive."[1] Curious's root, *cura-* means "to care or be careful" and "to cure or help," which is similar to the root of "curate," which embeds care with choice (Loveless 2019). Zurn (2018) draws attention to historical dangers in a spectrum of care in curiosity, identifying a sovereign curiosity that is both autopsic and therapeutic, in forms of circumscription, identification, and enclosure:

> whether curiosity constrains or confines, it does so to death. Autopsic curiosity is a matter of the "objectifying to death of the object." Therapeutic curiosity, on the other hand, "consists in enclosing, depriving of freedom of movement and, hence, of freedom itself, hence of power, or power to see, to know, to have beyond certain limits, and hence of sovereignty." (90)

This description illuminates curiosity's political character, which we may consider by simply asking which questions or topics may be posed, and by whom. In this sense, we can see a sovereign curiosity at work in settler colonialism, the horrors of medical history, and even the *Wunderkammer*. It is important to temper our desire to simply Romanticize curiosity, in light of its reemergence in popular culture and transdisciplinary scholarship that is often linked with notions of innovation and capitalist production. I address the residual effects of curiosity's troubled histories and potential dangers in Chapters 5 and 6.

Vital curiosity rejects purely teleologic values that are driven by narrow instrumental ends. More than functional, curiosity is at times aimless and unfocused, egoistic and distracted. Throughout the book, I introduce other concepts of curiosity to differentiate vital curiosity and to provide a spectrum of ways that curiosity takes form as a complex emotional connection. These iterations that include aesthetic, porous, sovereign, neoliberal, and collective illuminate curiosity's constitutive and emergent qualities that take form through situated and relational encounters to become biopolitical, sociocultural, ecological, pedagogical, and economic.

Vitality's Evolving Complexity

Similar to curiosity's spectrum of meanings that range from the instrumentalist to the strange and indefinable, vitality's roots trace historical debates between science and mysticism. The Latin root of "vital"—*vita*—means "life," or the animating principle of living beings. "Vital" is defined as essential, spirited, life's energy, and the electric current below individual life-forms. Vitality functions in nuanced ways throughout the chapters, echoing its multiplicity of historic meanings in which vital energy has been ascribed to magic, resistance, joy, and desire, animating bodies as a life-giving force and perceived in vital signs as corporeal expressions. Vitality implies movement and flow within bodies. Atmospheric vitality is registered through electric currents, intensive disturbances, lightning, and shifts in pressure. Moreover, vitality suggests fertility and dynamism, where aliveness is expressed in an openness to diversity and variation. Mitchell (2013) describes three eras of what he coins as "experimental vitalism" in art, science, and society: the Romantic period in literature at end of the eighteenth century; "neo-vitalisms" in philosophy, art, and the natural sciences at the end of the nineteenth century that included embryological and botanical experimentation along with the philosophical works of Nietzsche and Bergson; and the "vitalist turn" of the last fifty years that are embracing a renewed interest in the earlier philosophies and the potential they might hold for our critical global ecological crisis, born out of centuries of anthropocentric destruction and domination over the rest of life. Mitchell (2013) explains how vitalism, "in the sciences and humanities, in short, is a sense of life as *provocation*; for the various authors, life is not a self-evident fact that can be taken for granted but rather a source of complexity that demands new modes of concealment and practical experimentation" (2, emphasis in original).

My concept of vital curiosity is rooted in this third vitalist turn, and theories of vital materialism as an affective force, inspired and informed by historical philosophers (Bergson, Deleuze, Guattari, Nietzsche, Spinoza), as well as contemporary scholars and artists working with and across new materialisms and posthuman studies (Alaimo, Barad, Bennett, Braidotti, Brennan, Clough, Colebrook, Coole and Frost, Dolphijn and van der Tuin; Gregg and Seigworth, Manning, Massumi, Snaza et al., Springgay, Truman, Wallin). New materialist theories are not actually new, and posthuman studies do not eliminate the human but instead have revitalized ontological and epistemological questions to decenter the human, creating a radical departure from the humanist legacy within the social sciences, natural sciences, and humanities (Coole and Frost 2010; Dolphijn and Van der Tuin 2012; Snaza et al. 2016). Here, human relations are oriented to a shared vitality among living and inorganic matter in relation to biopolitical and bioethical conditions, where everyday experiences reveal geopolitical and socioeconomic entanglements (Bennett 2010). Within these two umbrella categories of posthuman and new materialism are a range of more specific areas of study that are addressed through specific experiences in the chapters, such as affect theory, biosocial studies, new vitalisms, and critical life studies.

In this articulation, vitality is more than energy. The concept of vital curiosity is inspired, in part, by Bergson's (1998) creative principles of *élan vital*, the imminent capacity and impulse to move toward increasing complexity, and hence evolution. I apply this form of vitality to explore curiosity's intensive force as a creative capacity, where "evolution does not mark out a solitary route, that it takes directions without aiming at ends, and that it remains inventive even in its adaptations" (Bergson 1998, 102). Creative evolution is driven by movement, transformation, and not-knowing, rather than a desire to create fixity and finality. This form of vital energy tends toward a harmonious joining in the future as a form of durational emergence and creative evolution. Moreover, Bergson (1998) suggested that this emergent tendency becomes a perpetually nascent state, a capacity to move with the will of youth as a "free passage to the full breath of life" (99). It is important to reinforce that Bergson differentiates élan vital from mere existence, that is, a tendency toward simplicity or a reproductive repetition. Élan vital is a tendency toward evolution and transformation, a mobile and active affirmation of complexity. Bergson (1998) argued that "the role of life is to insert some *indetermination* into matter. Indeterminate, i.e., unforeseeable, are the forms it creates in the course of its evolution. More and more indeterminate also, more and more free, is the activity to which these forms serve as the vehicle" (126, emphasis in original). This is critical to my notion of vital curiosity as not simply a desire to know through fixed definitions, mastery, or acquisition, but rather as a desire for learning as connection and collective emergence through life's uncertainty. The notion of freedom (referenced above) becomes an important theme in Chapter 8, in relation to the predetermined nature of curriculum in schooling. For Bergson, freedom was similarly limited by the ready-made problems and challenges created in advance by teachers for students to solve, as opposed to creating conditions for "true freedom [that] lies in the power to decide, to constitute problems themselves" (Deleuze 1988, 15). Curiosity, as a capacity and desire to ask new questions and follow indeterminate paths, relates to Bergson's notion of freedom as a tendency toward mobility and complexity.

Questions of vitality and variants of vitalism were historically at the root of modern science, physics, electricity, genetics and evolution, religious spiritualism, and Romantic fiction (Holmes 2008; Mitchell 2013). Historical critiques have minimized vitalism as a form of unscientific mysticism and spiritualism (Bennett 2001; Tuscano 2007). A renewed interest in Bergson's work along with vitalism broadly has yielded a range of new insights and warnings about the historical connections to Eugenics and exploitative experiments and tests on minoritized bodies, as well as fascisms in the first half of the twentieth century, and lingering echoes of some of essentializing and xenophobic sentiment in ecological movements today that continue to embrace a settler colonialist sentiment in their relationship to the environment (Bennett 2010; de Freitas 2018; Mitchell 2013; Sparrow 2019). Echoing some of the historical dangers of vitalism, new materialism has been critiqued by contemporary scholars for its potential essentializing and flattening effects, in a privileged positionality of whiteness and distance from the lived texture of social research (Ahmed 2004; Rousell and Cutter-Mackenzie-Knowles 2019; Sparrow 2019). Moreover, the contemporary vitalist turn in the sciences and humanities is critiqued as another form of neoliberal capitalism, which, like curiosity, is frequently linked to innovation in scientific research and entrepreneurialism (Mitchell 2013; Rose 2008; Sparrow 2019; Toscano 2007). But, as I hope to illuminate in this book, both curiosity and vitalism exceed innovation's domesticating force when the human is decentered (Zurn and Shankar 2020).

While acknowledging these historical dangers and contemporary weaknesses, I take up a critical posthuman, vital materialist approach that is embodied and embedded (Braidotti 2021), as well as aesthetic and affective to recover the creative forces that have been captured by capitalism, because, as Toscano (2007) asserts, "if capitalism really is practically existing idealism, then the most idealist stance might be the one which tries to promote a practical existence of a living materialism. In this regard, the phenomenological virtues of vitalism might be considerably greater than its critical or ontological ones" (88). I critically and creatively trace capitalism's vital forces through my curiosity into the practical aspects of daily life (Bennett 2010; Stewart 2007), finding the strange erasures and invisible exploitations hiding in plain sight, where "this style of thought and practice begins with an active search for what is perplexing and inscrutable in vital phenomena" (Mitchell 2013, 2–3). The vitality I ascribe to curiosity acts as a collective attraction (vital curiosity) and committed affection (curious vitality), where curious desire is met with care and responsibility. Vital curiosity embraces *élan vital's* tendency of movement toward uncertainty and indetermination, as a perpetually nascent state of emergence to embrace *the full breath of life*.

Vital Curiosity and Curious Vitality

Vital force is both internal and external, moving through currents of energy, registered as expressive signals of affection and connection, akin to the rhythmic pulse of a heartbeat (Bennett 2010, 2020; Deleuze 1990b). The vital force of curiosity breathes difference into the familiar, embracing uncertainty as the space of unknown potential (Bergson 1992, 1998). Energetic attractions enfold and are enfolded through aesthetic connections, forming a sort of Möbius strip from expressive force: a mutual, dynamic relationship between vital curiosity and curious vitality as an internal drive and an external re-composition, like the ebb and flow of breath (Barad 2015; Bennett 2020). One side acts as an exterior attraction and connection, or a kind of reaching out. The other folds in as an affective internalization, where curious connections are synthesized with memories, then metabolized as new connections. Vital curiosity is an attentive *and* distracted force that attracts and connects, akin to sympathy as "currents of 'affection' circulating in the atmosphere to connect different types of beings and things [...] as a contagious pain by which one is 'possessed' [...] which sends out 'mad filaments, ungovernable shoots' into a 'screaming electric' atmosphere" (Bennett 2020, 29).

Throughout the book, vitality is expressed through energy, resistance, transmission, transformation, and residues. These are combined and aligned with curiosity, as a thought-in-the-act, expressed through qualities of attraction, perception, affect, affirmation, and memory (Deleuze 1988, 2001b; Dimitrova 2018). Together they become thought's energy to affirmatively link up with the world. I map the movement of vital curiosity as durational change, often realized in moments of affective intensity, where affect becomes a stoppage point, a point of resistance in the energy circuit, transduced and transmitted into something else; revealing the evolution of curiosity's potential and diminished vitality in education. Using a vital materialist framework, expression becomes a more-than-human phenomenon rooted in concepts of force—force in the sense that something is pushing or pulling on something else. It is a more-than-human event that applies notions of expression to organic and in organic forms. The world expresses and attracts through *thing-power* (Bennett 2010), which activates a curious ability to see life where we failed to recognize it before, and a combinatory force to become something else as a process of creative evolution.

While vital materialism inspired my thinking about the exteriority of curiosity's force as more-than-human collective and connective potential, theories on thinking, affect, and embodiment shaped my ideas on the interiority of curiosity as radically intensive and aesthetic (Anderson 2012; Gregg and Siegworth 2010; Sedgwick 2003). Spinoza (1994) argues that the body is affected in the form of passions through experience in movement, "in which its power of acting is increased or diminished" (154). Here, affect acts as a passage from one state of being to another, where knowledge and intelligence emerge through embodied, affective, and "combinatory" processes of perception, relation, recollection, connection, and self-awareness. Spinoza describes three kinds of knowledge, the first of which is rooted in perception, and constituted through "shocks . . . as random affects determined by encounters, affective capture or contagion" (O'Sullivan 2012, 16). This idea of intensive shocks relates to curiosity as an appetite or aliveness to the unfamiliar in lived encounters. Here, the body enters into complex modes of relation registered in speed and slowness through sensory data, that are internalized as affective intensities or passions, which include, among others: joy/pleasure, pain/sorrow, desire/appetite (de Freitas 2018; Dimitrova 2018; Spinoza 1994).

Spinoza's second kind of knowledge exceeds the senses, gaining an abstract distance from the world to develop a conscious understanding of these relations and appetites. In the passage between the first and second kinds of knowledge, one develops intuitive capacities for attuning to the rhythms of life differently through intensive encounters (Coleman 2008; Deleuze 1988, Knudson and Stage 2015). The third form of knowledge is an awareness of what causes the relations, an active, conscious, and joyful intensity, as an active gesture and orientation to the world, different from the prior two more passive and reactive states through affirmation and connection between the body, mind, and experience (Spinoza 1994). This threefold process and concept aligns with the progression of curiosity across the book's three parts: Disruptive, Connective, and Collective. I take inspiration from Spinoza's concepts in the dispositional and process-oriented qualities of vital curiosity as embodied in learning encounters as expressive, aesthetic, affective, sticky, experimental, porous, and transversal described in the following sections.

Disruptive Postures: Divergent Orientation and Aesthetic Disposition

Vital curiosity is a radical disposition and orientation, taking form through a will to question and a sensitivity to root conditions (Fayn et al. 2015; Massumi 2002; Zurn 2021; Zurn and Shankar 2020). This aesthetic drive acts as a motor for attraction, as an open and divergent orientation to uncertainty, and an approach to learning that is both attentive and distracted, with an unexplainable desire to follow the unfamiliar. To follow our curiosities, we must be willing to flow with strange intuitions, embracing their unsettling, immanent potentialities.

I build on Lewis's (2012) concept of aesthetic curiosity, which is less about the cognitive than the sensual and affective, as a "creatively synesthetic moment where what can be sensed is sensed differently, in new permutations, and radically heterogenous chains of equivalence" (43). Distraction becomes a capacity for sensing and drifting with the unfamiliar or uncanny, rather than favoring the unifying nature of attentiveness (Lewis 2020). In this sense, curiosity's divergent tendency is enacted as a state of attentive distraction to other possibilities. In the classroom, this type of curiosity is often irritating, as it takes the class off-task. Curiosity may be minimally encouraged through open-ended questions in motivational classroom activities to gauge student interest, then often swept aside for *real* learning. Lewis (2020) addresses "a tendency to reduce [curiosity] to the level of a secondary, peripheral role of intentionality" in the phrase "I am just curious" (91). He (Lewis) argues that, rather than diminish the distractibility inherent in curious questioning, the ability to become distracted illuminates where "curiosity spreads out, swarms, and multiplies beyond centralized control" (104).

Vital curiosity becomes a collective attunement to what increasingly entangles and disrupts, a radically collective orientation, where "to be one is always to *become with* many" (Haraway 2007, 4, emphasis in original). While our orientation refers to that which we move toward (Ahmed 2006), dispositions are intuitive behaviors and qualities of mind, expressed through behaviors with enacted effects. Vital curiosity's aesthetic disposition becomes an electric current that attunes to expressive energy through a sensorial attentiveness beyond language. It is a mode of being more sensitive to life's creative evolution (Bergson 1998;

Guattari 1995), experienced as an urgency to "decipher what cannot be said, what is expressed otherwise than in verbal speech which nonetheless arouses the desire for words" (Zurn 2018, 88). As a pedagogical force, vital curiosity creates a radical tendency to test the pliability and porosity of established boundaries through direct and embodied experimentation (Mitchell 2013). Learning through curious experimentation creates an intensive drive toward complexity and change, "for life is tendency, and the essence of a tendency is to develop in the form of a sheaf, creating by its very growth, divergent directions among which its impetus is divided. This we observe in ourselves, in the evolution of that special tendency which we call our character" (Bergson 1998, 99). Here, tendencies become internalized conditions and character traits that are both established and primed for change. They imbue learning with a vital sensibility, where learners become contemplative souls and larval subjects (Deleuze 1994).

Connective Encounters: Affective Intensity and Existential Stickiness

Throughout the book, vital curiosity is attuned to affective intensities realized through an embodied and embedded inquiry process (Braidotti 2012), where affective vitality is affirmed in the relational intensity between bodies (Deleuze 2001a; Deleuze and Guattari 1987; Guattari 1995; O'Sullivan 2012; Spinoza 1994). Bodies, as a more-than-human landscape, become the milieu for learning as "our first and foremost, most immediate and intimately *felt* geography is the body, the site of emotional experience and expression *par excellence*" (Paterson 2009, 771, emphasis in original). Affect is more than simply shock or feeling, but instead, where intensity is perceived by the increase or decrease in the body's potential to act. Intensity animates the present moment and is the feeling by which "we sense the future animating the present moment" (de Freitas 2018, 301).

Curiosity's affective capacity creates a texture to experience, scratching the surface through sensual attraction and embodied vibrations that form an existential stickiness (Coats 2020; Guattari 1995; Massumi 2002; O'Sullivan 2010a). Affective stickiness becomes a medium and passageway for currents of connection that illuminate invisible, coded, and sedimented elements of the everyday. Curiosity becomes an ethico-aesthetic capacity to become affected, cultivating conditions of care and a durational response-ability to difference as a mode for living. Here, stickiness as a sensitivity becomes a passage and feedback loop, addressed by Massumi (2002): "Is not this enduring 'sensitivity' a connecting thread of affect meandering impersonally throughout the world? World-affect: life-glue of matter" (227). From a phenomenological perspective, Merleau-Ponty (2012) describes a sensation of intersubjective attraction in terms of "a vortex [that] forms around the perceived body into which my world is drawn and, so to speak, sucked in" (p. 369), and while I position the stickiness of vital curiosity as a more onto-epistemological event and capacity, the image of the worlding vortex paints a similar picture of the sticky affection.

Vital curiosity's stickiness creates a field of affective intensities that come into composition with the present as a "strange attractor," forming new relational coordinates between living beings (Guattari 1995). This stickiness is more than sympathy, which emerges from sincere care but can easily slip into pity, judgment, and infantilizing patronage, comparable to curiosity's dangerously unethical potential (Bennett 2020; Zurn 2021). Rather than a smooth flow of experience, it favors attentive distractions, where aesthetic energy resides between the sticky object and the affected body. Ahmed (2004) describes the affective texture and attractive force of stickiness of bodies and objects that emerges from the felt energy that emerges from a sensuous proximity. Intercorporeal encounters produce complex modes of relation registered in speed and slowness as sensory data, which are internalized as affective intensities, while at the same time, language and other forms of cultural significance can get stuck to bodies, where "what sticks 'shows us' where the object has traveled through what it has gathered onto its surface" (Ahmed 2004, 91). So, this notion of stickiness becomes an affective capacity and the fluid space of subjective sociocultural assemblage emerging from relationships between bodies (Coleman and Ringrose 2013; Kofoed and Ringrose 2012; O'Sullivan 2001). Bodies of land, animals, children, knowledge, and work become sites of labor, commodification, disturbance, mutation, resistance, affective eruption, connection, and transmission.

Collective Emergence: Experimental Inquiry and Processual Compositions

Curious vitality becomes a motor for ecologically oriented world-building through an embodied, active, and creatively attentive inquiry practice that often exceeds linguistic, disciplinary, and subjective boundaries. Distraction and attentiveness function as an affective ebb and flow with response-ability to set forth a choreography with the world through questions and experimentation that connect time and space by what Zurn (2018) describes as "unmooring curiosity—setting it adrift among plants, animals, human, and beyond" (100). My process echoes Zurn's description of setting curiosity adrift, enchanted by the unfamiliar, and driven through questioning.

Curiosity is often expressed through questions that activate movement toward uncertainty. Artful and experimental research practices can become a form of world-building, when we realize that "the crafting of a research question is the crafting of a story that is also the crafting of an ethics" (Loveless 2019, 14–15), which suggests we might spend more time developing the ability to ask questions—than to resolve them (Knudsen and Stage 2015). While I may answer some questions, I do not seek resolution; but, rather, the creative and emergent energy of curious indeterminacy.

Following sticky questions, curiosity connects with the unknown through movement and transformation that activates inquiry as "the aesthetic yield of experience in the making. Its power is in the way, in the *how* of a coming to form" (Manning 2020, 44). The inquiry process embraces curiosity's radically undutiful potential, forming attachments and following lines that may be unfaithful to established methods, boundaries, and hierarchies. I approach many chapters as forms of research-creation, which are

> curiosity-driven, inter- or transdisciplinary method(s) . . . that work not only across discursive fields but challenge the norms of those fields, producing boundary objects that insist on being undutiful . . . [and] insists that curiosity, in all its erotic pluripotency, be its guide, pushing us to tell new stories in the academy, stories that denaturalize singular disciplinary locations while nomadically claiming space within all of them; stories that unmake as much as they remake how we understand what we are doing as *maker-thinkers* in the—disciplined and disciplining—university today. (Loveless 2019, 37, emphasis in original)

Throughout the book, inquiry is activated in everyday experiences, revealing how "even the most familiar places become different in lieu of new understandings, perspectives, and changes in relationship with the landscape" (Wallin 2008, 318). Places become vital objects of knowledge production rather than innate byproducts of human making. As such, the transmission of knowledge is embodied and participatory. Human and nonhuman bodies serve as sites of inquiry and the stage for each narrative throughout the book. Space resides between places and bodies as a grounded, real, and lived environment in which stories weave together to constitute meaning (Pink 2009).

Curiosity comes alive through inquiry paths presented in a range of forms and contexts, where new constellations of connection form to reveal porous boundaries and recomposed relations. This book project started with bits of stories and moments that have stuck with me in their strangeness or affective intensity as confusion, excitement, discomfort, and surprise. While these emotions are frequently overlooked in traditional research because they fall outside the realm of quantitatively measurable or qualitatively representable data, they can signal deeper connections through a presence that exceeds common modes of understanding (Clough 2007; Crang 2003; Hickey-Moody 2013; Knight 2021; Knudsen and Stage 2015). St. Pierre (1997a, 1997b) argued that new knowledge requires new methods, such as dreams and sensual responses, where data resides in the folds of language, which can be mapped only by recognizing the shifting of subjectivity amid forces of bodily affect.

In parts, I apply arts-based and nonrepresentational approaches because they can often express the sense of *larval* experiences, where "the feeling around them is the feeling of creation and creativity . . . of something in motion, being incubated, about to happen, unfolding" (Nxumalo, Vintimilla, and Nelson 2018, 438). Combining historical and place-based research, visual and photographic methods, and experimental approaches to classroom teaching to evoke the sense of strange intuition, odd surprise, and percipient wonder, the stories trace the vitality of thought, pointing to subjective shifts that unfold through material encounters that are made strange through affective disruption.

Crafting Curious Stories through Strange Returns

In each chapter, I curiously return to stories that have stuck with me to see where they would go in the retelling. The narratives drift and leak, following bodily flows to consider how curiosity creates vectors of force on the porous boundaries between learning spaces and power structures, as bodies and questions stick, enfold, and resist. I have told and analyzed some of them many times, while others I have simply been ruminating on in my memory over time. Taking inspiration from the approach described by Deleuze and Guattari (1986), "We will be trying only to discover what other points our entrance connects to, what crossroads and galleries one passes through to link two points, what the map of the rhizome is and how the map is modified if one enters by another point" (3). This idea of discovering what other points of entrance might connect to is precisely my goal, where imaginatively returning to personal experiences creates new lines of connection and unexpected paths. I often did not know where chapters would go when I embarked on the questions and the writing. At some points, my surprise is expressed in pauses, or moments of shock with words, "Wait! . . ." or critical confusion, rhetorically questioning how some phenomena are accepted or overlooked. The past is recomposed upon return, where "creative repetitions, i.e., retelling, reconfiguring, and revisiting the concept, phenomenon, event, or location from different angles, [. . .] infuse it with a nomadic spin that establishes multiple connections and lines of interaction" (Braidotti 2012, 230). In this way, rewriting narratives becomes a way of worlding through fabulation as a form of myth-making akin to religion, where imagination creates fantastic tales that are not only utopian but also stir the senses (and the emotions) to think of a world that exists, but in a different fashion (Barone and Eisner 2011; Bergson 1935; Garoian 1999, 2013; Haraway 2016; Wallin 2011a).

Storytelling becomes a creative method of remaking reality in all its actuality, but in such a way that curiosity makes visible what was hiding in plain sight, "it is curiosity about what might be possible that enables us to imagine and create a different, more ethical existence. We made the existence we have—it is not 'natural.' We can think and make another, and that is the task of ethical experimentation" (St. Pierre, Jackson, and Mazzei 2016, 102). Curious narratives become a window into the actual world through a strange or curious filter, heeding Lewis's (2020) call for a curious form of educational philosophy that "wanders, that yields to the features of curiosity that ensure it remains curious . . . [with] stylistic quirks and or odd, carefree subject matter" (104). As a set of real-world narratives written with an urgency and expressive perplexity, the book invites readers to become curious through the materiality of everyday encounters.

Stories are followed by a contextualization and analysis of the topics that were initially important to the experiences as well as those that have emerged in my return. Together, they create a set of interwoven transdisciplinary, transtemporal, and transversal connections. In other words, I start with a strange memory, and then I follow my curiosity to research the context and historical conditions of the phenomena in question. The research process and moments of discovery are woven into the chapters, with a combination of elements intended to create a different intensity or sense of divergence, such as asides labeled "curious paths," images and date stamps, or a screenplay style within the primary narrative. I then draw connections across paths through movement, stickiness, and porosity. Curious stories explore how institutional education has coded learning into disciplinary and curricular constructs, how young bodies have become commodities in the service of educational fundraising, and what clay bodies might teach about colonialism and industrialization. Together, they consider how vital curiosity becomes a more-than-human and collectivizing capacity that might act *with* the world, rather than on it.

I analyze vital curiosity's collective force along a spectrum of openness and rigidity, where intensive shifts affect the porosity of boundaries. I consider curiosity's spectrum of effects as it presses against the boundaries of embodied territories to reveal connections, movements, seepages, and flows that in turn illuminate a collective, communal, dynamic, and residual potential. Some chapters draw on Guattari's (1996, 2000) use of an ecosophical analysis as well as his articulation of transversality to reflect on vital curiosity's potential in everyday and institutional contexts. I consider how vital curiosity produces "coefficients of transversality" (Guattari 1996, 15), which is the degree of openness to difference created through encounters. This question of openness is nuanced, because completely open flows are equivalent to something like apathy, where experience or information merely moves across with little sedimentary or residual impact or remains. My intention is not to create a dichotomy between open and closed but a qualitative spectrum of ways that the world sticks together.

Overview of Parts and Chapters

The book is divided into three parts that correspond with vital curiosity's qualities and effects: disruptive, connective, and collective. They also align with thought's movement and intensity, inspired by Spinoza described above, evolving from perceptual shocks, to relational connections, and into a collective entanglement of joyful intuition. Part I, "Disruptive Curiosity: Unsettling Education's Neoliberal Monoculture," explores a series of questions about the control, coding, and commodification of bodies in education, with each chapter emerging from experiences in an elementary school. Echoing the sense of shock and critical confusion that the inquiries in this section explore, the tone of the chapters is frenzied at times, expressing an anxious energy driven by the speed and intensity of my curiosity. These lines of thought are less about curiosity as a subject, and more about curiosity as a disruptive force to question habituated norms and conditions in education.

Chapter 1, "What Can GMOs Teach us about Curriculum Reform? Coding Pedagogical Vitality through Neoliberal Logics," introduces concepts that will reemerge throughout the book. This chapter opens with my friend and I harvesting seeds from plants brought from her home to start a pollinator garden at an elementary school. In the process, I realized the only process I had with gardening came from small seed packets at the grocery store or Home Depot—

paralleling the divide between learning through a standardized curriculum versus lived experience. Through a series of memories related to gardening, the chapter traces connections between the commodification and corporatization of agriculture and neoliberal reforms of public education. Ultimately, I question how our diminishing ecological diversity resulting from pesticides and GMOs is akin to a decline in curiosity, as thought's vital potential. Rather than viewing this effect as a kind of death, the chapter initiates ethical questions about how this foreclosure produces unanticipated mutations, modulations, resistance, and residue in the form of affective surplus, anxiety, and alienation that are explored in later chapters. By examining the concept of expression as thought and vitality, the chapter begins the book's trajectory that will move across the boundaries of institutional spaces and the natural environment. This sets the stage for the following chapters that move back and forth between learning in schools and noninstitutional contexts. Political connections are argued as actualizations of technologies of control made visible through experiences in and out of the institution.

Chapter 2, "What Did the Cafeteria Just Become? Educational Fundraising's Affective Intensity," opens by describing the affective intensity of a fundraising rally I witnessed in the elementary school cafeteria from Chapter 1. I explore the sensorial and affective registers of the rally, specifically how the barrage of popular music, visual marketing of cheap toys and expensive cars provoked an animalic response from the students, with their bodies shaking and writhing together on the cafeteria floor. Moreover, the rally replaced "specials" for the day, meaning art, music, library, and physical education were skipped to promote the consumption of cheap toys and processed foods. The circumstance illuminated how certain interests are invited to alter the disciplinary norms and environmental intensity of the school while others are perpetually muted and controlled. This event sparked my curiosity about school fundraising broadly, and how bodies are affected in the school's existential territory. I explore the affective modulation of the school as existential territory and how the institutional context itself—psychoanalytic or pedagogical—mediates a collective life (Deleuze and Guattari 1983, 1987; Genosko, 2009). It shifts our focus from controlling expression, in order to limit thought, to operationalizing expression for profit through the animation of environmental stimuli. Here, the vital spirit (Bennett 2001) that has been stripped away from learning to create the elementary school monoculture is replaced by manufactured vitality to generate a neoliberal curiosity (Shankar 2020). This energetic drive emerges not from the pollinator's complex fertility but from an atmosphere charged by an industry built on the lack of public-school funding.

Chapter 3, "What Can a Body Earn? School Fundraising as Immaterial Labor and Affective Currency," continues to investigate the growing industry around educational fundraising, focusing specifically on Fun Run events as an embodied curriculum and territorializing force. Using a rhetorical analysis of promotional videos, I question how the events become forms of affective labor (Hardt and Negri 2004), illuminating shifts in the human body's role in schooling, from intellectual and civic participation to forms of physical labor that generate vital affective intensities only to deaden them as profitable commodities. In response, I consider how vital curiosity might subvert or redirect the energy of these accepted forms of affective labor in schooling, articulating a set of examples that embrace the radical potential of walking in histories of social protest and gardening as creative affective counterattacks.

Part II, "Connective Curiosity: Permeating Thresholds through Transcorporeal Movement," takes up curiosity's energy through "footpaths, pathways, and footways, tracks trodden, and trails traced along lines of desire and discovery" (Zurn 2021, 199). The gap of complexity and the emergence of unpredictable forms of material expression expand, as movement, bodies, duration, and sedimentation are critical themes that shift the curious process from one of unsettling shock and competitive consumption in Part I, to realize a more-than-human vitality and transcorporeal interconnectedness. Several of the experiences emerge from my role as an art teacher and my interest in photography as a mode of inquiry. The intersection of art and curiosity raises questions about the vital potential of both, in a move toward increasingly complex ways of relating to and understanding the world, as bodies expand to the soil, plants and animals, disciplinary knowledge, modes and objects of art and craft, to acknowledge centuries of human interactions. Forms of bodily extraction shift from human-oriented affective labor to centuries of physical extraction and sedimentation of native land, indigenous populations, and cultural values.

Chapter 4, "What if We Dig It Ourselves? Mapping a Transcorporeal Inquiry across the Composition of Clay Bodies," takes place during a field trip with college students, visiting a local resident's home to dig clay for a ceramics project rather than purchasing it commercially. Starting with limited knowledge of clay bodies, the inquiry creates transcorporeal (Alaimo 2010) connections where history and culture are felt in layers of matter, composed through an ecology of practices that crossed disciplinary, geographic, and temporal boundaries. *What if we dig it ourselves* becomes a radically connective proposition to realize we are always *making-with* the world, activating a sympoietic pedagogy to realize that "earthlings are *never alone*" (Haraway 2016, 58). Over the course of the day, clay's sticky substance forms connections across the oil and gas industry, histories of DIY practices, intersections of colonization and capitalism, with questions of organized religion and mysticism. Vital curiosity's connective and collective potential is revealed as we attended to compositions of the land, tools, bodies, relationships, and community values, diminishing our bounded individualism and representational distance to rehabilitate a contact with the earth, and realize collective transcorporeal effects across life-forms.

Chapter 5, "What Else Could We Create by Suspending Our Reality? Traveling Isolation's Intensity as Frictions of Potential," takes a different form and covers a longer stretch of time than previous chapters, where duration is given texture through months of daily notes and written communications, tracing three months during the initial global Covid-19 shutdown and isolation period. This chapter becomes a diary of curiosities and anxieties through periodic voice notes, texts, social media posts, and other forms of communication over the spring of 2020. As I grapple with a spectrum of emotions that range from curious optimism for a new future to desperation, anxiety, and hopelessness, different textures of curiosity emerge. I follow circuits of movement and thought through bodies, screens, affect, hormones, and material residues from industrial mining while experiencing social isolation. Swirling questions and conditions of hope and fear, imagination and disillusionment expressed through a range of voices create connections to scientific, economic, religious, and institutional elements from previous chapters. Again, science and religion become a means for understanding and explaining—historical sources for resolving uncertainty, and illuminating core questions in the philosophical history of vitalism. The vital difference in our everyday physical encounters was eliminated, and the curious potential of a world we have never seen was captured by the negative affects of a world void of desire for difference and variation.

Chapter 6, "Is This Land Just Layers of Bodies? Mapping Spectral Flows across Skeletal Forms," follows a curious attraction to the term, cactus skeletons. Using a rhetorical inquiry into a range of definitions of the word, skeleton, the chapter curiously traces cactus bodies as a node for connecting colonialist histories of the American West, native tribes, gold mining, and contemporary suburban sprawl. The attunement to cactus bodies and their skeleton forms activates movement across land and time, merging the unblinkered awareness of Chapter 4 with the durational flow of Chapter 5 extended across histories of bodily extraction. Similar to my questions of rhetoric around DNA that opened the book, this chapter follows corporeal connections between cactus and human bodies, following layers of dead bodies that constitute the desert southwest of

Texas and Arizona. Curiosity's detrimental potential is illuminated, providing nuance to the utopian embrace of the unknown and the novelty of experimentation by illuminating how the stakes of such engagement vary depending on one's positionality. The chapter maps transcorporeal connections across thresholds of existence, histories of invasive spread and mutation, considering how death creeps across the landscape. I introduce the term "porous curiosity" to address the necessity of thinking beyond bounded individualism, embracing vital curiosity's connective stickiness illuminating how education might be redirected to a politically, creatively, and ecologically collective imagination for rehabilitation.

Part III, "Collective Curiosity: Affirming our Ethico-Aesthetic Potential," merges the affective capacities and aesthetic inquiry processes from previous chapters to consider how vital curiosity becomes a collective, ethico-aesthetic, and ecologically diverse mode for living. While Parts I and II can be viewed as forming a dichotomy between nature and culture, suggesting that the outside of the institution is the space of free thought, we realize that this is not true. Transcorporeal inquiries in Part II reveal the historical and biotechnological capture of vitality on the environment and multispecies populations through colonialism and capitalism that parallels impacts realized within the school in Part I, but on a durational global scale. Part III explores the importance of attunement and intuition as collective forms of knowing and connecting in schools and everyday experiences. The dichotomy between learning in school or nature is merged, and the boundary of the human itself becomes porous (Benjamin and Lacis 1925) through questions of trans-species, transcorporeal, and transmaterial expression that consider ways of "promoting a new art of living in society" (Guattari 1995, 21). Themes, concepts, and memories start to fold in on each other in Part III, building on concepts of monoculture and pollination, shock and manufactured affect in Part I, and the circuits of connection between sympoietic pedagogies and transcorporeal inquiry of Part II, to realize our embodied and embedded ecologies of connection in Part III. In these final chapters, curiosity activates and takes form through nesting, joy, affective attunement, multispecies signaling and transmission, and response-ability, activated in a durational lived curriculum across and between a series of narratives.

Chapter 7, "What Can a Body Express? Nesting as Collective Sociality," explores the multivalent concept of nesting as an affective capacity and collective multispecies practice for world-building by mapping a transcorporeal inquiry across forms of affective expression. Corporeal seepages and biochemical assemblages illuminate interspecies signaling, and they are woven together through conceptual art, personal experiences, and curriculum theory to trace collective compositions across Green Leaf Volatiles, climate activism, conceptual art, lactation, nests, and petrichor to explore multispecies affective expressions, transmissions, and responses. Finally, this chapter returns to the classroom to explore teaching as a collectively embodied and embedded nesting practice vitalized through affective relations and feedback loops. Through these curious paths, I propose that we take up our intuitive capacities for affective connection and responsiveness as a collective sociality, realizing the sticky and porous potential of the social domain.

Chapter 8, "How Might We Live as Pollinators? The Joyful, Strange, and Vital Uncertainty of a Pedagogical Life," returns to the garden from Chapter 1 to focus on the art teacher, Denise, as an undervalued enigma within the overdetermined school territory. Tracing ecological and sympoietic transformations across Denise's life through stories, objects, and shared experiences, this chapter considers how "the art of life-living is the enthusiastic taking up of the adventure that is an ethico-aesthetics" (Manning 2020, 101). The chapter examines her classroom practice and how it merged with her life beyond the boundaries of the school, and how her curious subjectivity has composed and evolved over a lifetime. Vitality takes on a mythical energy, as a joyful affirmative force, illuminating porous boundaries of social and cultural norms that are both externalized and internalized. We see that her unwillingness to yield to the individualizing norms and stultifying rigidity of an education system that is bereft of curiosity yields undisciplined and immeasurable vitality to her collective pedagogical practice.

Chapter 9, "What if We Learn This Together? Composing Collective Ecologies through Curiosity's Radical Interconnectedness," develops a thought experiment that maps a collective curriculum on sensorial attunement and affective transmission that vibrated in the background of the book. The circuitry of my strange curriculum zigzags through experiences that are collective, solitary, and ecological, where inquiry is crafted through a range of techniques, realizing how the world is co-composed through vital curiosity as a force for collective participation across years of experiences and experimentation around sensory attunement, where art, again, becomes a powerful conduit for curious attractions and the formation of mutant coordinates, affirming the complexity of the world through playful experimentation.

Part I

Disruptive Curiosity
Unsettling Education's Neoliberal Monoculture

Part I, "Disruptive Curiosity: Unsettling Education's Neoliberal Monoculture," explores a series of questions about the control, coding, and commodification of bodies in education, with each chapter emerging from experiences in an elementary school. Throughout these chapters, I critically question the effects of neoliberal policies applied in schooling and curricular reform. Activated by a curiosity around seed harvesting and broader biological processes, I examine how we might understand curiosity in school environments differently, as a form of vital energy (or lack thereof), if viewed through the lens of genetic modification and biotechnology. After laying the foundation of the school as monoculture, I curiously encounter ways that the landscape becomes ecologically diversified through forms of affective labor, witnessing the activation of young bodies by parasitic industries that thrive off of the lack-based logic of public schools.

The concept of the gap of uncertainty emerges as a fundamental aspect of curiosity's vital potential, as a site of translation, emergence, transformation, and capture across the first three chapters. Concepts of sovereign and neoliberal curiosity (Zurn & Shankar 2020) become important ways of articulating how curiosity is captured and expressed as another form of biotechnology. Finally, the tone and energy of Part I shifts in intensity to express the shock and critical confusion that the inquiries in this section explore. The tone is, at times, frenzied and anxious, driven by the speed and affective force of my curious uncertainty and confusion. In these moments, experiences are less about curiosity as a subject and more about curiosity as a disruptive force to question habituated norms and conditions in education.

1

What Can GMOs Teach Us about Curriculum Reform? Coding Pedagogical Vitality through Neoliberal Logics

We start with a seed. Planting a seed is an act of faith that a future life is possible. Curiosity is similarly a belief in something more: a life, world, or understanding that is beyond what you currently know. And while a seed appears to be teleologically oriented toward a predetermined end, perhaps its life is more like curiosity than we might at first expect, as a seed is open to any number of contingent paths that may or may not lead to germination. Perhaps a seed is equally curious about the world into which it is thrown.

This chapter sets out on a thought experiment that originated in an elementary art classroom harvesting seeds for a school garden. The seeds generated a curiosity about biotechnological treatments and genetic modifications, creating a sticky path, where I continually noticed how agricultural rhetoric and values around isolation, discipline, and reproduction sounded so similar to themes, discourses, and practices of education. Recognizing these parallels, I questioned if similar biotechnological connections might emerge as well. Using concepts of expression, invisibility, coding, diversity, and biopolitical control, I map a network of connection between the vital potential of seeds and that of curiosity.

Seeds from Dead Bodies

The bell rang for the third period to begin, which was our planning period. Denise closed the door and pulled out stalks of dried basil, milkweed, and zinnia that she brought from her garden at home. She had explained that these plants attract bees and butterflies, so they would be ideal for the pollinator garden we were planting with the fourth-grade classes. We needed to revitalize the garden plots behind the school that the Parent Teacher Organization (PTO) constructed a couple years earlier. The plots always dried up in the summer when school was out. First, we needed to extract the seeds, so we spread the dried stalks out across the tables in the art classroom. The petals and seed heads of the milkweed were painfully sharp and itchy, but I was impressed at the amount of seeds we were retrieving. The only experience I had with pulling seeds was helping my friends separate them out of marijuana plants in high school. I was mystified and somewhat skeptical that this process would work. It seemed too easy. Why weren't we all doing this to grow produce at our homes?

Prior to this moment, I associated gardening with the packets of seeds sold in the grocery store, where images of herbs or flowers on the cover provided a preview of what to expect, with step-by-step instructions for planting them on the back. My connection to seeds had nothing to do with their life-giving capacity. Frankly, I had no idea where the seeds in the packets came from, and from my limited experience gardening, the process of germination seemed kind of magical, or just so elemental that I took it for granted. The sun is just there, and the soil just works. As I harvested the seeds from Denise's dried plants, I realized that my limited understanding of seed reproduction had come from schooling, where biological processes were mapped onto decontextualized science diagrams labeled with discipline-specific vocabulary. In this standardized curriculum, the seed was isolated from its environmental context, which is one among many ways that bodies (human bodies as well as bodies of knowledge) are disciplined in school. I had taken years of science classes, and even grew a little plant placed in the window at school, but the content never really stuck. Science seemed to isolate knowledge *about* life from life itself.

Biology's Disciplined Visibility

Richard Doyle (1997) argued that, as a representational and rhetorical system of study, "biology's project was, in some sense, to make the invisibility of life visible or at least articulable" (113). Biology articulates life's energy in terms of functions, traits, expressions, and effects, which are then translated into lines, charts, measurements, and timetables. It simplifies the complex ecological elements and diverse interconnectivity between and among organic life in its lived context. The complex vitality of learning is similarly represented in terms of linear stages, with an emphasis on measurable or *articulable* outcomes. To facilitate learning transactions with easily articulated results, classroom content is simplified into elemental processes or functions, aiming for memorization, mastery, and recitation (Davis, Sumara, and Luce-Kapler 2000). Moreover, to create efficient learning transactions, the ecological complexity of educational content on living processes is minimized or phenomena are completely decontextualized from their place in everyday life. In this curriculum, seeds are reduced to plants' reproductive function, while learning (as the cultivation of knowledge for lifelong growth) equally becomes teleologically oriented toward prescribed outcomes. Seeding education becomes ceding to instrumentalized learning.

While "direct observation is naturally more vivid and vital" (Dewey 2007, 120) than decontextualized worksheets, exposure alone does not necessarily equate to thoughtful action. There is more to forming this relationship. Providing contextual data, connecting to prior understanding, and incorporating opportunities for physical experimentation creates conditions for students to form their own ideas and questions about the content at hand. Even though progressive educators have articulated the necessity of hands-on experimentation that connects disciplinary content to everyday life for over a century, many science classes in US public schools continue to be taught through representational formats aimed at "the accumulation and acquisition of information for purposes of reproduction in recitation and examination . . . due to a static cold-storage ideal of knowledge [which is] inimical to educative development . . . [that] swamps thinking" (Dewey 2007, 120). In my experience, science was swamped with simplified and decontextualized information aimed at accumulation rather than meaningful connection.

Curious Drift . . . the Gap of Uncertainty

Dewey (2007) importantly argued that the gap between the familiar and unfamiliar—the gap of uncertainty—in education is the space of imaginative and creative potential. It is important to understand that the gap is not a lack or deficiency, but instead, the site of unknown potential and the passageway of emergent translation. This gap is the place of meaning-making and connection, but if it is too large, connections will either be superficial or unmet. While, if the gap is too small, novel associations or the creative leap of new ideas will be stifled.

Let's imagine the gap of uncertainty in one's mind, where curiosity is sparked through confusion and attention to difference, where connective threads begin to vibrate, seeking out a familiar element to which they might attach this uncanny attraction. If that teeming energy of uncertainty is provided an answer too quickly, the vitality of the imagination is limited. At the same time, the unpredictable imagination might take too long or move in too many directions, becoming a vulnerability in overdetermined contexts that demand predictability, such as education and agriculture. In which case, the gap's potential must be constrained and ordered. This invisible gap seems to be the site of potential across a number of milieus, as I will explore throughout this chapter, where a vital indeterminate energy is primed for translation, anticipating movement toward an undecided future, the chaotic space of a "people to come" (Deleuze and Guattari 1994, 218). Might the gap be curiosity's space of energetic attraction to the unfamiliar—the site of desire? If so, then the gap contains the vital connection that determines what the body can do.

The Predictable Yield

As I stated earlier, prior to the experience harvesting seeds for the school garden, I associated the biological vitality of gardening with the images and instructions on small mass-produced seed packets. I thought of the few times I *had* attempted gardening, in terms of success or failure, rather than any relationship to biology. The first gardening experience I remember was at my grandmother's house.

Bright Yellow Squash

Grandma never had an elaborate vegetable garden, but she always had bright, colorful flowers throughout her front and back yards. No one in her suburban neighborhood seemed to have vegetable gardens. Dad was very skilled at lawn care—I mean, Grandma's lawn was the best-looking one for blocks around. It was a point of pride for the entire family, and the mowing, raking, trimming, and leaf collection were part of our family's Saturday ritual. In the summer, Dad would create a perfect checkerboard pattern in the yard with the lawnmower. It was a kind of art and science for him.

One year, we decided to make a small vegetable garden on the side of her house. I had never planted my own seeds, so I got to pick which ones we would grow from the selection of seed packets at the grocery store. I loved summer squash, and the bright yellow gourds stood out among the other cover photos of herbs and vegetables. My dad and grandfather prepared the plot, and I distributed the seeds once it was ready. When I returned two weeks later, the squash were enormous—far larger than any that I had seen in a grocery store. I had no idea how they had grown so much larger. In retrospect, I remember that Dad treated the grass with weed killer on the recommended cycle, and I bet he had added the right amount of fertilizer to the germinating squash.

Their bold yellow bodies stood out against the brick wall of her house—curiously calling out to me. Gardens don't remain bold and lush, though. Green and brown stalks and leaves fill the space over time, and the dense messiness of vegetation and the mixed growing cycles can create an aesthetic that is counter to the highly desired checkerboard suburban lawn. A garden might seem too unkempt, a little too natural. I don't remember what happened to that small garden, but it didn't last much longer than the cycle of those giant yellow squash.

The memory of the large yellow squash stuck with me, but it was not because I learned anything about gardening or seed germination. Our success in meeting the potential of the bright yellow squash, which was pictured in advance in the photograph on the outside of the seed packet, simply confirmed my prior understanding that gardens started from those little packets. Moreover, that association was nested within a much broader cultural context related to suburban lawns, my Grandma's house, and a nostalgia for summer. It was a success story that my dad and I shared. Unlike the science diagrams of seed germination and photosynthesis that decontextualized the processes, in Grandma's garden there was an actual plant, and I observed it meeting its potential. Importantly though, because learning science through worksheets and diagrams that omit the natural context, the experience at Grandma's house was able to fill in that contextual gap that school had omitted, creating a connection with gardening as an overdetermined process of following step-by-step instructions to achieve a successful outcome pictured in advance. Time and reproduction were prioritized, and in a few days or weeks, I might have a shiny yellow squash. And if not, oh well, I could try again next spring. While I touched the soil and distributed the seeds, I was not interested in how it was composed or what it might do beyond the outcome predicted on the packet.

Moreover, the convenience of purchasing a seemingly unlimited supply of seeds and other agricultural products in shopping centers also makes them easily disposable. I had never considered how I might replant them as we were preparing to do in Denise's classroom, because that would require a future. In my mind, they were dead. But that day, pulling the seeds from the dried stalks felt very different. The seeds were attached to a body. It housed them. The spikey milkweed pods pricked my hands as I tried to separate the seeds. These seeds had a past and a geographical context that made their potential pulsate differently, where a new set of questions and connections emerged.

Education mystifies nature on the one hand by eliminating firsthand experiences as inefficient or messy and oversimplifies it on the other by minimizing the complexity of nature so that it is taken for granted as a machine that can be mastered as well as manipulated. Dewey (2007) argued that educational content severed from thoughtful action created a "dead, mind-crushing load" (164). Could this dead, mind-crushing load be the elimination of the appreciation for life's interconnected vitality, and the elimination of curiosity's intense desire to know the world differently?

Coding Vitality's Invisible Force

While disciplinary techniques in education and agriculture have isolated, simplified, and standardized processes of production for predictability and efficiency, a different form of control has emerged in the last thirty years. Power relations shifted from modes of discipline to the development of biopolitical technologies in science and society that could expand modes of control.

> Whereas disciplinary techniques transform bodies, biopolitical technologies are aimed at a multiplicity inasmuch as it constitutes a global mass, invested with overall processes that are specific to life—such as birth, death, production, and illness. Disciplinary techniques only know the body and the individual, while biopower targets the population. (Lazzarato 2006, 178–9)

Here, biopower targets the organization of life itself, where the fertility, reproduction, and expression of an entire species is subject to new modes of control that intersect across life-forms, seeds being one example (Rose 2008).

The Treated Garlic

A few weeks after we harvested the seeds, Denise invited me to her house to see her "backyard ecosystem," as she described it. She was in the process of turning over the garden for the winter crops. The early stems of a number of plants peeked out above the soil. Denise pointed to garlic bulbs growing on one side of the plot and told a story of her trip to San Francisco, where friends gave her a bulb from Gilroy, California. I had actually been to Gilroy about fifteen years earlier, and I remembered my surprise at the smell of garlic in the air.

But, wait, was she saying that the garlic bulb in her garden was the one that her friend gave her? Or that they had continued to grow them from it? Even though we had spent an hour in her classroom prepping seeds for the pollinator garden, garlic seemed different because I was familiar with it, unlike the milkweed. Could I just take any of my common kitchen vegetables and plant them in my backyard?

I asked her why we all weren't just replanting our vegetables from the grocery store. Denise explained that they might grow if they haven't been treated: "Well, I've heard that if they've been treated they won't produce. Yeah Monsanto. . . . If they don't want you to grow your own potatoes, you won't grow another potato—you have to get these little starters. I'm learning a lot every day with this garden."

What did she mean by *treated*? I had heard people talk about issues with Monsanto and genetically modified organisms (GMOs), but I never really understood any of it. I had seen foods labeled "non-GMO," but I always thought it was the same as farmers mixing different breeds to create new varieties. The invisibility of the processes, in nature, on the farm, or in a lab, made it easy to conflate them all. Large-scale monocrop farming practices have maximized production and efficient yield at great environmental cost (Shiva 2016). These practices have disciplined crops' life cycles into predictable growth patterns and production yields by isolating and reproducing a single plant, stripping the surrounding soil of nutrients over time. While monocrop farming practices have been common for over a century, genetic modification is different. The danger of genetics expands the disciplinary coding of vitality to the modulation of its force.

Like biology, the field of genetics emerged, in part, from an interest in mapping (making visible) how dominant and recessive traits are passed on through heredity. This knowledge was quickly applied to predicting and controlling genetic expression, which determined and modified a plant's vital capacities and ecological variability. Scientists at multinational agricultural corporations developed biotechnologies that control the functionality of organic life-forms, thus harnessing the mystical force of vitality in the interest of science partnered with industry (Shiva 2016). Monsanto (the multinational agrochemical and agricultural biology corporation mentioned in the story about garlic) is a commonly referenced industry example. Monsanto was one of the first agricultural companies to genetically modify seeds. They developed the process in conjunction with their herbicide, Roundup, which is one part of a line of products that the company patented to withstand pesticides in large-scale agricultural production—including genetically modified seeds (Pollan 2001). These products would ultimately alter the entire global agricultural landscape, which includes small-scale operations like Denise's garden.

Denise had mentioned "treatment" where the genetic modification of seeds has a twofold effect. As part of the Roundup line of products, the seeds are resistant to the toxins in the chemical herbicide, so farmers buy the herbicide to eliminate pests in their crop production, along with seeds that will not be affected by the herbicide. The genetic advancements in the treatment of seeds limited plants' ability to naturally respond to environmental elements, and created a vulnerable dependence on pesticides and fertilizers. The other effect of the seeds' genetic modification is that the seeds are made sterile and only live through one growth cycle. In other words, plants are stripped of their natural responsive and reproductive capacities. They lack the capacity to become affected by and connected to their environment, genetically isolated from their ecological context to serve their singular productive function. At the same time, the modifications also kill the detrimental "pests" (i.e., weeds, insects, pollinators, caterpillars) that try to eat the crops. This, in turn, expands the circle of destruction to future cross-pollination of plants and other life-forms nearby. These biotechnologies not only affect the body and future of that crop and its surrounding soil; GMOs affect the future of all surrounding life-forms.

In recent years, Monsanto has reorganized and been purchased, but the promotional justifications for GMOs is common across the industry. They claim that the biotechnological innovation creates stronger seeds and more resilient crops that require fewer resources. Nature is articulated as a threat, where pests, weather, weeds, and disease are challenges to be withstood. They claim to address these challenges by minimizing environmental impacts that would affect future crop growth. This industry rhetoric suggests that technological innovation empowers farmers, strengthens seeds, and provides needed protection from environmental pests. This is false.

They fail to mention that this biotechnological modification addresses environmental challenges by eliminating surrounding plant and insect species, diminishing ecological variability and complexity, and that future crop species are protected by manufacturing seeds that only survive one life cycle, so they cannot evolve in unpredictable ways. Their autopoietic capacity has been eliminated, so seeds can no longer reproduce. Preserving the singular function of the crop in this way creates a dependency on these agricultural products among farmers and seeds alike, because their ability to become self-sustaining has been genetically eliminated. The exponential impacts on the organic interspecies symbiosis and complex biodiversity of its entire ecological community are dire (Moore, 2015; Pierce 2013; Pollan 2001; Shiva 2016).

Vitality as Intellectual Property

Public awareness about the potential dangers of biotechnology and detrimental effects of GMOs is growing. At the same time, the challenge of meeting the agricultural demands of an ever-increasing human population allows the industry to justify their practices in the eyes of the public and policymakers. The year 1998 marked a critical moment in public policy when the genetic code of specific seeds became a matter of intellectual and commercial property:

> In March 1998, patent number 5,723,765, describing a novel method for the "control of plant gene expression," was granted jointly to the U.S. Department of Agriculture and a cottonseed company called Delta and Pine Land. The bland language of the patent obscures a radical new genetic technology: introduced into any plant, the gene in question causes the seeds that plant makes to become sterile—to no longer do what seeds have always done.... Genetic engineers have discovered how to stop on command the most elemental of nature's processes, the plant-seed-plant-seed cycle by which plants reproduce and evolve. The ancient logic of the seed—to freely make more of itself ad infinitum, to serve as both food and the means of making more food in the future—has yielded to the modern logic of capitalism. Now viable seeds will come not from plants but from corporations. (Pollan 2001, 231–2)

This quote illuminates a critical shift from the *ancient logic of the seed* to the *modern logic of capitalism* through the biotechnological control of expression and reproduction. Patent number 5,723,765 protected a method of coding that diminished farmers' ability to count on nature's autopoietic capacity to reproduce. Instead, the modified seeds produce a short-term yield and do not regenerate. Companies like Monsanto control and commodify nature's fundamental capacity to live, connect, and diversify, claiming that this novel method for controlling plant gene expression is their own invention, patented as intellectual property (Pollan 2001; Shiva 2016).

Biotechnology's control over gene expression and reproduction becomes the site of contestation and profit as well as the space of potential for revitalization. If, as Pollan describes in the quote above, Delta and Pine Land's patent allows the control of "plant gene expression," then Delta and Pine Land controls plant variability. To put it simply, gene expression determines what a cell can do. As Doyle (1997) explained, a gene is expressed as a set of information or instructions in DNA, which is converted or translated into functional products, such as protein. The gap between DNA and proteins is the site of translation and conversion, where the plant's vital potential for connection and expression is determined.

Revisiting the curious drift about the gap of uncertainty above, the invisible gap of movement and translation made articulable by biology, and which parallels the gap of curious drift and meaning-making in learning, we see in the example of GMOs, how biotechnologies territorialize the critical site of potential and capitalize on the control of genetic expression. *Again, the gap contains the vital connection that determines what the body can do.* By controlling the gap, you control expression, and expression is vitality. I explore this gap for the remainder of the chapter, returning to my question above about curiosity's desiring force in the gap of uncertainty as a space of potential in the biopolitics of schooling.

Fragmenting Connection, Redirecting Desire, and Sterilizing Thought

In the following sections, I transpose the analysis of genetic manipulation of seeds onto the vital force of thought in schooling to consider how educational ecologies reveal parallel effects as those in agriculture. Like DNA, curriculum could be considered a machine of expression and thought within schools, which has been similarly manipulated as a tool for isolation and coding to reduce variability and guarantee predictable reproduction through disciplinary order and efficient pedagogical processes (Pinar 2012). The "education marketplace" is now populated by multinational corporations whose prioritization of profit has operationalized similar biopolitical technologies to control expression and limit variability (Pierce 2013).

Like the seed packets, standardized curriculum packages information into small sets of decontextualized data that is simplified and converted into education's products to be applied at scale. Both seed packets and school curricula isolate the radical and reproductive vitality of difference and variability. Students learn to think of disciplinary content in isolation from diverse connections and organic variability, which limits their understanding of life's complex ecological interconnectedness. Moreover, the fragmentation of subject areas into disciplinary bodies of knowledge functions similarly to a monocrop approach to farming that disciplines crops' life cycles into predictable growth patterns and production yields by isolating and reproducing a single plant, stripping the surrounding soil of nutrients over time. Similarly, in the curriculum-as-plan (Aoki 1986; Pinar and Irwin 2005), the desired outcome of education is articulated in advance through measurement devices calibrated to capture specific outputs, creating an image of thought, where the ability to think outside of those measurements is discouraged. As Jason Wallin (2011b) argues:

> Born of opposition and negation, the curriculum-as-plan halts the lines of movement between virtual (unthought) and actual, severing itself from the embryonic field of relations herein dubbed the curriculum. In this way, the

curriculum-as-plan is synonymous with the lauded institutional ideals of predictability, organization, and prescription. (294)

Like the genetically modified seed's inability to respond to ecological variability, the curriculum-as-plan has disconnected the potential of the yet unknown from the embryonic field of relations. Here, the embryonic field of relations is the gap of uncertainty, translation, and connection.[1]

Similar to the agriculture industry's rhetoric that fallaciously suggests it empowers farmers and strengthens seeds, neoliberal curriculum reforms are normalized through claims that they support teachers and strengthen students' learning through testing cycles, quantifiable outcomes, ARD (admission, review, and dismissal) processes, and AYP (adequate yearly progress) figures, which have become a monolingual system functioning like the DNA of the US public school system. These tools, embedded in the curriculum-as-plan, code intellectual and pedagogical expression and create a sense that learning only exists within the boundaries of the system. Education policy, in tandem with the educational marketplace, creates an image of educational life, isolating, decontextualizing, and commodifying information; where, like seed germination, thinking itself is articulated in terms of a narrow set of numerical data (Lewis and Hyland 2022). This normalization of learning articulated as data, and data as truth, becomes a kind of conditioning for consensus and diminished response-ability, where Colebrook (2008) argues that

> the very idea of truth, as that towards which thought ought to be led, was responsible for a politics of normalisation. We no longer actively question what our life ought to become so much as aim to know, discover, manage and communicate the facts or data of life. The allure of *not-thinking*, of being led by an image of man, of failing to think. (36, emphasis in original)

In this case, *not-thinking* rigidifies a desire and ethics born elsewhere, where life and its ethical uncertainty are resolved in advance, and simply need to be ordered. It begs the question, is the force of public education actually to encourage the population to *not think*?

Curiosity's Vulnerability and Vitality

This chapter opened by setting forth a thought experiment to map connections across the coded lives of agriculture and education. In this final section, I connect the control of the seed to the modulation of curiosity, becoming at times, a desire for disciplinary mastery and at others, a vital capacity for connection. Doyle's (1997) assertion about the gap of untranslatable vital connection between DNA and protein is the critical site of potential for imagining the open space of undetermined desire, where schooling overdetermines the translation between curious expressions and functional outcomes (redirecting a potential drive toward complexity to predetermined ends). In this scenario, the gap of untranslatable vitality in curious expression is coded and directed to a devastating split that allows a standardized illusion of the body, knowledge, and seed to fragment nature's complex processes into discrete bits of data stripped of substance, directed only at testing outcomes. It prioritizes short-term yield over long-term sustainability.

As I contemplated garlic bulbs in Denise's garden, I realized how genetic modification eliminated seeds' regenerative capacity and life-giving potential, which was different from pulling the seeds for the garden and planting squash. The seeds' connection to vitality was minimized, isolated, and decontextualized in schooling through simplified representations of organic processes. By pulling seeds from dead bodies, I discovered how natural processes are made invisible through mass production, where convenience and packaging diminishes a desire to engage in nature's time and complexity. Learning as a complex, connective process, is reduced to an illusory quantification akin to the seed's diminished capacity to "freely make more of itself ad infinitum" (Pollan 2001, 232).

While disciplinary isolation and decontextualization can inhibit students' understanding of ecological complexity, a decontextualized curriculum that determines meanings and connections in advance might be even more dangerous. The second experience—planting bright yellow squash—illuminates how setting forth an image of life in advance can increase a consensual desire to follow *that toward which thought ought to be led*, like the photograph on the cover of the seed packet, which predicted the squash's potential. The image of life on the seed packet promotes only certain desirable traits as a form of commodification that narrowly informed my understanding of vegetation and seed vitality to an existence linked only to its capitalist teleology. By suggesting that there is one right answer or a specific path to follow without allowing students freely create their own values or ideas, making *more of them ad infinitum*, students' capacity for imaginative thought, individual connection, and idea formation is stifled.

The curriculum-as-plan affirms the politics of normalization, where value is assigned to an image of life provided in advance, safely isolated from the complexity of lived environmental conditions (Wallin 2010). Similar to the dependence on fertilizers in the corporate agricultural monoculture, students begin to rely on the predetermined curriculum as the primary driver of their educational vitality. This organic life-and-death connection between learning and control is echoed in Freire's (2000) use of the concept, biophilia, as a love of life, inspired by Erick Fromm. Freire applied it to curiosity as a biophilic relationship to learning. Moreover, Freire applies its opposite, a necrophilic relationship to knowledge and learning, a love and desirous longing for death, which is rooted in control and possession. The neoliberal educational landscape diminishes and directs curiosity's biophilic capacity to form attractions and build connections. In this barren landscape, curiosity finds other forms of expression to carry forward, redirecting the desire toward mastery and judgment, as forces of sovereign power cultivated and normalized in the system driven by consensus and accountability. Here, sovereign curiosity (Zurn 2018) emerges as a necrophilic form or *treatment* to curiosity's biophilic potential.

Curiosity's creative mobility toward the unfamiliar is redirected toward a consensus, reinforced through normalization as an ethics of sameness. Curiosity's pesty expressions with unpredictable offshoots become a nuisance, muted by negative reception and affectively discouraged through disciplinary norms in schools. Similar to the unkempt garden in the manicured suburban landscape, curious attunement can be perceived as being off-track, unfocused, or causing distractions, behaviors that are treated as pests and weeds in monocultural classroom ecologies. In addition to a diminished capacity for attuning to difference, educational monocultures intentionally strip variability created through curiosity's critical capacity expressed in questions. Like the pesticide that kills both weeds and pollinators, questions can express distraction in schools, as a sign of curious drift (pollination) to be eliminated through discipline, guilt, and anxiety (techniques for controlling responsiveness and variability). Such pedagogical pesticides blunt responsiveness to the complexity of ecological connections, diminishing students' criticality as a curious capacity. Freire (1998) described questioning's critical vitality in learning,

> Curiosity as restless questioning, as movement toward the revelation of something hidden, as a question verbalized or not, as search for clarity, as a moment of attention, suggestion, and vigilance, constitutes an integral part of the phenomenon of being alive. There could be no creativity without the curiosity that moves us and sets us patiently impatient before a world that we did not make, to add to it something of our own making. (37–8)

Freire's articulation of curiosity as forms of movement, attention, and being alive underscores the creative force I attribute to vital curiosity, pollinating connections, expanding variation, and fostering biodiversity as a form of movement toward the *embryonic field of relations*.

Through the process of this thought experiment, I have realized that rather than viewing the sterilization of thought as death, thinking can instead become a form of *bio nullius* or empty life (Shiva 2016), illuminated in both the garden and the school, where nature's creativity and diversity have been stripped from its embodied expression, creating a void and a longing (explored further in Chapters 2 and 3). Shiva (2016) argues: "every seed is an embodiment of millennia of nature's evolution and centuries of farmers' breeding. It is the distilled expression of the intelligence of the Earth and of farming communities" (xviii). As I will explore in Part III of this book, curiosity becomes a more-than-human, affective, and intuitive capacity that connects with the intelligence of the earth and ecological complexity, a biophilic drive toward vitality and variability. Like the modification of the seeds' expression, the consensual force of education acts as an affective biopower (Anderson 2012), diminishing the complex, drifting, cross-pollinating, and dynamic mutational desire that drives curiosity's vital intensity, which is born out of movement, memory, and connection with the world. Vital curiosity can be fragile, vulnerable to toxic ecological conditions, like those faced by the butterflies and bees we hoped to attract in our pollinator garden, but the key is the gap of uncertainty, the invisible force of movement toward nature's creativity, embracing ecological diversity, and connection to the embryonic field of relations.

2

What Did the Cafeteria Just Become? Educational Fundraising's Affective Intensity

This chapter returns to the elementary school and describes my experience witnessing a fundraising rally in the cafeteria, which sparked my curiosity about school fundraising broadly, and how bodies are affected in the school's existential territory. I explore the sensorial and affective registers of the rally, specifically considering the barrage of popular music, with visual marketing of cheap toys and expensive cars that innervated students' bodies. This energetic drive emerges from an atmosphere charged by an industry built on the lack of public school funding. Using Guattari's (2000) ecosophic approach, I attune to the material and immaterial elements within the school's existential territory, mapping how the intensity of the social, mental, and environmental vectors are modulated to alter students' affective responses (de Freitas 2014). The experience enlivened my curiosity about ways that certain interests are invited to disrupt the school's disciplinary norms while others are perpetually muted and controlled.

The Big Kahuna

It was my last day student teaching, and Denise had the day off. She told me that the Big Kahuna would be coming and the schedule would be different, but she didn't say much else. I was instructed to bring the fifth-grade class to the cafeteria at the first bell. When the bell rang, Principal Parker's voice filled the classroom: "Third, fourth, and fifth graders now need to move to the cafeteria." Several of the students in the three back rows quickly looked up: "Oh yeah, Ms. Coats! Today is the Big Kahuna!" John, Ashley, and Ryan hurried to the doorway to be at the front of the line. I opened the door and let in the clamor of other lines forming in the music room and library down the hall.

We filed out to merge with the slow-moving stream of bodies flowing toward the cafeteria. The most efficient path was to head out the exterior door and back into the cafeteria from the car drop-off area. When the sun hit the kids' skin outside, the slow shuffling of their legs turned into skips and their silence shifted quickly to giggles and squeals as they saw other friends entering the building. We entered the cafeteria, where loud dance music filled the room. Teachers flanked the walls, ushering students into rows on the floor. As they were corralled together, teachers yelled for the children to sit on their hands, but that would only keep them calm momentarily. The students seemed to know what was about to happen. Their growing bodies fidgeted with excitement, packed tightly next to each other, trying awkwardly to sit cross-legged and cheek-to-cheek. The principal stepped up to the microphone:

> Okay, let's calm down. We all know it's a big day that you all look forward to. As you know, we are going to be starting our annual fundraiser. I know that many of you get excited about the prizes that you may be able to win, but I want you to know how important your contribution is to our entire school. So let's start it off strong this year. Let's give a big applause for our visitor—you all see him year after year, and he is going to tell you about the great new items you can sell and the prizes you may be able to win.

On cue, the loud bass of a popular dance song shook the cafeteria. The kids could no longer contain themselves. The room erupted in a roar of screams and cheers as the sea of young bodies began to gyrate. They had clearly seen this before (anticipation and predictability). I looked around, disturbed by the screaming kids who I had just seen yawning in my classroom. In the two months that I had been at Roosevelt Elementary, I had not witnessed this kind of energy in any other space. These were the same kids who had walked into my art room less than an hour earlier, half asleep, with heavily lidded eyes. A man dressed in slacks and a tie (not even a Hawaiian shirt!) approached the stage. This was the Big Kahuna? He walked to the microphone:

> OK, OK, I know we are excited for a new year. As you know I am here from the Big Kahuna, and we are going to raise more profits this year than we ever have! Am I right? I can tell that this group is ready to win! Because as you know, we are number one in student incentives. We spend more on the best prizes to motivate all of you to sell and do your best to raise money for your school! In the last year, the Big Kahuna has netted more profits from school fundraisers than any previous year!

Was this not strange to the other adults in the room? He was pitching this to a group of eight- to ten-year-olds. The Big Kahuna continued:

> As always, we have our best-selling cookie dough!!! Yes, I know all of your families look forward to this every year! But this year, we also have new packs

of soup that your parents can easily take to work or that you can pop in the microwave after school!

Now, we know it's never a good idea to go alone to strangers' houses to sell these items, right? A better idea might be to have your parents take the catalog to work or church or ask relatives. Your school will receive a percentage of everything that you sell. And if your parents or relatives don't want to buy from the catalog, they can just give a money donation. As I said, your school will get a portion of all of the revenue earned.

Wait. What? The school only gets a portion of the earnings, even if people just donate money without buying the company's products? Does this not seem strange to anyone else? I looked across the cafeteria, shocked and disgusted, at the sea of children whose bodies writhed uncontrollably, rubbing against each other and screaming, with spittle and froth forming at their lips while the loud bass pumped from speakers on the stage and a loop of images of toys and pizza played on the screen. The Big Kahuna began again:

Yes, that's right, look at all of the prizes you can win this year! For selling just three items, you can win Space Slime!! And for just twelve items, you can win Minion Goggles!!! And finally, the grand finale: the Hummer Limo Ride with Pizza Party!

The students roared with cheers again. As the bass thumped, a bold yellow background flashed on the screen, and the image in the center was a long Hummer limousine with pizzas edited in all around it. It was the most popular prize, and with this image the room once again erupted. The kids began to reach forward, screaming and jeering. The Grand Prize Hummer Limo Pizza Party had clearly earned an important status among the kids. The crowd of children ecstatically waved their arms in the air, looking at each other squealing at what seemed to be the highlight of the fall semester. Students and their families would sell over $300 worth of products, not to mention the time and effort put into this process, to ride in a Hummer limo and eat pizza one afternoon during school hours. This in addition to the blatant advertising for yet another disgustingly wasteful commodity: the Hummer.

Atmospheric Intensities, Bodily Contagion, and Affective Attraction

A new atmospheric intensity was moving through the school, territorializing the cafeteria, hallways, and students' bodies, which had been vibrating differently since the early announcement to come to the cafeteria. As they excitedly filed into the room, the energy began to shift. Most of the kids had attended similar rallies in the past—their memory created anticipation as an attraction to the familiar with a layer of excitement in the small gap of uncertainty. It was a space of curious unpredictability, where memory functions differently than in Chapter 1. There, my memories of the squash and garlic affirmed my understanding of them via representation. Here, the students' memory of the Big Kahuna was associated with a break from schooling, which was an emotional connection that meant a new experience was imminent. The energy of this anticipation was met with the barrage of dance music filling the space, where the electronic rhythmic bass required us to yell, amplifying the vibrations so that students' squeals, screams, and laughter were not as audible as they might be in the normal sonic atmosphere of the school (Brennan 2004; de Freitas 2018).

The experience resonated with Barad's (2015) description of atmospheric anticipation just before lightning strikes: "Desire builds, as the air crackles with anticipation. Lightning bolts are born of such yearnings. Branching expressions of prolonged longing, barely visible filamentary gestures, disjointed tentative luminous doodlings—each faint excitation of this desiring field is a contingent and suggestive inkling of the light show yet to come" (387). The crackles of anticipation, which increased as we filed in and sat down, contagiously merged across the bodies corralled on the floor. It may at first appear a purely pragmatic choice to fit as many students in the space as possible, but they were touching on the floor rather than separated in chairs around tables as they would have been at lunch. The disciplinary norms that controlled the movement and isolation of bodies were disrupted. The students were in direct contact with each other and with the ground, thumping from the intensity of the bass coming from the large speakers at the front of the room (de Freitas 2014; Knight 2016).

Next, the principal approached the stage, further modulating the intensity of the room as she welcomed the corporate fundraising representative, anticipating the roar of the children crowded on the floor. She prepared the intensive shift, her preemptive strike of sorts, inviting a new force into the space of the school. Next, the auditory and haptic assault of the song "Gangnam Style" ruptured the space to ignite students' frenzied responses. The loop of flashing images of cheap, plastic toys and expensive cars locked in the children's affective desire, provoking an animalic longing as their bodies shook and writhed together on the cafeteria floor. And then the corporate rep, the Big Kahuna, stepped up on the stage. I was amazed at how much control the man had over them at that moment. He could have said anything.

Corporate Parasites

This event illuminated ways that students' values are produced and reified through neoliberal shifts that have corporatized public school funding. In Chapter 1, I discussed Colebrook's (2008) description of a life produced in advance, that simply needs to be ordered, creating an ethics of *not-thinking*, as a way in which one ought to live. In my experience with the fundraising rally, the idea of not thinking and the notion of an ethics framed by entrepreneurial values were operationalized. While my initial shock at the cafeteria scene related to its modulation of the intensive registers of the space, my curiosity quickly turned to the effects on the children and the disinterestedness of all the adults in the room.

The attraction of the Big Kahuna event came from a complex assemblage of sociopolitical conditions that deprive schools of necessary resources, then infuse the culture with a belief that the conditions are of their own making and that they should bear the individual responsibility of remedying the situation (Ravitch 2013). The normalization of capitalist values and this lack-based subjectivity directs the community's desire, justifying the need and celebration of the fundraising event to interrupt the rest of the curricular composition. As a supposed expression of self-reliance and entrepreneurial agency, fundraising is framed as an ethical responsibility of all members of the school community. The experience of collectivity and the affective surge that is generated in the school environment is mediated by competition for individual prizes in the fundraising campaign. It aligns with the broader accountability culture in schools, that creates a desire bound to externally determined measurements and outcomes that are then tied to state budgetary formulas, which direct the system's choices, movement, time, and priorities. Within this system, the substance of schooling is composed around capitalist logics, which is imbued in the educational content produced and consumed within it (i.e., math, reading, science, history).

Fundraising practices have now emerged into a parasitic industry of its own, relying on communities' internalization of the lack-based narrative. Think about that idea of the parasite: an outcropping on the side of the body, taking from it. The affective vitality of learning driven by curiosity and connection has been replaced by assessment anxiety. As parasites, fundraising industries recognize this emotional terrain, where enthusiasm for learning has turned to stress and boredom. Fundraising events like the one in the cafeteria, act as modes of affective exploitation, extracting the emotional energy that has been repressed in schools, then redirecting the emotional registers toward entrepreneurial values (Anderson 2012; Lazzarato 1996). They feed the lack-based narrative to produce an image of the students as entrepreneurial fundraising heroes. By intervening in the overcoded educational landscape (Davies 1982, 2000) with a vitality produced in the rally, they exploit students' need for positive energy, and direct their desire toward the same neoliberal capitalist values that have created a lack of funding for public schooling in the first place.

Thing-Power as a Force for Desire and Enchantment

I watched this atmospheric shift emerge as the Big Kahuna approached the microphone. His body activated a strange attraction. The students' sensitivity to a shift in the ordering conditions of the school created tangible effects and revealed their openness to receiving a new educational vitality. The drought of energetic variation made the students particularly receptive to ecological diversity, similar to the seed made vulnerable by its limited exposure to environmental stimuli (Chapter 1). The production and control of desire in the cafeteria that day was ingenious. The students' extreme excitement about the rupturing of their everyday institutional assemblage through the corporate fundraising rally reveals the value of the emotional intensity within the environment. The production of affect was the company's commodity, realizing how "affect names the intensive quality of life," the event modulated "the risings and fallings, the movement, from one state of being to another, the *becomings*" of students' emotional registers (O'Sullivan 2010b, 198, emphasis in original). As another form of biotechnology, the students' affective vitality was redirected to create embodied expressions in stark contrast to the common rhythms of school life. The students became enchanted by the sensory and spatial stimuli, expressing a yearning for a different intensity within the educational monoculture.

Art and design have long been employed to promote and entertain, a primary tactic for marketing. In opposition to the historical mechanistic view of capitalist materialism, where popular culture acts as an opiate, tactically controlled by the ruling class to create a consensual blindness (Adorno 1991); Bennett (2001, 2010) argues that the enchantment of popular culture is about more than just consumption, and instead illuminates *thing-power* as an attraction and a form of love. Thing-power affirms the potential of nonliving elements to elicit visceral feelings of enchantment that infuse mystical, animate, and occult vitality to materiality and media. Capitalist marketing has long recognized how the active participation of nonhuman forces creates a mystical effect, and the rally in the cafeteria evidenced the exploitation of this enchantment, in light of its void within educational territories (Collu 2019; Lazzarato 1996). Bennett (2001) suggests that political theory needs to do a better job at recognizing this affective weapon of expression and question how it should be taken back. I agree with Bennett, and view it as particularly pressing in education.

Replacing the Vitality of "Specials" with Affective Fertilizer

While I was initially shocked by the spectacle of the cafeteria experience, I then grew intensely curious about how the event took the place of "specials" classes that day, which are art, music, physical education, and library. The school seemed to value the content taught in the specials less than the fundraising rally. Bennett's (2001) suggestion to take back enchantment as an affective weapon illuminates how the power of those classes, which are spaces for movement, expression, and connection through art, physical activity, and personal interest in reading, is overlooked and misunderstood. The specials breed variation, dynamism, and nonverbal expression into the curriculum, but they often have indeterminate outcomes and lack immediate, measurable results. Hence, they are devalued within the educational monoculture, where learning and curiosity as knowledge-emotions become tethered to success within a market logic (Shankar 2020; Zurn and Shankar 2020).

Experiences unrelated to predetermined neoliberal values are dismissed as idle curiosity and a waste of time, aligning with Shankar's (2020) notion of "a neoliberal curiosity" related to knowledge acquisition in schools, where "particular forms of knowledge are considered especially valuable within social settings, while others are not" (110). This is exemplified by replacing art and music with the fundraising rally, where the complex thinking that might emerge from the former is rerouted and applied to measurable, monetary, or quantifiable outcomes in the service of entrepreneurialism and profit in the later. The students were removed from their specials, which invite vitality and diversity, to redirect their attention to selling useless products. The routinized schedule and control of bodily movement and behavior that typically structure the school environment were disrupted to generate a desire to fulfill the guiding values of the educational community: market success and entrepreneurialism. So, it is not that the school has killed curiosity, but, rather, that it has created a different form of it: a neoliberal curiosity that tears away experiences and knowledge that have historically strengthened personal and collective expression (art and music), independent learning (library), and physical health (PE). This practice creates a pesticide (Chapter 1) effect by replacing organic stimuli (specials) with designer marketing products (like a synthetic fertilizer in relation to the focus of Chapter 1).

The children's passionate responses, combined with the teachers and administrators' lack of affect and criticality, demonstrated how the ordering force of accountability culture operates through technologies at a distance to capture the community's affective registers in a range of ways (Brennan 2004; Coleman and Ringrose 2013; Lazzarato 2006). Market-based values of commodification, competition, and individualism have captured modes of expression in the educational monoculture around logics and language of accountability (de Freitas 2014; Toscano 2007). The life-denying force of assessment culture does not kill life but redirects that force around a different set of values. The monocultural effects within the school ecology are similar to Round Up's impacts in agricultural ecologies (Chapter 1), where the herbicide kills the ecological variation created from weeds, butterflies, and insects to prioritize only a limited set of agricultural traits; the monocultural effects that value predetermined outcomes expressed in a narrow set of potential directions for learning by limiting open movement and direct experimentation with a variety of tools and resources (Boldt 2020; Engel 2011).

Transversalizing Ritual of Locust Formation

In closing, I wonder if the students' locust-like physical responses (see Prelude) are the site of potential. Rather than seeing them as subject to an oppressive, consensual dependence on consumption, let's consider how we might create other disturbances in the institutional territory. Guattari (2015) argued that to maintain institutional order, a variable amount of blinkering must occur: "think of a field," he wrote, "with a fence around it in which there are horses with adjustable blinkers: the adjustment of their blinkers is the 'coefficient of transversality'" (112–13). Here, the coefficient of transversality is the degree of blindness of everyone present. If the blinkers are opened too quickly, a form of affective trauma could occur. Guattari suggested that any modification must be in terms of a structural redefinition of each person's role and a reorientation of the whole institution.

When the cafeteria became a carnivalesque rally, it deterritorialized the stratified institutional codes that order body, movement, language, sound, and vision and restructured the spatial, mental, and social elements in the elementary school assemblage. By extending the sensorial field outside of that conditioned in that space, the multisensory vectors of force opened the students' blinkers to a degree that produced a nearly affective trauma (Guattari 2015). Moreover, the existential terrain of mass media entertainment exploded the perceptual field into one that was recognizable to students but deeply counter to the sensorially deadening force of the established institutional conditions. The Big Kahuna formed a new assemblage through the multisensory, corporate intervention as an embodied form of marketing television (Anderson 2012). The event caused a shift in the existential terrain of the school that reordered its social hierarchies. The principal ceded her authority to the Big Kahuna, but, more importantly, the students' affective force was recognized as the source of power—rather than disciplined and controlled, it was temporarily innervated and embraced (de Freitas 2018; Lazzarato 1996). It makes me wonder if it was actually a kind of transversal ritual that reoriented the students' institutional role to a responsibility akin to the household breadwinner. Let's stay with that. Capitalists appropriate art's power to enchant, but it can be taken back. The substance at the root of education, which I identify as a yearning to connect with the unending dynamism of the world, can be reclaimed by turning to the vital curiosity that pulsates in the "embryonic field" of the unknown and is always present (Wallin 2011b). Rather than students being subjected to the effects of the consumerist opiate, what if the event revealed their potential to be reoriented to their vital response-ability, the radical force of the locust and the pollinator?

3

What Can a Body Earn? School Fundraising as Immaterial Labor and Affective Currency

Rather than opening with a curious moment, this chapter starts from the image of the fundraising rally that has stuck in my memory (Chapter 2). From a distance, the scene in the cafeteria that day resembled a pep rally. The kids seemingly enjoyed it, and the teachers got a break while the corporate rep took over the room for a while. But as I revisited this story in my mind, the children's bodies continually bothered me, becoming stuck on this critical connection between the young body and the collective potential of affective response-ability. In Chapter 2, I explored the link between affect and corporeality, as the driving force behind hiring the company to take over the cafeteria that day.

I wonder if it is easier to stir affection in schools because the territory is so barren of affective spirit, care, compassion, and intimacy (Shankar 2020). Could the students' locust-like response be linked to this lack of spirit, creating a desperate desire for diversity, variation, and connections to any other signs of life? The event disrupted the norms and routines of the school with students' ecstatic screaming and movement, energizing the space with images of toys and thumping dance music. So, if the company was brought in to provoke an affective response in the children, I am curious: What can a body earn? For me, this question emerges from Deleuze's (1990b) work on Spinoza, asking, what can a body do?

In this chapter, I continue to question the commodification of affect, exploring how educational fundraising extracts affective labor and redistributes its vital connective force toward profit. The chapter concludes with an affirmative pivot to which I hinted at the end of Chapters 1 and 2, suggesting our potential for taking back curiosity's vital force through a collective counterattack that realizes our radical gap of potential to reconnect to the embryonic field, pollinating the seed and the soil toward a fecund culture of curiosity.

Visible Young Bodies and the Fun Run

After the cafeteria rally, I began to explore the larger social practices embedded in educational fundraising. Young people raising money for schools and recreational organizations is not new. You may have seen a sales catalog passed around by parents at work or children selling magazine subscriptions or cookies in front of the grocery store. These practices are bolstered by a discourse related to entrepreneurialism and community-building. For those of us in education, it also means giving up class time to promote what seems like a necessary evil in many districts, as public education is continually under attack (Ravitch 2013).

My lingering curiosity about the school fundraising rally had as much to do with the students' physical reactions as the industry around it, so I started to look for other ways that young bodies are used in the service of educational fundraising. In my community, the school dance team stands on the sidewalk in front of What-a-Burger every Wednesday to persuade drivers to stop there; the team receives a percentage of that day's sales. Car washes are another common example of community-oriented fundraising activities. Every fall, I see the high school cheerleaders standing on the side of Main Street with posters directing people into a parking lot to wash their car. The visibility of their bodies seems to function similarly to the images of toys flashing in the cafeteria (Chapter 2), creating transmissions of desire that flow from the student planning a sporting competition to the community member paying to watch their car be washed by a teenage girl. In both of these scenarios, there is an exchange of currency for goods and services, and the visibility of the body (or toy) acts as a mode of persuasion. Recently, though, fundraising efforts have shifted away from car washes and cookie sales to a focus on events, such as the Fun Run.

In Fun Runs (which have broadened into color runs and other, more spectacular events), students solicit monetary pledges from family, friends, and the community to run a certain distance. For example, I can pledge to pay $5 for each lap my son runs around the school gym in twenty minutes. The pledge form operates like the old candy catalog—but rather than candy, I am buying a lap around the gym. Students are organized by grade level, and they run for a set amount of time, cheered on by the school and community members. Let's say my neighbors and relatives also pledge for my son to run laps around the gym. Ben is potentially earning quite a bit of money for each lap he is able to run. For me, this immediately brought to mind images of betting on boxing matches or dog fights. And let us not forget the disabled body that may not be able to run in circles. What does that body become in relation to this neoliberal chariot race?

This is different from a sporting event or gym class or a talent show or bake sale. The kids' bodies are put to work to perform a repeated task at the service of educational funding, but it is not a task that requires skill or is imbued with meaning besides monetary value.

Exploiting Collective Spirit through Affective Labor

Fun Run events are promoted as raising school spirit, improving physical fitness, inspiring teamwork and participation, and encouraging individuality and entrepreneurship. Initially, people doubted that these events would succeed; because there is no object to receive in return for the monetary pledge; parents and administrators were concerned that teamwork and school resources may not be enough motivation for donations. Instead, the Fun Run became an ideal form of *immaterial labor*, about which Hardt and Negri (2004) explain: "in the final decades of the 20th century, industrial labor lost its hegemony and in its stead emerged 'immaterial labor,' that is labor that creates immaterial products, such as knowledge, information, communication, a relationship, or an emotional response" (108). They go on to describe one form of immaterial labor as *affective labor*, which "produces or manipulates affects such as feeling of ease, well-being, satisfaction, excitement, or passion" (Hardt and Negri 2004, 108). In school fundraising, the commodity is no longer a tin of cookies, but instead the body and an affective response. As a reminder, affect registers in our bodies as an intensive shift from one experiential state to another. Our capacity to affect and be affected is a vulnerability to intensive force that results in the increase or decrease of one's potential to act and, in turn, to connect (Deleuze and Guattari 1987; Massumi 2002; Spinoza 1994).

Conceptual Aside . . . Affective Surplus

As I explored in Chapters 1 and 2, affect becomes a productive surplus in the biopolitical economies of education and agriculture (Anderson 2012). Here, I consider how affective labor mediates relational connections in schooling. In a very simplistic way, capitalism operates through external exchanges of commodities and currency. Feelings and relationships create a different kind of exchange than that of common goods and services and are at times overlooked as simply a relational or emotional surplus. For instance, if you took your car in for a repair, you may strike up a nice conversation with the technician, but the primary exchange was the cost of services related to the skill and labor they applied to your car. The friendly conversation was an emotional or affective surplus. But now, events like the Fun Run have turned affective connections—derived from relationships, cognition, excitement, and care—into *the* commodity, manufactured for profit (de Freitas 2014; Rose 2008).

Like vital curiosity, affective labor is both intensive and extensive, as it commodifies the connections created from emotions, responsiveness, and the relationships (between bodies) from which they emerge (Lazzarato 1996). That potential for connection is the space of emergent variation and is critical to increasing vitality, akin to the gap of translation in DNA (Chapter 1). If the goal of capitalism is to extract the maximum amount of surplus value, then the common concern that capitalism alienates individuals from the fruits of their labor poses an exponential danger with affective labor, leaving little else beyond a transactional existence. In certain relational occupations, such as teaching, a biopolitics of affect emerges where the invisible energy that connects teachers to their students and gives life to the classroom is extracted as a resource and assigned exchange value (Rose 2008; Wallin 2014). Treating that energy as a resource to mine strips the relational connections of their spirit, creating the conditions for classrooms as *bio nullius* or empty life (Shiva 2016).

Ritualizing an Entrepreneurial Spirit

As I explored in Chapter 2, the fundraising industry has formed a parasitic and even predatory relationship to the public school system by creating events that exploit a desire to become affected. As my interest in this fundraising industry increased, I looked for images and videos of rallies at other schools. I wondered if they might have the same effect if I wasn't present and if students at other sites responded similarly to those in my experience. In my research, I discovered that the fundraising industry has shifted. It no longer invests in these rallies to motivate students to sell products. Rather, they focus solely on the event itself and figures like the Big Kahuna who energize the students to generate affective responses, expressed as spirited competition and the physical excitement that I witnessed. Rather than affect as surplus, affect is the primary commodity.

I discovered a set of promotional and training videos, curiously examining possible evidence of my interests in affective surplus, paying close attention to the visual, performative, and discursive aspects of one particular video[1] by a company called, Apex Leadership. The video opens with a series of quick clips of company representatives, who lead the school rallies. In it, they're wearing sports jerseys and responding to questions about working for the company; I refer to them here as cheerleaders. First, let's look at the company's rhetoric, as expressed in the cheerleaders' responses, considering how it relates to the commodification of affective relations and the cultivation of spirit as both energy and entrepreneurialism. It starts with a montage of their responses when asked to describe the company in one word: awesome, leadership, epic, exciting, exhilarating, inspiring, inspirational, and legendary. Then, they are asked what a typical day is like, with responses that refer to: prepping pledge reports, arriving up bright and early, first to arrive and last to leave, and "hittin" five to ten classrooms.

Their responses combine notions of energy with commerce, where the affective spirit expressed in their first set of responses is commodified and quantified in the second, characterizing the life of their workday, in terms of time and labor through the pledge reports that account for classrooms "hit." Rather than sending catalog books home, the classroom becomes the marketplace. All of the cheerleaders wear the company jersey, which also seems to serve as a costume that creates a kind of celebrity status. It plays on so many images within entertainment culture for young people: "Once you put this orange jersey on, you're a superhero for life, that's what it is, and you play that role from then on, you go into a grocery store and a kid sees you, '[hey!] what's up!'" They become sticky objects that form attachments with the kids as a sign of leadership, health, and hero status.

The performative nature of the job is illustrated throughout the video, as one person practices enunciation exercises ("red leather, yellow leather") in the same way a theater performer might. The cheerleaders are pictured in classrooms, gymnasiums, and cafeterias, wearing their jerseys and flanked by colorful company banners and other promotional materials. Groups of kids cheer as they volley beach balls through the air. In one scene, the cheerleaders perform stretches as the kids sit on the floor mirroring their movements. This idea of mirroring to evoke collective energy is evidenced in a couple scenes. In one, the cheerleaders perform the company's stock phrase in unison, and the kids are taught to repeat parts back as a form of call and response. Their bodily instructions to "stand up! stand up!" and the collective verbal utterances are critical because there is no other substance at the root of this venture. Music, decorations, words, and time are all incorporated to make money off of the body. Sensorial stimuli drive the energy, from the colorful jersey and associated banners to the music and cheering that fill the rooms. Even while wearing matching jerseys, the cheerleaders emphasize that the performance is a form of individual expression, suggesting: "You make it your own, it's personal. Everybody does it their own way, they've got their own flare." So, while the company's objective is to generate collective energy, cheerleaders maintain their individualism as a fundamental neoliberal value.

Fabricating Relationships

But the spirit is not developed from sensory stimuli and bodily movements alone. Cheerleaders describe how emotional relationships form through these transactions, explaining that it is more than a job due to the relationships that they build at the schools, as one explains: "It's all about showing love and spreading love." One of the most awkward scenes in the video shows a cheerleader who appears to get choked up as he describes his meetings with countless PTO (parent teacher organization) moms, where, "they'll start tearing up and they'll give me a huge hug. And it's the most amazing, rewarding experience." References to affection and bodily connection occur throughout the video as the cheerleaders describe loving the kids or loving what they do. This attraction is intensified by the physical contact of hugs and high fives, making this last statement an affective climax with the tears of PTO moms.

Affective labor is materialized in tears, hero worship, and mirroring, all of which is intended to produce excitement, passion, emotion, and desire. These come together in one comment:

> It's so awesome going to work every day in this jersey, and the kids treat you like a celebrity, it's insane, they love you, they wanna be you, they respect you, and they want to do everything that you wanna do, so you're able to teach them things and show them how to become a true leader.

The video illustrates how our current celebrity-obsessed culture is exploited to create ecstatic energy, where one is identified as an impactful leader based on superficial performative gestures. Comments that describe making a difference and changing the world, such as fun, play, and build leaders, high fives, and autographs are equated to embodying the brand. The experience the cheerleaders describe attempts to affect the social, mental, and environmental registers of the school as the gym, cafeteria, and classroom are territorialized by the performativity (Sedgwick 2003) of the rally, and the performers who embody a brand and manufacture affective desire through their costumes, cheers, movement, and affection.

The Neoliberal Curriculum as Ethical Imperative

I learned that Covid-19 surprisingly resulted in companies expanding their affective services, including pep rallies and motivational events delivered through digital platforms that lead up to in-person events like the Fun Run. Intensifying the curricular implications of replacing the "specials" with a fundraising rally (as I explored in Chapter 2), some companies also provide a curriculum on topics, such as character building and leadership, that schools can implement alongside the fundraising campaigns. So beyond simply invading the school environment and taking time away from the established school curriculum, leadership and character become primary learning outcomes, developed and demonstrated in these lessons through participation in the fundraising campaign, completing pledge reports, expressing adequate competitive drive, and expressing entrepreneurial spirit. Moreover, the ethical implications of demonstrating this type of "character" is extended to teachers, who are described as having "skin in the game," as they too are expected to bear responsibility for school fundraising. Not only does this add to the teachers' already overextended responsibilities, but it suggests that they do not already have "skin in the game."

Through this inquiry, I realized how affective labor is also built into the weeks leading up to the campaign or Fun Run event, where daily and weekly reminders promote competition, generating anxiety and shame for teachers and families who have not adequately participated. The connection between curriculum, character, and emotion illuminates the ethical implications of this scheme, which determines what students and teachers *ought* to teach, where interest *should* be directed, and how one *should* demonstrate good character through their commitment to neoliberal values (Wallin 2014). While the public school curriculum continues to echo a Fordist model of mass reproduction and standardization, these examples of informal education that operate within schools situate students as productive subjects within a neoliberal economy. The body, the gym/track, the policies, the social norms, the character building, the affective force of competition, anxiety, excitement, and fatigue become entangled. The existential terrain of the public school environment shifts, and the young body becomes the site of affective labor and bears responsibility for potential educational resources (Walling 2014). So, if we return to Guattari's (2015) concern with the reconfiguring of the institutional terrain via a shift in social practices (described in Chapter 2), the affective response to fundraising is one example of systemic forces that shape students' and teachers' subjective relationship to institutionalized education.

Neoliberal Curiosity and Entrepreneurial Spirit

As an emotional state, curiosity is also subject to types of affective manipulation that cultivate and constrain desire toward what one *ought* to want. These marketing campaigns aimed at developing spirit and cultivating character infect the thought and desire of the entire educational community, narrowing curiosity's complex and emergent attractions to those aligned with capitalist values, creating a form of "neoliberal curiosity," which Shankar (2020) describes as a knowledge-emotion "that is instrumentalized toward questions that pertain only to monetary success and value as defined by corporate-State interests, carrying gendered, sexualized, and racialized norms in the form of competitive 'drive'" (107). Shankar further explains that "As a result, students continue to experience an increase in the distance between what they want to know [i.e., a self-motivated curiosity] and what they ought to want to know [neoliberal curiosity], which in turn tears them from themselves, producing anxiety, depression, and the like" (108). The "tear" from one's self or personally motivated desire is a critical point in understanding how the fundraising rally is symptomatic of neoliberalism's effects on subjectivity in schooling.

In Chapter 2, I witnessed students' expressions of desire through physical exaltation in response to the Big Kahuna event's haptic intensity, which was also a break from education's anxiety-inducing labor. The term "haptic" technically references the sensory perception of touch, but in this context, it refers to the perception of forces or vibrations often made recognizable by affective responses. The haptic nature of the school rallies is intended to elicit an emotional and unreasonable attraction through sensual perceptions, playing on the paternalistic mind/body divide often attributed to children, women, and "primitive" subjects (Braidotti 2012; Grosz 2004; Tolia-Kelly 2010). But this is not a way of separating the reasonable mind from the sensuous body. Instead, the stirring of the spirit becomes another technique for isolating and capitalizing on the invisible gap of vitality that connects us (Collu 2019; Toscano 2007). The notion of the spirit has historically been associated with gods, mysticism, and the soul—similar to curiosity's vital connective force, which has been operationalized for neoliberal values. The experiences in Chapter 2 and the examples explored in this chapter illustrate how affective expression is extracted through environmental stimuli. Here, the vital spirit (Bennett 2001) that has been stripped away from learning to create the elementary school monoculture (Chapter 1) is replaced by manufactured vitality to generate neoliberal desire around school fundraising as a form of entrepreneurialism (Rose 2008; Wallin 2014). The cheerleaders operationalize the children's affective capacity, and their emotional response becomes a virtuous expression of the entrepreneurial spirit that is the defining characteristic of a valuable member of the community.

Moreover, this connection to a tear from one's self echoes the fracturing of connections between educational knowledge and its context in the world (Chapter 1). It seems that anxiety and depression could be one form of the "dead, mind-crushing load" that Dewey (2007) described as a result of information severed from thoughtful action. Anxiety and depression are pervasive in schools and across higher-income countries today, in part because the substance of life, to which we connect and through which we form relationships, has been severed. Thoughtful action has been replaced by meaningless competition, learning is equated with assessment, and the substance of the world has been abstracted into representations, as I explored in Chapter 1.

In schools, curiosity's emotional connection and attraction to learning has been redirected to the acquisition of information in a prepackaged curriculum, where the complex potential of learning with the world is emptied out and expressed, instead, as a grade. In this sense, grades have become a currency that mediates exchanges of knowledge, relationships between members of the learning community, and their personal connection to the learning process. This raises interesting questions about connections between affect and accountability, where the former is a commodity to be extracted, as well as a capacity that is exploited within accountability culture, to activate feelings of anxiety connected to the acquisition of grades as a currency in the educational sociopolitical landscape of indebtedness (Harney and Moten 2013).

Moreover, the link between affect and curiosity becomes critical when anxiety is the overriding negative emotion associated with learning. Anxiety emerges from uncertainty, making curiosity's connection to uncertainty feel dangerous. The curious excitement that fuels an interest in learning has been overcome by an anxious uncertainty grounded in fear about grades and standardized outcomes. Fear of the unknown is antithetical to a vital curiosity that longs for and is drawn toward the unfamiliar. Anxiety, as a fear of not knowing, constrains curiosity's vital attraction to the unfamiliar, strange, or indeterminate. That does not mean that curiosity is eliminated, but that its desire and capacity for attraction has been narrowed or modified into a neoliberal curiosity.

Untethered Affective Connection

What else might we do together in schools, where bodies move together through a barrage of sounds, images, and smells every day? The collective innervation that I witnessed in the cafeteria rally (Chapter 2) may also hold radical potential through the contagious or infectious movement of energy that ignites the imagination as the opening up of an unknown future, and opens the self through the formative power of expressive movement toward an experience of familiarity with an unknown future (Benjamin (1935, 1999; Hansen 1999). In this case, the vital connectivity of innervation and the aesthetic intensity of the burgeoning imagination become sites of radical political potential (Hansen 1999).

In relation to the fundraising industry in schools, a new image of the life of schools was envisioned by the PTO, who were permitted to disrupt the habituated control of time, space, and bodies in the school's existential landscape with the corporate fundraising campaign. Using the idea of the innervation of the masses (Benjamin 1999), we can see how the cheerleaders' elicitation of mimesis from the children, in the form of collective utterances and the repetition of movements, created a shared time-space experience, where students might also embody the spirit of the "brand" (Hansen 1999). The notion of innervation as an affective force raises questions for the revolutionary potential of taking up the performative biopolitical technologies of collective movement differently, as a creative counterforce to the fundraising industry's exploitation of affective labor in the service of neoliberal market values that have territorialized the space and curriculum of public schooling.

How might we affirmatively harness "the active discharge of emotion, the counterattack... [where] affects are projectiles just like weapons... weapons are affects and affects weapons" (Deleuze and Guattari 1987, 400) to create a different kind of energy and set of conditions in schools? Marketing and entertainment industries are built on the innervative power of modulating affective force for profit and persuasion. The fundraising industry has realized the profit potential of increasing affectivities, and its cost continues to be revealed in a range of effects. Braidotti (2006) acknowledged this potential when asking: "How can one increase affectivities as the capacity to invent or capture affect and look after the affected bodies? In other words, what is the 'cost' of the capacity to be affected which allows us to be the vehicle of creation?" (12). Inspired by Deleuze's (1992) suggestion that "there is no need to fear or hope, but only to look for new weapons" (4), how might we activate the examples in these first three chapters differently to create counter-codes and counter-projects that shift flows away from capitalist values?

To address these questions, I conclude this chapter by revisiting the pollinator garden in Chapter 1 and rethinking the potential of collective walks like the Fun Run. Guattari (2015) argued that while institutional change can happen from the bottom, the group with most power ultimately controls the degree of transversal intensity. In each of these scenarios, the PTO organized the campaigns and provided the financial resources. Fundraising company websites even appeal to school PTO members as collaborators on its website, playing to their desire for efficiency by promoting the fundraising campaigns as hassle-free and financially successful. But this desire for efficiency often overlooks the fundraising parasite's financial gain. One company charges schools an initial service fee of $2,000 for starting the campaign and then takes 48 percent of the proceeds. So just think about that. People donate to watch their child run in a circle, and the company not only charges $2,000 off the top but then also takes nearly half of the monies pledged. This racket reveals the absurdity of the system, where a desire for efficiency above all else is actually wasting the school's natural, intellectual, emotional, and monetary resources. But there is another way.

Digging in the Dirt

I thought back to the pollinator garden that we had built with the fourth graders a week earlier, thinking about ways that a transversal shift that embedded the students in an ecology with nature might create new lines of affective connection with the same force as that of the rally in the cafeteria. In fact, the PTO had initially paid for the garden plots. The students were so excited to be outside, working in the soil. Williams and Brown (2012) explain:

> For children, learning gardens provide an excellent place to commune with nature. In particular, the living soil of learning gardens connects children to the life below their feet . . . develop[ing] intimate connections with plants, animals, insects, wind, and water through awakening their curiosity, wonder, critical thinking skills, and imagination in commune with the soil directly and indirectly. (41–2)

This intimate contact with the vitality of soil is a slow and reciprocal communion that activates curiosity. The seeds planted form a relationship that grows literally and figuratively, invigorating a transcorporeal connection to the "embryonic field of relations" (Wallin 2011b) that might evoke a different kind of spirit, where thought and curiosity can be untethered from capitalist values. This organic contact might create new intensive flows of energy that "redesign the mindscape: from domination to compassion, from competition to cooperation, and from mechanical relationships to ecological relationships" (Williams and Brown 44). By seeding the curriculum differently, connections in nature can modify the bodily flows within the institution, resisting the sedimentary force of "lifeless ringing of bells, the ticking of clocks, and the rigidity of curriculum aligned with linear development" (Williams and Brown 48). We could affirmatively alter school rhythms to align with the earth's temporal flows and cycles. Investing more time in natural spaces during school, such as school gardens, can transform students' relationship with learning as a process of connection to ecological vitality and change. As opposed to the superficial participation of blindly running in a circle; incorporating opportunities for taking care of other forms of life creates a more specific sense of responsibility and responsiveness, with the potential of cultivating a collective consciousness among all members of the school and broader community (Gibson-Graham, Cameron, and Healy 2013).

I recall the difference in affective intensity, between the barrage of sounds and images in the cafeteria and the slower pace of collective planning, digging, and planting, and I wonder how that difference might translate into students' relationship with food, particularly because both spaces are intended to bring groups together for collective nourishment. The curriculum might also reconnect to traditional forms of knowledge sharing—incorporating seed banks made fugitive when seeds became intellectual property (Shiva 2016)—and realize the radical ancestral potential of the seed. If taken seriously, the garden unsettles educational monocultures, pollinates diversity and variation, curiously embraces unknown potential, and revitalizes the complex interdependence of the school environment as a more-than-human collective.

Walking a Different Course

Moreover, if we value the collectivizing potential of the Fun Run, we might reclaim the energy that has been commodified by placing young bodies in a predetermined, repetitive loop. Walking has been a collective show of solidarity for civil and labor rights, cancer research and survivor solidarity, and political protest (Solnit 2000). With the Fun Run, the shared movement of walking together creates a different kind of relationship through physical proximity, open connection, and mutual visibility because "Walking 'alone' does not exist.

Walking in/with the world [is] the only kind of walking" (Manning 2012, 29). Corporate parasites have capitalized on communities' connective capacity and collective spirit, but families can just donate the funds directly to the school and walk together. The visual stimulation of toys and cheerleaders can be redirected to a public display of solidarity as a community moving together at shared and differential paces, realizing the radical potential of just being together.

Each of the experiences in these first three chapters reveals both the ways that capitalism has colonized and commodified our connection to the vital force of the natural world and the radical potential that exists at the root of our everyday lives (Waxman 2017). My intention is not to diminish the potential good of activities like a Fun Run or other forms of charitable collective action. Instead, I am suggesting that we don't need to intervene in school time with this sort of activity. From a very practical perspective, we can just let kids go to their physical education class to run laps. The energy diverted to these fundraising activities could remain in the classrooms, giving teachers more time to design thoughtful experiences that create new associations with learning. In other words, if we would just leave it alone, we might recognize the fundamental resources that are already around us all the time.

While collective forms of running and walking might innervate a new understanding of social, political, and environmental connection, walking as a form of curious mobility takes up attentiveness that is more akin to dwelling (Ingold 2011), and perhaps a sensorial attunement to the minor in our everyday encounters (Manning 2012). How might this difference between the shift in temporal, perceptual, and affective registers also create a different understanding of curriculum as a course to be run. While the collective action of the Fun Run, with its predetermined path and competitive justification, still holds potential for a revolutionary innervation in the educational commons, it might also need to be imbued with the potential of a vital curiosity that can generate creative energies and imaginative movements that dissolve the well-worn ruts of established curricular pathways (Wallin 2013). Engaging in gardening and walking thoughtfully illuminates the radical and transversal potential to revitalize our relationships to each other and the world. These minor gestures resist biopolitical isolation, coding, and sterilization to embrace a more-than-human collectivization that might mend the tears from ourselves and the substance of the world. Perhaps this radical simplification nourishes (rather than codes) the invisible gap of vitality that activates affective intensity, stimulates thinking, and charges a field of attraction as the vital and virtual space of becoming (Barad 2015).

Part II

Connective Curiosity

Permeating Thresholds through Transcorporeal Movement

Part II, "Connective Curiosity: Permeating Thresholds, through Transcorporeal Movement," shifts from the disruptive potential of curiosity's affective force in Part I to gain some distance from the sensorial shock of experience and to develop a durational consciousness of life's transcorporeal interconnectedness. Part II becomes a middle passage of the book and a turning point, a transition from predetermined outcomes and production in Part I to increasingly unpredictable encounters in the natural environment. Forms of bodily extraction shift from human-oriented affective labor (Chapters 2–3) to centuries of physical extraction and sedimentation of native land, indigenous people, and cultural values.

Bodies of knowledge are unsettled through the movement across different territories of existence, where natural environmental elements become vectors of force, as the body takes on a different set of relations and expanded forms, realizing it is "always already a multiplicity of different bodies ... open to the most diverse fields of alterity" (Guattari 1995, 118). Transcorporeality is a critical concept in Part II:

> By emphasizing the movement across bodies, trans-corporeality reveals the interchanges and interconnections between various bodily natures. But by underscoring that trans indicates movement across different sites, trans-corporeality also opens up a mobile space that acknowledges the often unpredictable and unwanted actions of human bodies, nonhuman creatures, ecological systems, chemical agents, and other actors. Emphasizing the material interconnections of human corporeality with the more-than-human world—and, at the same time, acknowledging that material agency necessitates more

capacious epistemologies—it allows us to forge ethical and political positions that can contend with numerous late twentieth- and early twenty-first-century realities in which "human" and "environment" can by no means be considered as separate. (Alaimo 2010, 2)

These transcorporeal interchanges across bodies are realized on footpaths and pathways, as the milieus of all three chapters in Part II, where curiosity is taken up through experiences of walking as research, moving along paths of desire to realize sedimented locations of power, which become visible, felt, and hidden in environments affected by patterns of colonial and capitalist destruction.

Walking becomes the primary mode of encounter in all three chapters of Part II, with experiences revealing the transcorporeal entanglements of our everyday lives and environments. Walking produces a different mode and rhythm of perception, as we move outdoors and away from the institutional space. Time slows and elongates, as environments become open fields of sedimented history, expressed through layers of culture, technology, and economic development. Unlike the institutional blinkers that direct movement and narrow attention in schools, learning takes on a new pace or vibration and requires a different kind of focus and sensitivity to discern the myriad organic and inorganic expressions of the world.

Walking has a historical importance in philosophy, social protest and cultural expression, artistic experimentation, and cultural geographies (Ingold 2011; Solnit 2000; Waxman 2017). Springgay and Truman (2018) identify four major concepts common to walking methodologies in research: place, sensory inquiry, embodiment, and rhythm, which they expanded "to be accountable to an ethics and politics of the more-than-human: *Land and geos, affect, transmaterial, and movement*" (2). Each of these concepts, initial and expanded, aligns with the ethico-aesthetic nature of vital curiosity, as an embodied and sensual, affective and transcorporeal, and emergent within embodied encounters.

A wide range of attractors draw me in through a class field trip at a local residence, a hike across a historical landmark, and daily notes from the first three months of isolation during the Covid-19 pandemic. Moreover, the stories take on new forms, styles, and media in the form of photographs, digital notes, and alternative modes of expression and communication—diversifying now only the context but the content.

4

What if We Dig It Ourselves? Mapping a Transcorporeal Inquiry across the Composition of Clay Bodies

In this chapter, I return to an unresolved project from a course that I taught several years ago with art education students. I was curious how we might understand ceramics differently if we sourced our own clay by digging it locally rather than purchasing it commercially. The chapter follows a single day where we left campus to dig clay at a local resident's home. We set out together, uncertain of what we might find, and driven by the connective force of vital curiosity. Starting with an interest in clay bodies, the inquiry creates transcorporeal connections where history and culture are felt in layers of matter, composed through an ecology of practices that crossed disciplinary, geographic, and temporal boundaries. *What if we dig it ourselves* (the title of the chapter) becomes a radically connective proposition to realize we are always *making-with* the world, activating a sympoietic pedagogy to realize that "earthlings are *never alone*" (Haraway 2016, 58, emphasis in original). Moving away from our habituated relationships and processes of school, our local community became a strange stage for discovering our vast geographical and historical lines of connections through a pedagogical encounter in the fold (Stengers, Manning, and Massumi 2009), where memories, histories, experience are all folded in, not just among humans, but with those of the rocks, land, tools, grasses, and the clay (Pacini-Ketchabaw, Kind, and Kocher 2017).

Driving Out—Nervous Energy and the Strange Presence

It was the third week of the fall semester, and Jennifer, a new student in the art program, entered the classroom beaming with excitement to tell us about a woman she met over the weekend. I had tasked a team of students to research local soil compositions and try to identify a place where we could dig our own clay as an experiment. Rather than "wasting time" (Dewey 2007) by preparing their own clay, most ceramics instructors buy bags of clay that have been processed to successfully fire in common kilns. This choice makes sense, because their focus is typically on developing artistic techniques with the clay, as opposed to developing the clay itself, similar to painters buying tube paint rather than making it. Prior to this experience, I too had only used commercially packaged clay, but I wondered what else we might learn if we dug and processed the clay ourselves. Like Pacini-Ketchabaw, Kind, and Kocher (2017), I wondered, "how might clay ecologies relate, entangle, interlink to world making, sense making, change making?" (60).

I thought of sneaking down to a spot by the creek adjacent to campus and hoping for the best, but an invitation to a local home seemed safer with a group of students that I didn't know very well yet. The students searched local maps and the state park website for information. Jennifer, who was a ball of energy from day one, started talking about the project with locals. She met Carol, who taught classes at the Native Plant Center nearby. Carol owned a large plot of land about 15 miles outside of town and was intrigued by our project. She welcomed us out to dig clay and shared stories with Jennifer about how her daughters made figures from clay on her land when they were young. I was exhilarated.

The following Tuesday, we all met in the parking lot by the art building. It was a cool, crisp February morning, with a light frost glistening on the grass around the school. The excitement of a field trip was tangible. Even though all of the students were in their twenties, piling into cars to drive to an unfamiliar home and looking for something we were uncertain of finding felt adventurous. We took three cars. I drove the two ceramics graduate students, who had been informally helping out with the class because they were equally intrigued by the process. The younger students rode in the other two cars, giggling loudly as we pulled away from the university.

The college town was remote—two to three hours from any metropolitan area. A 5-mile loop circled the commercial Main Street and residential areas. On the other side of the loop was an expanse of farms and large rural plots, accessible by winding, two-lane roads lined with fences and large pine trees. As we drove out, the school and town were out of sight within minutes. A heavy weight of responsibility came over me, but I tried to keep the atmosphere light and playful. There were very few road signs, and the internet was spotty in the countryside, so I measured the distance we'd traveled by Carol's approximation in her instructions.

We came around a sharp bend, and a tall white figure appeared on the right side of the road. We were going about 50 miles an hour, with the others following behind, so I was reluctant to break too fast.

"Did you just see that?" I exclaimed to Erik and Mike.
"What the hell was that?" Mike responded.
"Was that a crucifix?" Erik asked. "But it was weird—like an alien or something."

I kept going to stay on track with the timeframe we gave Carol. The trace of the strange white figure intensified my anxiousness about where we were going. It definitely seemed to reference the Crucifixion, but the body was completely void of facial identifiers, and the cross on which it was mounted had large points on each end. Was this a harbinger of something odd in the community we were about to enter?

Pulling Up and Setting Out

We reached an opening in the long fence associated with her address and drove through the gate down a dirt path carpeted with pine needles. We passed a large barn, then an open shed, and arrived at a two-story, wood-framed home. It was Plantation style, with gray siding, common in Louisiana and rural areas throughout the Midwest. A large ladder was extended to the roof, resting beside the front entrance. Carol opened the door before we could knock. She explained that they were fixing the roof and that we had to be careful of the ladder. We briefly stepped into the entranceway. The rustic interior was cozy, with large, exposed-wood beams, like a cabin. Layers of history and knowledge filled the kitchen, with handmade tile decorations above the old stove, rustic furniture, and family photos throughout. Carol explained that she and her husband built the home themselves forty years earlier, using lumber cut from trees on the property. She pointed out the smaller one-story cabin close by, which they built first and lived in while constructing the larger home. Carol grabbed her coat, and we walked back out.

She led us toward the shed that we drove past on the way in. One side, in the process of being extended, was covered with a large brown tarp. The grasses and pine needles had been cleared away for the construction, and the ground around it was a bright, smooth, rust-colored clay that appeared like a quiet pool around the structure. The color stood out boldly against the pale browns and greens of the fallen leaves that covered the rest of the area. Red clay is common in the southeastern United States and other humid and tropical areas, as a result of the accumulation of iron oxide (rust) from the moist atmospheric conditions.

Figure 4.1 Digging by the shed. Photograph courtesy of author.

We had brought four large plastic buckets, assuming that would give us enough clay for the small vessels we planned to make in class. We had three shovels, so the students took turns digging (see Figure 4.1). Several students did not know how to use a large shovel and giggled nervously as they tried to get the shovel into the ground. The tools visible in the open shed seemed to vibrate with a different life than these awkward, large shovels—with a dense texture that "offered information about how, substantively, historically, materially [they] came into being" (Sedgwick 2003, 14). The fresh dirt and visible construction on the shed animated Carol's stories of building the structures over the previous four decades. The energy of her tools, clearly still in use, created an ironic contrast as the students struggled, flinging clay into the air with their large shovels. A couple students complained about the blisters starting to form on their palms, quickly handing off the shovels and offering to carry the buckets instead. Their inexperience clearly caused them some embarrassment, but the clay that slowly accumulated in the first bucket bore a kind of magic as the result of their labor.

Curious Path . . . Clay's Geological Composition and Historical Residue

Clay is essentially rock that has washed down mountains and is deposited in valleys below. Over time, the sediment combines with other organic materials to form geographically specific "clay bodies," which is the term for its composition of material properties. Although clay bodies are as varied as the ecological conditions from which they emerge, the three most common categories are earthenware, stoneware, and porcelain. They are differentiated by their properties and applications in pottery, with the most significant factors being: temperature, workability, and color. Most clay manufacturers process the raw materials with other minerals to increase malleability and plasticity for more successful firing.

Clay's color is described in terms of purity—for instance, porcelain is considered the purest clay body because of its high level of kaolin, found at the highest global elevations. It is purer than clay compositions from lower altitudes, which is referred to as earthenware, such as terra cotta. Earthenware can be found in creek beds and contains more impurities from the accumulated sedimentation at lower altitudes. It has the lowest firing temperature and is more porous and less durable than the other forms.

When researching the different types and compositions, I was struck by how the descriptions of clay bodies seemed to express value judgments. They echoed centuries of rhetoric that (de)values human bodies, linking skin color and purity, elevating certain bodies based on their geographic origin and diminishing others due to their diverse physical characteristics and cultural background. The racist undertones registered, in part, because we were located in Deep East Texas, near the Louisiana border, with high humidity and swampland throughout the region. Within an hour's drive were antebellum plantations with slaves' quarters that had become tourist sites. The historical residue lingered in the air and on the land. I wondered how this residual history was sedimented into the layers of clay across the region.

Mapping Ecological Threads on Unsettled Lands

We walked farther from the house, and the land began to slope upward. We came to a long, wide clearing in the trees (see Figure 4.2), where you could see beyond Carol's land. Unlike the short grasses and pine needles that covered the ground around her home, the clearing was matted with mounds of long brown grasses that looked like piles of hay. Carol explained that the trees were cleared when the land was acquired to lay a gas pipeline about twenty years earlier. In Texas, pipeline operators are granted eminent domain rights, because gas is considered a public utility. Private landowners can negotiate with the oil companies on some of the terms, but the Texas Railroad Commission (TRC), which is identified as

Figure 4.2 Walking along the pipeline clearing. Photograph courtesy of author.

"the state agency with primary regulatory jurisdiction over the oil and natural gas industry, pipeline transporters, natural gas and hazardous liquid pipeline industry, and natural gas utilities."[1] Even as the primary regulatory body for the state, the TRC has no authority over the process of taking citizens' private property to lay pipelines across it.

In the clearing process, companies cut down miles of trees. After the pipeline was finished, Carol and her husband attempted to rehabilitate the land by laying new seeds to grow the thick grasses I noticed when we first walked up. The grasses provided a stronger foundation that limits the flooding or wash across the now-barren soil. The new grasses also attracted different bird species and other wildlife, creating a more diverse ecology. We dug into the cleared area for the second bucket of clay. Unlike the bold rust color by the shed, this clay was a greenish gray. It occurred to me that our walk across Carol's property transported us far more than the two hundred yards or so that our bodies moved. We traversed centuries together because when the company excavated the soil, it displaced the layers of sedimentation that had formed several feet below the surface, and provided access to centuries-old clay bodies.

Next, we moved only a few feet away from the gas line clearing, back into the trees, and dug again. This time, the clay was red again, but slightly less intense than that near the house, illuminating the sharp line of excavation. The land

Figure 4.3 Buckets with clay. Photograph courtesy of author.

had been overturned to transfer natural gas, which itself is an effect of fractured sediment stimulating flows of energy from the earth. I was stunned at the literal and metaphorical layers of time, knowledge, bodily matter, and evolution composing in this moment. Ultimately, we found four different clay bodies on the property, creating a spectrum from red to gray to green (see Figure 4.3)

Returning to the God(dess) Figures

We walked back to Carol's home, where she provided refreshments. She showed us around the house and pointed out the small clay figures that her children had made years earlier. There were four objects: a rounded, dark-gray pinch pot; a palm-size, dark-gray, anthropomorphic figure with a smiley face drawn on the head; a larger, seated figure with more facial details that had some kind of white glaze over it; and a columnar form that seemed like a vase or a cracked, standing goddess. The smallest figure reminded me of the archaic *Venus of Willendorf*. It lacked physical details, but it could be held in the palm of your hand like a talisman. The larger white seated form was about four inches tall, and eyes with bold lashes had been etched into it, expressing the imagination of a young girl that gave life to the earthenware form. The taller, cracked vase goddess evoked something else, like a centuries-old vessel unearthed from an archaeology dig (see Figure 4.4). Its surface bore cracks and porous holes around the belly of the form, atop a wider base shaped by small hands, evidenced through traces of fingerprints and indentations. This relic echoed the energy that vibrated across their land. It was an assemblage of so many elements we encountered that day: made by the children who grew up on this land, using organic material from which their world was composed. The goddess expressed the duration of this domestic ecology, standing on the kitchen table in their home, which was a structure made from the trees that surrounded it, and built by their parents using tools that held centuries of handed-down skill and labor.

As we loaded up the buckets of clay and prepared to leave, we asked Carol about the crucifixion statue on the road, and she told us it was made by a local artist who lived in the next town. He had a whole house and more Jesus sculptures right on the main square. Our curiosity was piqued, so we quickly drove a few miles farther on and found the house she had described. It bore pointy spikes similar to those on, what we dubbed "Alien Jesus" on the drive out. There were other crucifixion sculptures that were far more detailed than the one on the road, but the eeriness of the original resonated differently. We stopped at it on the way back, and I felt a strange sense of danger and an unsettling ghostliness. It was an anthropomorphic figure covered with a white plaster exterior, void of distinguishing features and attached to the wooden cross with ends that looked like stakes. It was haunting, but different from the mystical connection I felt to the clay goddess at the house. The figure on the side of the road felt like a warning—a sign of an invasive presence. The figure seemed like

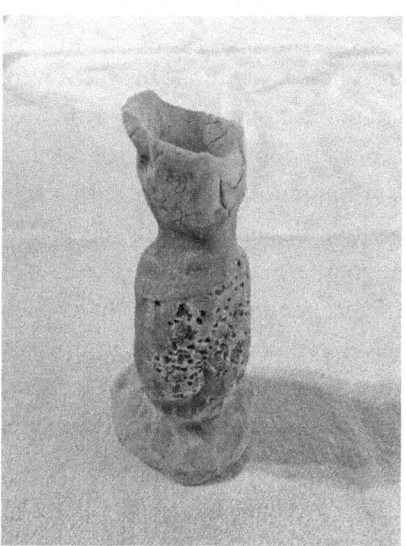

Figure 4.4 Single clay figure. Photograph courtesy of author.

a strange beacon, amplified by the fact that we were on Highway 21, which had served as the Caddo Trail two centuries earlier. The Caddo Trail's official name is El Camino Real de las Tejas National Historic Trail. It was a primary trade route for native populations, connecting tribes from the eastern United States to those in New Mexico and then eventually to the Pima Tribes in what is now Phoenix, Arizona. It later became the primary overland route for Spanish colonization:

> Linking a variety of cultural and linguistic groups, the royal road served as an agent for cultural diffusion, biological exchange, and communication and as a conduit for exploration, trade, migration, settlement, and livestock drives. Spanish, Mexican, French, American, Black, and American Indian travelers along El Camino Real de los Tejas created a mix of traditions, laws, and cultures that is reflected in the people, landscapes, place names, languages, music, and arts of Texas and Louisiana today.[2]

We had just seen the small earth goddess at Carol's house, made with the land by children's hands. The porous fragility of that piece created an intense contrast to this figure, made of artificial materials and standing atop the residual layers of culture, bodies, and violence that spread across the area. "Alien Jesus" became an abstraction of a centuries-old symbol used to justify colonial conquests and the destructive domination of the environment as Manifest Destiny, human progress, and the promise of a better world beyond (Moore 2015).

Curious Path . . . Global Information System's Haunting Metadata

Retracing this experience now (four years later), my memory is filtered through the atmosphere of the environment, relationships, and unanticipated excitement of that day. I had a vague idea of where her house was located, but I have since moved away from the town. I found eight photographs that I had saved on an old hard drive. The image from the moment we saw the clearing for the pipeline (Figure 4.2) lingered with me the strongest, and now the glow (MacLure 2013) of the experience came into sharp focus.

Wait, the metadata on the photos! I realized the photos might tell much more of this story. If I could find exactly where we were, then I might also find the pipeline and better understand these lingering questions. The coordinates on the photo yielded only a general area on the map, but the aerial view online did not reveal the difference in the land that we were able to see while walking. I searched the internet for oil and gas pipelines in East Texas, which took me to the TRC website. The commission provides GIS (global information system) maps with different-colored lines, signifying all of the pipelines across the state. The area around Carol's house showed a network of green lines, with labels that identified the different companies that owned them (see Figure 4.5 of images overlapping).

I found it! It was her exact plot of land, with a green line that cuts straight through it. It's a natural gas pipeline labeled "Energy Transfer Company" (ET). I had to pause for a moment. My mom had worked for this company for fifteen years when I was younger. I searched for when ET laid gas pipelines in East Texas to see if I could dig deeper. The company's website states that it formed in 1996 and laid 200 miles of gas pipelines in East Texas. Mom started working there in the late 1990s, and I remember her talking about all of this development. I didn't know much about oil and gas at the time, and I did not live near there, so it was all kind of invisible and just seemed to align with the long history of oil in Texas. I was haunted, looking at these glowing green lines on the GIS map beside the photos from that day. I am part of these layers.

Since that time, Energy Transfer has grown into a multinational corporation that has been embroiled in controversy—most notably, the decade-long battle over the Keystone XL and Dakota Access Pipelines, which garnered international attention with the protests by the Standing Rock Sioux Tribe in North Dakota. This story became the epicenter of, and a public education on, the effects of the

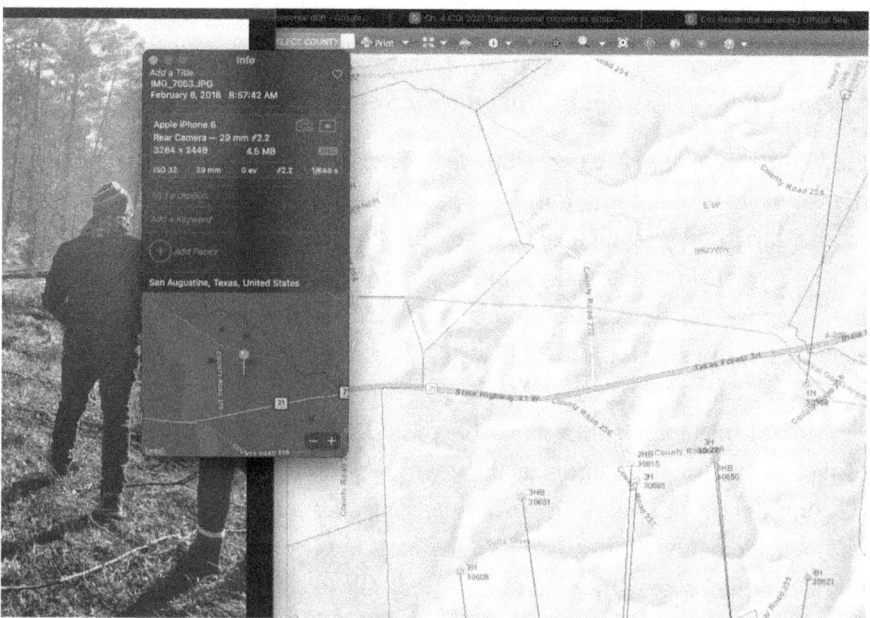

Figure 4.5 Overlapping images with GIS map. Photograph courtesy of author.

oil and gas industry that connect the land and people across the entire North American continent (Denchak and Lendwall 2022). I noticed that even just a few days prior to writing this, the company was convicted of criminal charges in Pennsylvania for water contamination across several counties due to leaks from pipelines (Grinapol 2022).

Collective Encounters in a Sympoietic Pedagogy

What if we dig it ourselves? This question is radically simple and profoundly complex. The primacy of digging in the dirt and of reorienting our values toward durational understanding, rather than convenience and efficiency, connected this single class day to centuries of knowledge, skill, history, and evolution. In this analysis, I unpack and thread together desire, movement, encounter, and connection to better understand how our collective travel beyond the institution illuminated the entanglement of so many lives and bodies through a sympoietic pedagogy driven by the connective force of vital curiosity. Inspired by Haraway's (2016) curious practice, as the

> energetic work use of holding open the possibility that surprises are in store, that something interesting is about to happen, but only if one cultivates the virtue of letting those one visits intra-actively shape what occurs. (127)

Our curiously sympoietic field trip to dig clay revealed the complex layers of *making-with* that compose our world, through surprises with those we visited, shaping what occurred that day to realize we are never alone in our education and everyday life. The collective virtue that Haraway describes is akin to conditioning for a vital curiosity, as a disposition of critical inquisitiveness and creative experimentation.

Recomposing with and through Tools

The experience disrupted our habituated educational values away from a need for prescribed outcomes with predetermined roles, instead prioritizing collective exchanges and emergent relationships between all of the contributing actors in the process—human and nonhuman (Trafi-Prats 2017). Rather than inert objects, tools became vectors for connecting our bodies to centuries of sedimented minerals. Tools and technology are often bound to a telos or purpose that defines and is defined by the boundaries of that function. Because most art classes focus on artistic skill-building and making individual art objects, they often bypass the material composition of their tools, rarely asking what was disrupted so that they might come into being. As a result, the materiality of art media, as "a multispecies event" (Pacini-Ketchabaw, Kind, and Kocher 2017, 57) is flattened. Their origin and history are overlooked, as the material is appreciated for its predetermined function alone.

Approaching tools curiously can unsettle their limited appreciation and expand increasingly common justifications for curiosity in research and education that are limited to notions of innovation and efficiency. Innovation, too often, domesticates curiosity through its designated telos and clear objective (Zurn and Shankar 2020). Art making can create unusual relationships with tools and media because it isn't bound to a telos in the same way as design or engineering. Tools may take on different functions where transversal openings may become more tangible when makers drift across domains of knowledge and practice. When artists partner with tools and natural materials to realize expressive capacities, a more-than-human connection can emerge (Coats 2019; Dean and Berling 2020; Hofsess 2018; Hood and Kraehe 2017).

Coming Alive with the Land

The connection between our experimental dig driven by our collective curiosity and that required to lay the pipeline bothered me. After all, like experimentation, curiosity can lead to detrimental capitalist exploitation (described in previous chapters). Moreover, rhetoric glorifying experimentation has been rightly critiqued for overlooking the erasure of its historic dangers in science (Nxumalo, Vintimilla, and Nelson 2018). Our intention to extract organic material to use for human-centered purposes, even if our process was embedded in a sincere respect for the land, still resonated with the settler colonialist history of acquisition and displacement to the extractive capitalist exploitation that has spread across that territory for centuries—too often justified by a desire to cultivate other populations in the image of some form of human exceptionalism (Moore 2015). Unfortunately, curiosity's unpredictable relationship with experimentation is historically susceptible to becoming "sovereign" (Zurn 2018) or appealing to those with fascist tendencies (Mitchell 2013).

While I recognize those historical resonances, in our experience, the dig became a sympoietic process that linked up with other elements in the world, creating potential for "rehabilitation (making livable again) and sustainability amid the porous tissues and open edges of damaged but still ongoing living worlds" (Haraway 2016, 33). The digging and weeks of processing the clay rehabilitated our distance from the earth and from organic processes of transformation, which capitalism has extracted and exploited to the extreme (Lippard 2014*)*. The clay told stories of sedimented land-use policies that favor industries who exploit and pollute the environment for profit.

My interest in getting to the root of the materiality embedded in teaching ceramics drove us to an unfamiliar space, where the all-too-familiar power relations embedded in capitalism and colonialism were layered across this property, expressing their force in the clay's range of colors, the ecological transformation, and the juxtaposition of the goddess figure and "Alien Jesus." The impurities of the earthenware we collected bore the impacts of colonialism, capitalism, and the degradation of our environment. A *geostory* emerged through a commitment to "situated work and play in the middle of messy living and dying" (Haraway 2016, 42).

These stories matter differently when you touch them directly, as opposed to reading about them from a distance. Learning by collectively walking and digging in the dirt created an affection for each other and the place through a physical labor that education has replaced with repetition, representation, and reproduction (explored in Chapter 1). Focusing on the materiality of the body in artistic production, as well as the agency inherent in occupying space, illuminates the potential of touch as a sticky pedagogy, where "transformations abound through the process of working the clay: Clay adheres to branches, disappears when immersed in water, and rolls through the forest humus picking up its leaf litter" (Pacini-Ketchabaw, Kind, and Kocher 2017, 57). Springgay (2010) argues that learning through corporeal acts of resistance creates fluid and complex connections, no longer rooted in a singular subculture or issue but as a mode of life that weaves various scenes together, where learning becomes relational, participatory, performative, and experimental. Curiosity drove the transcorporeal inquiry, unsettling layers of connections through an ecology of practices that taught us how history and culture moved across and intervened in the land.

Curiously Attuning to the Haunting of Unresolved Potential

In addition to learning through a direct engagement with the land, we witnessed a different kind of rehabilitation, where Carol and her husband sought to repair the damage wrought by an industry with more rights than the state or its citizens. They reseeded the excavated bodies to create a renewed, more diverse ecology that embraced its sympoietic potential. Recognizing the vital potential of new formations, even in the face of destruction, attuned optimism activates the affirmative power of a porous curiosity. What I mean by this is an openness to receiving others' flows of energy and transforming with them, cultivating the curious virtue (Haraway 2016) of co-creative malleability. Carol and her husband's entire history of working with the vital potential of the materials with which they cohabitate told a story of optimistic attunement and sympoietic porosity.

For years, I have thought that this project was a failure because over the weeks that followed, nothing really worked as it would have with a more controlled and prepackaged curriculum. But perhaps, instead, it was a form of research-creation, which "so regularly fails to resolve clearly into 'art' or 'scholarship,' and in the ways that it so regularly renders its makers illegible from one perspective or another, often unpredictably, is, at its most interesting, a decidedly uncanny practice" (Loveless 2019, 47). The uncanny practice enlivened through vital curiosity also emerges through a haunting attunement to unexpected expression and strange emergence. Unearthing the clay bodies shed light on capitalist effects that are often made invisible to those not immediately affected. But another kind of haunting energy emerged from dual encounters with the eerie "Alien Jesus" form and the small earthen figures that the children created. The experience created an earthbound, compositionist practice, "eschew[ing] the dubious pleasures of transcendent plots of modernity and the purifying division of society and nature" (Haraway 2016, 41). By engaging directly with the land, new facts emerge, and the reseeding of the ground left from the state/industrial excavation illuminates a different kind of compositionist potential—teaching us "how a common world, how collectives, are built-with each other, where all the builders are not human beings" (Haraway 2016, 41).

Finally, the lack of resolution left the class and experience open for nomadic and durational returns over the years since. Its lingering hold on my mind revealed how learning germinates indiscernibly and how curiosity sticks, creating longing to revisit relationships left idle. New tools and different connections emerged as I revisited the experience. I realized that my memory stuck to the moments of shock and surprise, like when Carol told us about the pipeline and how they had reseeded it, or when we observed the differences in the clay bodies, and when we returned to "Alien Jesus." The course was inspired by a desire to unsettle simplistic understanding of our classroom tools and create direct contact with our sensory perception and bodily force.

But upon return, a different set of sensing tools brought new life to the experience. I initially photographed parts of the day as evidence of our experience, without thinking about how much more information digital photos contain. Because digital technologies retain layers of data, I was able to precisely find Carol's house. My excitement about the complex connections to oil and gas had existed as a kind of narrative fiction that became exponentially real and personal with the help of GIS technologies that use sensors and cameras to map, connect, and organize all kinds of data, including from government and industry. As Alaimo (2010) suggests, "understanding material interchanges between bodies (both human and nonhuman) and the wider environment often requires the mediation of scientific information" (16). Now, I saw how this piece of land had connections to my family and to the ongoing contamination of tribal lands across North America. The shock of seeing the words, Energy Transfer, created a haunting affective fold (Stengers, Manning, and Massumi 2009), while at the same time, the multivalent connection of the words, *energy transfer*, also references the process of innervation, as a movement of energy across a nerve pathway. How ironic this seemed that this field trip became an aesthetic encounter that innervated lines of connection as transfers of affective, temporal, pedagogical, historical, and material energy—as another way of considering the revolutionary potential of mobilizing the imagination (Chapter 3).

Curiosity's haunting attunement is a kind of intuition that requires a commitment to following purposeless hunches that create a different circuit of energy and knowledge with strange and unpredictable inputs and outputs (explored further in Chapter 9). It is an energetic connection to the world, with roots in historical, pagan, and spiritual concepts of vitalism as life's invisible force. Clay's sticky assemblage of water, minerals, time, and force formed transcorporeal connections as "the transit between body and environment" across land, time, and history, "reveal[ing] global networks of social injustice, law regulations, and environmental degradation" (Alaimo 2010, 15). The porosity of the dirt, as well as the geographic and temporal boundaries, was dilated. They created a kind of uncanny mobility where human and more-than-human energy and materiality interpenetrated, revealing thresholds for connecting with the unknown and calling attention to the magic of the everyday sites all around us (Bennett 2001). Time coalesced to reveal porous borders between the material property and land rights that govern it, between sedimentation and extraction, art and science, and nature and culture. Alaimo (2010) argued viscous porosity epitomizes transcorporeality, "with its emphasis on mediating membranes, which may be biological, social, and political, [as] a powerful model for understanding material interactions in scientific/ethical/political terms" (15).

Through an initial interest in better understanding clay compositions as the fundamental resource used in ceramics, we learned what was available in our local community. This looking again, or *re-searching* for the source of our common tools, revealed layers of connections that were previously invisible. Through a collective uncertainty, traveling together in unfamiliar terrain, the experience created a sympoietic pedagogy driven by vital curiosity. Our profound interconnectedness was revealed as we attended to compositions of the land, tools, bodies, relationships, and community values, diminishing our bounded individualism and representational distance to rehabilitate a contact with the earth and realize collective transcorporeal effects across life-forms. This project's lingering subjective and collective residues illuminate the powerful educational potential of every day, which are composed of so many moments where a life of learning crests in contact with all of the other lifetimes of experiences (humans' and nonhumans').

5

What Else Could We Create by Suspending Our Reality? Traveling Isolation's Intensity as Frictions of Potential

Unlike previous chapters that travel with a singular question or phenomenon to realize their infinite connections, here I confront an existential uncertainty, tracing evolving questions and spiraling realizations. This chapter takes on a different temporality, following the first three months of the Covid-19 shutdown in the United States through a timeline of phone notes, emails, social media posts, text messages, and personal reflections on daily events. As with previous chapters, curiosity is activated by material objects, language, and organic matter that appear as expressive signals (appearing in bold) that activate changes in my perception and perspective, and illuminate historical power relations connected to isolation, bodies, and control. Over three months, fundamental vital themes emerge around questions of life and death, certainty and confusion, existence and representation, biology and chemistry, hormonal development, proximity, and transmission. Like Chapter 4, walking is critical for activating my curiosity in a landscape of isolation and uncertainty. Among the walking research concepts introduced in the introduction to Part II, land/geos, transmateriality, and movement (Springgay and Truman 2018) are primary to the many emergent questions and evolving perspectives recorded and shared as "walking notes" throughout the chapter.

The paradoxical immediacy and duration of the date-stamped posts express the precarity of the moment. They act as traces of the past, coursing between work, school, travel, home, walks, daily routines, and popular culture. As the weeks pass, my posts express a spectrum of curiosity, from hope and optimistic speculation to anxiety, denial, and dismay. The contextualization and analysis reveal historical, philosophical, and political arguments around questions of truth, science, and religion; ethical questions between individualism and collective well-being; and stages of grief, moving through denial, bargaining, anger, and eventual hopelessness. Again, we see how curiosity, anxiety, and imagination emerge in the gap of uncertainty, but the affective expression of that uncertainty composes differently based on the conditions of emergence.

The Covid Landscape Forming

Tuesday, February 11, 2020. First feeling. Traveling to a conference in Chicago.
*A man sat in the corner at the airport, wearing a **mask** and **coughing incessantly**. I walked to the water fountain for a drink, looked at the **public faucet**, and **paused**. I bought a bottle of water instead.*

Saturday, March 7. Phone notes: List of wants/needs for spring and summer.
cruiser bike; dental work; tires for truck; couch; kids' summer camp; kayaks

March 8–15. Spring Break. The shutdown begins.

Wednesday, March 11. Facebook post: "There really is no toilet paper at any of the grocery stores."
*The **tension** in grocery stores had grown **palpable** over basic goods.*

News coverage of the coronavirus increased over the fall of 2019. First in China, then in Europe, and then, by February, came reports of a limited number of cases in coastal cities of the United States. Many government leaders were in denial publicly and encouraged more focus on physical hygiene in public spaces. I traveled to Chicago for a conference, where I felt my first sense of personal anxiety about contagion. The loud, incessant coughing by the man in the corner changed the atmosphere of the lobby. Masks had not yet become common, so his signaled awareness of a vulnerability. My above posts, from the second week of March, illuminate how oblivious we were to what would emerge. For instance, looking back on my plan for how we might spend our tax return on "wants/needs," it is clear how consumption was a way of providing some certainty and structure to life. During that week, we were informed that none of us would return to school or work, and those "wants" took on a very different significance. I bought the cruiser bike that had been at the top of the list over Spring Break. All of the other items turned out to be unnecessary and then impossible to access. I did not realize then that the bike would become a life raft to escape my home for short periods of time.

Over the coming months, the word "essential" took on a very different meaning—vital in terms of desire and necessary to keep the world running, but also anonymous and invisible, substituted as a moral imperative. My March 11 Facebook post about the grocery store marks a threshold, teetering between hope and despair. Up to this point, the virus was an abstraction. The news talked about it constantly, and the university had a social, political, and potentially legal obligation to limit their liability for spreading the virus among students, faculty, and staff. But that all just felt like prudent policy and political speculation, not reality. This day revealed something else. The material effects were beginning to appear in everyday spaces as the shelves in the grocery store were emptied of "essential" goods, like toilet paper and cleaning products. Signs went up about rationing meat and poultry—at first as a suggestion and then as a rule. But the physical absence of products and the introduction of procedures was only one side of the material shift. Our collective fear and shared anxiety turned into suspicion and competition. The disappearance of the toilet paper signaled a different atmospheric intensity in public spaces. Our relationships changed as strangers surveilled each other. Those who were hoarding specific products walked boldly through the grocery store, testing other patrons and cashiers to question their purchases or try to take them away.

A Taste of New Habits—Lifeline for a Different Future

Monday, March 16. Walking notes: Classes immediately go online.
I can do this. It will be an easy and kind of fun **transition**. *I am tired of this semester, anyway. It is a relief not to have to go to work. We are all at home working together, conscientious of each other's space and needs. We will have a daily work schedule for each of us, with lunches and walks together. I can finally finish the manuscripts that have been building dust, and I will make art and lose some weight with the restaurants all closed and food supplies limited. We will create a different* **lifestyle**.

Friday, March 20. Walking Notes: Daily walks and cactus blooms.
Daily walks around the neighborhood have become my social life beyond the house. The neighborhood's entrance gates, which I used to find irritating and alienating, now seem to keep the stories on the news at bay. The cacti are in bloom, and I have been documenting their changes every day as a way of studying and collecting, marking time and transformation. They create a kind of accountability, or maybe they validate my existence in some way, like something is still progressing as expected. It's strange how I still seem to long for something outside of myself to account for my existence. They make me think that my normal stress and **anxiety**,

and so many of the actions that fill my time, are just a **waste of energy** brought on by pressure to produce through **meaningless** busywork. *As these responsibilities and obligations disappear, other **forms of life are becoming visible**.*

Saturday, March 28. Walking Notes: Suspending and recomposing.
*How is the world **recomposing**? What unimaginable territories will emerge from the **suspension** of these established **flows**? What will life become?*

Sunday, March 29. Debt Relief Plan.
The government is sending out relief checks. I have been concerned about our finances since we moved here, and now a glimpse of a different life is emerging. We changed many of our daily habits out of necessity, and now, the possibility of having less debt becomes a lifeline to a different kind of future.

We were now home together all the time, as work and school all went online. With grocery store shelves emptying, I began inventorying our food and other consumable goods. I planned meals that could be stretched out and looked up recipes for foods that remained on shelves because they were less desirable. I got a sense of what rationing in previous crises might have felt like, and it felt good. It was liberating and empowering to make other choices and create different habits—possibly even create a different kind of life, and maybe even a different society. I thought for a moment, we might realize Guattari's (2000) assertion that

> it is no longer possible to claim to be opposed to capitalist power only from the outside, through trade unions and traditional politics. It is equally imperative to confront capitalism's effects in the domain of mental ecology in everyday life: individual, domestic, material, neighborly, creative, or in one's own personal ethics. Rather than looking for a stupefying and infantilizing consensus, it will be a question in the future of cultivating a dissensus and the singular production of existence. (50)

Our collective sentiment illuminated a growing potential for confronting capitalism's alienating and exploitative power in our everyday lives, and the sense that something might change was palpable.

My daily walking circuit around our neighborhood provided a sense of certainty and predictability, as the spring cactus blossoms signaled resilience and rebirth. While the path of the walk remained the same, the vital differences became noticeable in the environmental transformations among nonhuman species. Their bold, colorful variations expressed a world of potential that I had passed and ignored in previous years. Nature didn't seem to be affected by the pandemic, which affirmed that so many of the social practices and norms being suspended by our isolation were not actually necessary to live. The creative vitality of nature was amplified due to the newly realized capacities for attuning within the muted anthropocentric landscape. Then, it became clear that the environment *was* also being affected by the virus—but for the better. The lack of global travel, traffic, and tourism was measurably improving air and water quality. What else would become visible, as the world was on pause?

Cynical Curiosity Emerges

Thursday, April 2. Walking Notes: Who else is going to benefit from this?
We **converted** our classes to an online format **overnight**, and my kids' school district is in the process of doing the same. We are willingly **accommodating** changes that have been promoted for years by parties interested in **dismantling** public education. Who will **benefit** from and even exploit this crisis to implement changes that would have taken exponentially longer otherwise?

Saturday, April 4. Text to a friend: The campus as a future carcass.
I'm at school getting books and art supplies. The **lifeless** buildings are like skeletons. I wonder what they will become after this virus. How will their **lifeblood mutate**? The **deafening silence** of the vacant campus amplifies the sound of rustling leaves as they dance on empty cement walkways. The **desert** landscape beyond campus feels **more present** as nature thrives with spring blossoms. Shadows cast from trees onto the buildings are a reminder of the **native territories** occupied by the university. They create an eerie sense of a past and future folded together in isolation.

Monday, April 6. Email from a student: A bit more irritating than originally planned.
Hello Prof. Coats,
Unit 12 is proving to be a bit more **irritating** than originally **planned**. There is **no way to copy** and paste info as the units don't allow it. In addition, completing each unit **takes** a good amount of **time**. This is due to the fact that you **can't skip** pages and have to **complete** all of the **repetitive activities** to move on. I was wondering if there is an easier way to obtain the info since having to type out **everything seems really tedious**.
Best Regards, A

Tuesday, April 7. Message to mom and friends: Survive or flourish?

This is revealing how much energy we waste on useless activities we thought were necessary. We have a chance to live differently. We altered our entire lives overnight, trying to hold everything in the balance. Let's say no, **slow down,** *create* **new connections, pay attention differently,** *and deepen our* **relationships that matter.**

Wednesday, April 8. Newsletter I wrote to my field: A gap and a threshold.
Covid-19 has revealed a **threshold** *for* **change** *and* **illuminated** *the profound* **interconnectedness** *of life on our planet. The physical virus* **spread** *rapidly, moving between bodies and through the air; while a psychological virus moved through a drip, drip, drip of data, news, social media, and confusion.* **Testing** *has become the* **index** *for* **existence,** *and* **screens** *are more thoroughly entrenched as the* **lifeblood** *of global* **culture and communication.** *While many of us are experiencing profound levels of* **anxiety,** *we are also witnessing a* **collective ethos** *of compassion, sacrifice, and sharing among communities. Witnessing a reality that we thought was* **unattainable** *makes me ask what else might be possible. For those of you who rapidly changed your curriculum to an online delivery, what did it feel like? How did you adjust? What did you realize about yourself or about teaching art? While I am always impressed with teachers' resilience, this moment of* **openness** *to change can go a number of ways. What might the voluntary and mandatory* **constraints** *created by the virus* **enable***? The* **imagination** *is sparked by a* **gap** *between what is known and the unfamiliar. This unexpected break created by the virus might be just that kind of gap.*

Something else was changing. The novelty was beginning to wear off, and it was clear that radical change could be a threat to certain industries and institutions. My curious optimism diminished by the beginning of April, as the novelty wore off and the potential for making beneficial changes started to feel unlikely. The world was changing, and I felt I was sitting on a precipice. Up to this point, I had been running in circles to stay busy as a mode of survival rather than stepping back to consider what might be possible. If I could just keep planning, making, doing, then I wouldn't have to face the detrimental impacts of the pandemic.

We were notified that we would not return to school for the rest of the year, making the performance of normalcy or smooth adaptation seem silly. I had given up on trying to make the online version of my classes resemble the in-person experience and turned the majority of the content into independent work. Students also sought the most efficient path, exemplified by the student's message expressing irritation at being unable to skim, copy, or skip through the tedium of her schoolwork. Many people felt a similar desire to jump ahead in time to the end of the pandemic. We all just had to go through it, while longing to return to our normal lives and move on. Now, in the growing gap of the unfamiliar, norms and desires for "normal life" expressed a longing for predictability and familiarity.

I, too, had a shift in subjectivity, as my curious optimism turned to speculative pessimism. Growing wary and fearful, I wondered what would emerge and thrive in the end. The campus, as a body of land that structured the vitality of learning, now lay dormant as a sign of an uncertain future. Returning here after developing new patterns at home merged the world of my life prior to Covid-19 with my new routines, intensifying my questions about how these changes would be dangerously exploited. I didn't want to sit idly by while those with more power drove the machinery that further benefited neoliberal values of profit, individualization, competition, and efficiency, like the parasites in Chapters 2 and 3. Realizing the growing desire to just get on with life as usual, I began to overtly call out for others to recognize that we had an opportunity to do something else, but we would have to recognize our potential to direct energy toward our collective benefit. This call to action was an effort to slow the wave I could feel coming—trying to point out what was visible at that moment before the stronger forces took over.

The Death of the Human Is Preferable to the Death of Human Consumption

I had come to the critical realization that the struggle would be more difficult than I thought. My calls for change felt futile, and I was no longer in denial. Now, my curiosity turned to finding historical connections by attuning to traces of cultural and systemic patterns, where bodies of land and outmoded technology expressed dormant histories of extracted energy and collective myths. The effects I had realized during the clay dig two years earlier (Chapter 4) reemerged on a hike to a closed copper mine in the desert.

Easter Sunday, April 12. Walking Notes on a hike to a closed copper mine.
Purple and yellow blossoms cover the cuts in the cliff from the road that we are walking on.
The presence of the mine on the trail has been grown over.

*It's Easter Sunday, and the flowers make me think of the "**He is risen**" signs around my neighborhood.*
*Didn't Easter start as a pagan celebration of the **reemergence of nature** each Spring?*

*Looking up and out over the vast expanse of the mountain range, I realize I have been looking down, **lost in the immediacy of the trail.***
Danger sign. Burnt log. Dead animal? I am at the mine.
There's a strange, dark opening in the mountain—the shadow cast inside the passageway down is too foreboding to enter.

Turquoise** blue rocks surround the entrance. Is it an **effect** of the mining process? This would be a good question for science. **How do we reconcile science and religion?

*There's a change upon the return. The **novelty and wonder dissipate**.*
*My focus is more critical as the light, heat, and flies become **irritating**. The grasses make me **itch**.*
The effects of colonization and capitalism are again made present, this time through signs, cuts, boundaries, language, walls, trash, and the remnants of dead technology.
The buzz of the fly is more irritating, and the shadow created by a vulture flying above my head makes me feel like red meat.
I could die, but like this dead mine, the human habits that made mining possible will carry on.
The death of the human is way less threatening than the death of human consumption.

The Easter Sunday walk echoed the feelings I had been processing over the previous weeks. The initial sense of curious hope and anticipation had dissipated. I began to doubt that we could change the world for the better through this crisis. My curiosity about historical precedents illuminated transdisciplinary and transcorporeal connections about mythologies constructed to make sense of natural patterns. On the walk out, I was open to unexpected connections between history, technology, nature, and religion as I looked down at details and then out at the expanse of the landscape. On the way back, my body became more present, and my sense of awe diminished, as I critically recognized patterns of physical violence to bodies of land and realized how cultural mythologies of Manifest Destiny and the glorification of technological innovation at any cost justified the mine's detrimental effects (Alamo 2010; Moore 2015; Tsing 2015).

Nature's resilience, expressed in the grasses and flowers growing over the trails, reminded me that the energy remained, but in another form, while historical scars were visible in the cuts and discolored flows of chemicals on the rocks and recompositions of the land. I thought again about the clay dig, the renewed ecology of the strip of land with the gas pipe, and Alien Jesus (Chapter 4).

The change in my attitude and perspective during the walk paralleled the transformation in my perspective on the world over the previous two months. The hike was a turning point to broader, systemic realizations about ways that the land and bodies are used in the name of progress, technology, innovation, and production. My shifting state of mind about the pandemic converged with my interest in art, science, and philosophy at that moment. Together, they framed, focused, and colored my perspective about the echoes of our pandemic life left in traces on the deserted path to the old copper mine.

Philosophies of vitalism have historically traced a pendulum swing, back and forth, between mysticism and science. Lightning and magnetism were initially attributed to mystical forces or the will of gods and later explained scientifically by gravity and electricity, at times associated with religious spiritualism, and then with the magnetic pull of the earth and electricity, while vitality is now associated with consumption as our shared cultural worship as life's innervating force (Benjamin 1999; Bennett 2001; Mitchell 2013; Toscano 2007). The desire to hold open the possibility of an immeasurable force has consistently been met with a desire to name, control, and operationalize it. But what might it mean to hold open that unknown potential for a vital curiosity that attracts and lingers, without the desire to circumscribe and master it? I was left with the haunting thought that ended the last entry: **The death of the human is way less threatening than the death of human consumption.**

Invisibility, Proximity, Transmission, and Death

Monday, April 13. Message to mom and friends: Our moral imperative.
*No one is asking if this is an imposition on parents or teachers. We get a little nod, but ultimately the public discourse seems to be that it is **our moral imperative to be flexible and make it work**. In faculty meetings, all we talk about are student outcomes and support. At home, it is all about helping the children adapt and accommodating their needs in this difficult transition. We are **made** into the **invisible** and unbreakable funnel of support. No one cares about our needs, our challenges, and what we might need to "effectively transition."*

Friday, April 17. Walking Notes: Hormones and the future.
*If we are isolating bodies because they are **vectors** for the **contagion**, transmitted through **proximity**, how is this **isolation from other bodies** diminishing other corporeal transmissions? My teenage son is only able to experience his peers through screens and devices, but physical proximity creates a whole spectrum of **hormonal reactions** at his age—what will happen to those? Does the relationship of bodies **mediated by screens** create a different kind of **chemical response**? Is this affecting his hormonal development? How is he **mutating** through this **lack of stimulation**? I would think that widespread hormonal changes would reverberate for **generations** and ripple out to all other **life-forms**.*

Saturday, April 18. Walking Notes: Suspension, existence, and death.
*Is this lack of physical contact a kind of death? Culturally, we tend to **alienate** ourselves from the reality of death. **Now death lies on the side of buildings as our social roles are suspended.** The closed doors and windows to houses of death are held open and overflowing. We see the images day after day. And at the same time, the churning wheels of **factory production** and cars driving to work are **halted**, and the **natural environment can be felt and seen again**. The suspension of our normal lives has converged with an exposure to death, and it makes me ask **why our bodies are not enough. Maybe they are actually too much.***

Tuesday, April 21. Revealing what was there all along.
*An article called "No Room of One's Own" (Flaherty 2020) was published in the Inside Higher Ed journal, describing how Covid-19 was hurting female professors' research productivity because the **fragile supports** that **female faculty** typically rely on to balance their obligations at home and work **were now gone**.*

May 6. Message to mom and friends: I can do all of it again as usual.
*We are having a rough couple of days here. My husband has gone back to the office, which is sort of fine, I get it. But I can't go back to my office. I still have to work full-time, and the kids still have to be here doing school full-time. So, **what was a team effort** is, now again, me being a full-time mother and full-time professor because it is easier for him to get his work done in the office. Well, me too! But I can do all of it again as usual. Sorry, just ranting and frustrated.*

May 11. Walking notes: Rhythms of teaching.
*Spontaneity is the **lifeblood** of my **classroom**. It emerges from discussions, **relationships**, questions, curiosity, and **rhythms** between me and my students. Now, we are interfacing through **screens** and online content. I used to worry that I may have offended someone with an off-the-cuff remark, but that **honesty** created*

meaningful moments and invited students to become **vulnerable** *in response. Now I am talking to a black screen where students'* **faces aren't visible, wishing** *people would mute their background noise,* **confusedly** *trying to figure out what was said through the* **lag,** *awkwardly* **waiting** *for the next person to start talking before I do, and apologizing to let someone else talk. It is exhausting.* **This distance and mediation kills our vital and rhythmic chemistries.**

It became clear that this shutdown was not sustainable, and that certain people were carrying more of the burden than others, just as the environment carries the burden of human progress. I realized that teachers and other essential workers were becoming disposable tools. Like the seed bought in the package (Chapter 1), teachers, nurses, and other service workers were isolated and made anonymous, serving their singular function as a moral imperative (Agamben 2021). I began to wonder how the invisibility of "essential" workers illuminated what counted as life in schooling and local economies (Rose 2008). Like the "character" lessons in the fundraising rallies (Chapter 3), there was a morality to making it work in the most efficient way possible. We "ought" to be honored to be called "essential" while overlooked and sacrificed. This seemed so similar to the coding of life in other domains—that vital force, isolated, quantified, and operationalized for predictable outcomes (Agamben 2021; Anderson 2012). Later, the *Inside Higher Ed* article about the work/life balance inequities faced by female faculty confirmed not only that essential workers were carrying society in a number of ways but also that it has always been like this. It's just that the pause in so much of the world's activity finally made these inequities more visible. It was like this all along, and the final post about my husband returning to the office was really just a return to normalcy—the idea of having more help at home had actually been a novelty.

While I had grown deeply cynical about the illusion of caring about essential workers, a new curiosity emerged about bodies and transmissions through so much fear of contagion (Brennan 2004). I wondered: What contagions are necessary for development? How would pubescent hormones develop differently through this digital mediation? My son did not have a lot of friends at school, so the shift to online learning was actually better for his confidence and the development of peer groups based on gaming and social media. The competition and judgment so pervasive in teen life at schools had been a real struggle for him, whereas life across screens allowed him to determine his identity and exposure. It provided control and predictability, along with a new sense of self-confidence. He was shielded from the toxicity of youth culture.

The suspension had allowed me to be more attuned to my body and spend more time engaging with the natural environment, but for my son, social distancing strengthened his belief in the security of screens and the ability to simply log off when circumstances become uneasy. At school he was bullied, neglected, and alienated, so social isolation was comforting. Distance learning allowed him to control and predict his connections, limiting the potential for difference and variation. At the same time, I was on the other side of this experience in my classes. A different intensity had emerged in the online classroom. It was anxious and awkward, lacking any organic rhythms, a discordant exchange broken by lags and interruptions. The space of curiosity that could drive a lively conversation in person had become an experience marked with gaps of silence and confusion, lags and glitches, dark screens and loud backgrounds. Our worlds had become hyperpresent and completely absent. Unlike my son, I longed for the chemistry of physical contact, the hormonal tensions stirred by proximity, and the attraction generated from curious energy (Ahmed 2004, 2006). But so many of my students opted for the comfort of anonymity, efficiency, and predictability. The connection went cold.

These two paths of curiosity that related to essential workers' invisibility and the desire for online anonymity aligned for me in the frequent news stories about bodies being stacked in cooled trucks on the sides of hospitals in New York and other cities, while less affluent countries were burning bodies in the streets. As a culture, we tend to shield ourselves from death and dying. Not so much from the image of death-as-fiction, violently depicted in games and popular culture, but from death as a process of aging or loss. Death and dying are hidden, while we prioritize perceptions of youth and vitality as measures of value.

Perhaps thinking about essential workers' pain was too much to bear, just as my son's withdrawal from the emotional difficulty of teen life was easier than trying to cope with its complexity. As death lay all around us, we remained isolated behind screens and gates. Our capacity for connection diminished, like the treated crops incapable of responding to environmental pests (Chapter 1). At the same time, the decrease in industrial manufacturing was improving the quality of air and water around the globe. I wonder if there is any connection to be made between the factory production halted during isolation and the affective labor that replaced it? There seems to be an important paradox in the simultaneous increase of toxicity in human relations, while the toxicity of the natural environment decreased (Alaimo 2010; Moore 2015; Roussel and Cutter-Mackenzie-Knowles 2019). The solution is not isolation from difference, but the creation of conditions for a collective biodiversity to flourish (Anderson 2012; Braidotti 2021; Manning 2020; Mitchell 2013).

The Condition Has Spread

May 26. George Floyd was killed in Minneapolis by a police officer who kneeled on his neck to restrain him for over eight minutes while three others held him down.

May 27. The condition has spread.
*I woke up with **burning** hands. I could not stop the **itching** in my palms, and then the **heat spread** to my neck, ears, scalp, groin, armpits, and feet. The condition spread throughout the day. I had not eaten anything new nor introduced any new products to my daily regimen. What was **my body reacting** to?*

May 28. Birthday.
*This morning my **eyes** were nearly **swollen shut**, and my **breathing** was **strained**. The doctor gave me a steroid shot and prescribed antihistamines.*
The pandemic has moved to the backburner on the news cycle as riots, protesting the killing of George Floyd, have spread across the nation. Overnight, protesters had burned down the 3rd Precinct in Minneapolis, where the police officers who killed him were stationed.

May 29. It is in everything.
***The allergic condition remains.** I told my girlfriend, who lives in Ohio, about the outbreak. She informed me that she had a **similar reaction** a couple of days earlier. We speculated about the **water** or some toxins in the **air** but wondered how it could be **across the country simultaneously**.*

It *is* in the air. It has seeped into all living bodies. Our global condition is toxic. A threshold is coming. It reached my body—I could no longer simply bottle this stress, anxiety, and pain. How will this threshold register for the plurality of our global body? What will be on the other side?

In the end, of course, it was our bodies. While this seems terribly obvious, it is also critical to understanding how the desire to halt transmission of the virus, creating isolation from other bodies, only reduced certain kinds of transmission. Isolation narrowed the modes of relation to a flattened and primarily signified existence through digital interfaces, but contagious toxicity still flowed across the distance through a range of media sources (de Freitas 2018; Toscano 2007).

Social distancing did not change our profound interconnectedness, but it diminished our aesthetic capacity for finding rhythms with other bodies as a collective response-ability to "diverse fields of alterity" (Guattari 1995, 118). I longed for the return of an aesthetic classroom energy, embracing the sensations and intensities between and across our bodies.

Like the disciplining of knowledge and elimination of context in schooling, the isolation of bodies and the desire for efficient certainty during the pandemic limited our capacity and desire for experiencing complexity, variation, and difference. Not only was the distance felt physically, but by the end of the semester, students had turned off their screens as well. Now, there were not even facial expressions to provide a means of more-than-linguistic connections. Moreover, the pervasive desire to isolate our bodies also created a separation of the body from itself. In the final entries above, I experience a corporeal and existential threshold. My mind could no longer rationalize away what my body was feeling. It was expressed on my skin, in my throat, over my eyes, and in my lungs (de Freitas 2018). Perhaps the vital energy that had initially produced a flood of ideas and possibilities for what the world might become had turned inward through my growing pessimism. The force of despair and the frustrated drive to hold it all together created a turgid surge of toxins that could no longer be contained.

The three months that I explore through this chapter illuminate a range of curiosities, where the uncertainty of the original shutdown created infinite potential for change, where we could imagine new narratives about what life is and can be. The gap of uncertainty emerged from a reality that many living today had never experienced, as we witnessed collective efforts to ration foods, to people singing on their balconies at the same time of day, as a temporary global ethos and realization of our shared reality. But here the question of duration became critical—because as more time passed, the vital openness of curious and imaginative movement turned into repetitive flows, and the all-too-familiar began to fill in that gap. The virtual potential for life as something else turned into virtual learning spaces where everything is predetermined. The vital difference in our everyday physical encounters was eliminated, and the curious potential of a world we have never experienced was captured by the negative affects of a world void of desire for difference and variation (Agamben 2021).

Each day became a repetitive loop driven by a desire for certainty and a fear of the unknown. Even as the natural environment expressed new potential, with temporary clearing of atmospheric toxicity, the pervasive media messages and the deep longing for solutions, finitude, and a return to familiar habits and norms turned my curious energy to one of pessimism. I wonder: Did the inability of most of the population to remember a time when collective values mattered also feed into the fear? Memory could not fill in the gap of potential; narratives of threats and danger took over the imagination instead, creating a curiosity smothered by anxiety. The multiplicity that would normally characterize duration was muted and filled instead with a continuously homogeneous routine, where dreaming turned to automation. The elimination of the body, and the attentive movements that create encounters with difference, also limited the possibility of disturbances and dynamism that engender a vital curiosity. There was, and is still, the potential to engender the other tendency of life's vital force, which Bergson (1998) summed in this way:

> The role of life is to insert some *indetermination* into matter. Indeterminate, *i.e.* unforeseeable, are the forms it creates in the course of its evolution. More and more indeterminate also, more and more free, is the activity to which these forms serve as the vehicle (126) [. . .] Life in general is mobility itself. (128)

This conclusion is not intended to end so negatively, but to recognize the necessity of our bodily relations as a vital response-ability to each other. The potential of a different future existed, but we tended instead for the familiar and stagnation out of a longing for certainty and fixity.

6

Is This Land Just Layers of Bodies? Mapping Spectral Flows across Skeletal Forms

In this chapter, I follow an attraction to hauntingly beautiful cactus skeletons through a transcorporeal inquiry (a concept introduced in the introduction to Part II of the book), where a curious porosity emerges, as I think with cactus skeletons across a history of colonization in the American West and forms of displacement caused by contemporary suburban sprawl. This chapter takes a less immediate tone than others, reflecting the slowness of this inquiry, forming worlds around cactus bodies, as "stories are fleshed-out natural histories" (Alaimo 2010, 83). My family and I moved to Arizona in 2018, and like so many other transplants, we became enchanted by the desert. Having just left the piney forests and wetlands of Deep East Texas, the desert seemed mysteriously barren and eerily teeming with life—like walking into a ghost town, where the residents knew what was invisible to the rest of the world.

Mapping a transcorporeal inquiry that emerges over months of exploring, unlike the single day in Chapters 2 and 4, my relationship with cactus evolves through rhetoric, geography, popular culture, history, and folklore to realize our profound interconnectedness. I use the varying definitions of the word, skeleton, as a framing device for each section, following an emergent porosity (Benjamin and Lacis 1925) in its meaning, like that of the skeleton, forming multispecies connections and illuminating centuries of interconnected impacts of colonialism and then capitalism across bodies of human populations, bodies of land and nonhuman species, and bodies of knowledge and their evolution over time.

Skeletal Attraction

Every weekend, we visited a different park, venturing increasingly farther from home. On one of our first overnight camping trips, my son returned to the tent with a puffy green cactus ball stuck to his back. He didn't realize it was there, but as we tried to pull it off, the plant's tenacity struck me. The little "jumping cholla" was sneaky and kind of cute. Ben was surprised and slightly embarrassed, and we referred to the chollas as his little friends from that day forward. Looking more closely at the sneaky, detachable "jumping" joints on the cholla, I noticed areas where its exterior had dried up and fallen to the ground. Inside, the delicate, lacy fibers of its frame formed a flowing lattice of teardrop shapes, as seen in Figure 6.1. Was water stored in those amoeba-like pockets?

An intimacy with the cacti developed as the wounds on their skin became openings (see Figure 6.2), intensifying my attunement to their strange and spectral sense of lost futures and haunted pasts (Fisher 2014). I could feel the vulnerability of the cactus skeleton as its fluid vitality was drying into rigidity and crossing a threshold between life and death (see Figure 6.3). Attuning to the plants' differences amplified the landscape's signs of damage, drought, and death. Skeletons took on a spectral and speculative force as the desert became a cemetery or, more aptly, a crematorium. As we encountered more cactus species, they developed individual personalities. The established and iconic saguaro look over the wily cholla, while the tall flowering stalks of the agave signal their final burst of energy before passing, and prickly pears' spring blossoms attract a wide range of pollinators.

Figure 6.1 Close-up of cholla cactus. Photograph courtesy of author.

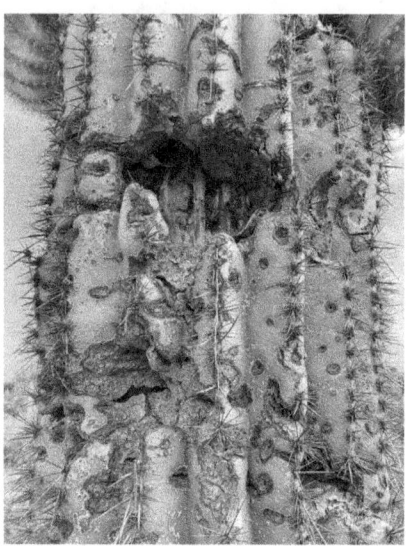

Figure 6.2 Peering inside saguaro. Photograph courtesy of author.

Figure 6.3 Cactus skeleton on the ground. Photograph courtesy of author.

I started photographing cacti that I would pass in my neighborhood and across the Western United States over a series of months. My photographic searches for skeletons changed, as the plants' dying elements allowed me to peer inside of them like the saguaro in Figure 6.2, seeing their beautifully complex, fluid vulnerability. I began to look more closely, gauging the varying degrees of decay when we hiked in different areas. At one point, I overheard someone describing the "ribs" of the saguaro. Were cacti bodies described in anatomical terms? Whereas so many of my curiosities exceeded language, now the word "skeletons" stuck with me, forming a node and an ecology, intensifying my interest in our mutual vulnerability (Colebrook 2014).

In the inquiry that I follow for the rest of this chapter, I enter the relationship with cacti from a series of openings, both bodily and linguistic. Sections are framed through a range of definitions of "skeleton," testing how their rhetorical variation creates a stickiness that transforms the worlds around the organic bodies (Ahmed 2004). A skeleton is first defined as "a usually rigid supportive or protective structure or framework of an organism *especially*: the bony or more or less cartilaginous framework supporting the soft tissues and protecting the internal organs of a vertebrate."[1] This definition aligns with my initial idea of skeletons, but the relationship between a rigid skeletal support and soft internal organs seems to be the opposite in the lacy, fluid, cholla skeleton, covered by its firm, protective, spiked exterior.

The Complex Life of Saguaro

Skeleton definition 2: "something reduced to its minimum form or essential parts."

Like so many other curious paths, my initial familiarity with cacti emerged from popular culture. I hadn't thought a lot about cacti before moving to Arizona; it may be cliché, but most of what I had seen before then was the prickly pear in Texas lawns or roadsides. Cacti never really interested me; like the packaged seeds (Chapter 1), they seemed lifeless. As we prepared to move to Phoenix, I became more aware of references to the desert in the news or other popular media and particularly to references to saguaro cactus. I thought of the saguaro as a kitschy symbol of the American West, so pervasive on keychains and in tourist marketing. There was a home insurance commercial that aired frequently during the summer we moved; it showed a saguaro falling on a house and described how the cactus can reach 250 years old. It seemed like a fun piece of trivia, but not actually possible.

Saguaros carry ecological, legal, cultural, ritual, and structural significance. The Saguaro National Park is called a "forest," but I never thought of cacti like trees. In Arizona, damaging or removing a saguaro is a class 4 felony that carries significant fines. While removing living saguaro is illegal, removing the dead is not. Like many cactus species, the saguaro's body serves a range of purposes, alive and dead. The ribs of dead saguaro are used to make harvesting tools, roofing materials, and furniture. Their spines have been used as sewing needles. You can find chairs, tables, and bed frames made from saguaro ribs at restaurants and markets across the Southwest. Saguaros stand like altars (see Figure 6.4) throughout the Sonoran Desert, which is facing a new wave of colonization, this time by suburban sprawl (pictured behind saguaro in Figure 6.5) and snowbirds from the northern states of the United States.

Figure 6.4 Saguaro on a mountain. Photograph courtesy of author.

Figure 6.5 Saguaro with an encroaching suburban community. Photograph courtesy of author.

Saguaros have historically played an important role in native ceremonies. The Tohono O'odham people "have long revered the saguaro cactus as a being with personhood—a belief that is congruous with the recent rights-of-nature movement" (Upholt 2022, n.p.). It is a sacred plant and a food source, bearing fruit that is eaten and prepared as a ceremonial juice. The plant is both a singular life and an ecology that carries worlds, as its body houses other species, exemplifying how "companion species infect each other all the time. . . . Bodily ethical and political obligations are infectious, or they should be" (Haraway 2016, 29). Gila woodpeckers create holes, called *boots*, with their beaks and build nests deep in the saguaros' cavities. The nests are hidden from view and left for other bird species to use in the future. The boots are created from callus tissue that forms over the wound. In recent years, early-breeding, nonnative birds have aggressively taken over many of the nests, to the detriment of the later-breeding and nesting elf owls.

Saguaros exist in a sympoietic relationship with the other life-forms in their ecology, making a home with the Gila woodpecker and providing space for collective and future-oriented nesting practices. The saguaro's body serves as a ceremonial altar, and its ribs become frames for other homes—human and nonhuman—in their passing. And while removing dead bodies does not carry the same legal punishment as removing living saguaros, removing the dead ribs damages the future habitats, populations, and plant seedlings of the fragile desert environment. The skeleton's organic content, vital to the biodiversity of its environment, is stripped to make chairs and tables for tourists.

The Bodily Strata at Massacre Falls

Skeleton definition 3: "something shameful and kept secret (as in a family)—often used in the phrase *skeleton in the closet.*"

Attunement to cactus skeletons intensified a haunting awareness of the area's darker histories. During the Covid-19 shutdown, we could hike local areas with far less tourists and even local traffic. With the quiet of isolation, the desert's barren surface created a strange intensity during our hikes, revealing scars born from how the human stories (Chapter 5) as surreal global mortality statistics were updated daily on the news. The land holds stories camouflaged by convenient myths that justify violent histories. But the hidden pasts are secreted through fluid hints and overgrown wounds.

My favorite hiking trails near Phoenix are in the Superstition Mountains. The area gained this name because of the interwoven stories connected to each area of the range, as well as myths, falsehoods, and spiritual beliefs attributed to Apache and other Indigenous tribes, Spanish and Dutch colonizers, historical settlers and surveyors, military outposts, and gold diggers. On our drive out to a hike one day, I learned that the trail we would visit was called, Massacre Grounds Trail. It gained its name from a North Mexican family of prospectors, the Peraltas, who were supposedly ambushed by Apache Indians in the 1840s. The story is part of the larger mythology around the search for goldmines during the colonization and settlement of the American West and has been portrayed in movies, popular TV shows, and documentaries about this region. My interest in this blurry line between the actual stories and fabulation echoed Haraway's (2016) practice of looking for "real stories that are also speculative fabulations and speculative realisms. These are stories in which multispecies players who are enmeshed in partial and flawed translations across difference, redo ways of living and dying attuned to still possible finite flourishings, still possible recuperations" (10). Like the hike to the closed copper mine (Chapter 5), Massacre Grounds Trail reveals local skeletons that connect centuries of living and dying, where the massacre continues through new technologies and earth's ongoing struggle with human desire for capture and innovation.

Myths and superstition are two sides of the same coin, providing explanations for that which is beyond our capacity to understand. They help us cope or provide safety from an uncomfortable reality. The story of the Peralta Massacre is told in a number of ways, but all follow the same tired tropes of "savage natives" brutally attacking enterprising settlers. Most accounts are told from the perspective of the Peralta family: independent, entrepreneurial prospectors unfairly ambushed by mounted Apache Indians, who drove them over a sheer cliff where the trail culminates at a waterfall. Historians have dispelled much of the Peralta Massacre story. But the prejudice against native peoples resonates. Their histories are deeply bound to the land, and the justifications for violence against Apache and other indigenous people echo a disregard for the environment as a disposable resource, whose significance is tied to use-value alone.

Invasive Thresholds

Skeleton definition 4: "an emaciated person or animal"

Once we arrived at the site, we realized that the trailhead is no longer accessible by car. We parked about a half mile out and hiked to a rusty old fence that opens to the original path. The terrain rapidly changed, as flat, open washes turned into narrow paths and winding ravines. The story of the massacre animated the trail as I looked for clues and hiding places, imagining where one might get trapped and stuck. As we stepped across a shallow stream of water, my husband stopped with a jolt. A cholla had grabbed his leg. The cactus was nearly invisible, buried under the overgrown grasses that lined the trail and surrounding hills. The invasive grasses emerged in part from decades of cattle ranching and monocrop farming, affecting the landscape throughout the Southwest. As cattle ranchers have moved across the area over decades, they feed cattle invasive grasses, such as buffelgrass, whose seeds spread rapidly and grow into tall, dry straws that choke out the native species. The grasses (seen in Figure 6.6) have increased the spread and impact of wildfires, in tandem with increasing temperatures due to climate change. The clinging cholla brought our attention to cactus skeletons lying on the ground around us (seen in Figure 6.3), some burnt by wildfires and others blanketed by dry grasses as they decomposed.

We continued on to the waterfall and walked a little faster on the return. The sun was setting, and shadows from the hills made the winding path more dangerous. As we descended into another shallow stream, my foot became stuck in the clay soil from the previous day's rain. I had been so focused on the cactus and grasses that I had not considered the ground itself. The moist, sticky clay clung to my foot, forming a threshold that took me back to digging clay with my students in Texas (Chapter 4). There, the property that we explored lay adjacent to the historic Caddo Trail, which served as a primary trade route connecting native tribes in the eastern and western areas of the United States.

Figure 6.6 Overgrown grasses along the trail. Photograph courtesy of author.

Curious Path... Bodies at the Border

The invasive grasses made me think about all of the nonnative invaders in Phoenix—like the snowbirds who migrate to the city every October to April from the upper Midwestern United States. My neighborhood is full of transient snowbirds. I have been confused by these folks, who are always grumpy at the grocery store. They seem so similar to the early-breeding, aggressive, nonnative birds that have taken over the nests in the saguaro boots at local elf owls' expense. The sprawling suburban neighborhoods expand, in part, to accommodate the transient populations, and they butt up against the tribal lands that surround Phoenix. Those native territories have been subject to centuries of treaties and settler rules that determine geographical demarcations. But the buffelgrass tells a different story: the burnt bodies of cacti, strangled by this invasive weed, remind us that those settled boundary lines are just another myth that compromises the lives of indigenous populations. I have heard neighbors complain of the migrants coming across the border from Mexico, 200 miles to the south. But my neighbors' primary homes in Minnesota and Michigan are 2,000 miles away. How can they describe the migrants as more invasive than themselves?

Weeks before the Massacre Falls hike, there was a news story about impacts of the Mexican border wall's construction on the ecosystem at Organ Pipe Cactus National Monument (Reese 2021). The wall was running through the national park, separating species that were dependent on one another. A video posted online went viral, showing bulldozers knocking down Organ Pipe cacti and hauling the bodies into large mounds to clear the land. The government downplayed the severity of the issue, claiming that the cacti could just be replanted. This idea that bodies can just be relocated and replanted echoes through history.

The bulldozed mound of cactus bodies reminded me of the Caddo Indian burial mounds near my home in East Texas. Throughout the early twentieth century, Caddo graves and burial mounds, which held human skeletal remains as well as pottery vessels and other funerary offerings, were destroyed and looted by farmers, archeologists, and graverobbers who often used large bulldozers—such as the archeologists who "for many decades [...] treated Caddo graves with little awareness of the feelings of living Caddo peoples. Taking a Western scientific perspective, [they] regarded human remains and grave offerings as mere evidence."[2] There is documentation of looted artifacts, including human skeletal remains, displayed on the mantles of private homes as decorative ornaments. The video of the bulldozer piling the large cactus bodies at Organ Pipe National Park brought back the story of the Caddo mounds and the image of human bones displayed as decoration that has always haunted me.

Transcorporeal Stickiness

In this chapter, my attraction to the rhetorical fluidity of skeletons and the realization that cactus forms are often described in anatomical language created a different kind of inquiry. The intentionality of my curiosity created a distance from this study, unlike the immediacy and shock that initiated most of the other chapters. The intrigue that the strangeness of skeletons held for me intensified as it spread to multispecies bodies sedimenting on the deserts that surround me. I began to see how the multivalent nature of language enfolded the anatomical, geological, and social, while bodily strata composed the desert landscape across a history bound up in creating stratified social groups as the American West was colonized.

Once again, moving across land as a form of walking research (see Part II introduction) connected histories of political, economic, geological, and cultural transformations. As I traced skeleton connections, the cactus body formed transcorporeal entanglements with invasive life-forms, realized through biased histories, cultural myths, and generations of migrations. Leaving the Massacre Grounds Trail that day, I felt the porosity of the clay soil, and how our contact with cactus bodies was obscured by invasive grasses. Attuning to skeletal connections embraced "trans-corporeality as the transit between body and environment [which] is exceedingly local, [where] tracing a toxic substance from production to consumption often reveals global networks of social injustice, lax regulations, and environmental degradation" (Alaimo 2010, 15). The transcorporeal inquiry was driven by an uncanny attraction to cactus skeletons, where vital curiosity diminished the geographic and temporal boundaries between the burnt jumping cholla, the exhumed Caddo graves, and the mound of Organ Pipe cacti.

Was it the language, beauty, or policy that first attracted me? It was all of them. Each unsettled my story of cactus, skeletons, and the desert. What I had thought was dead or purely symbolic became visible. Its vitality affected me. Looking across the mountains, the saguaros stood erect (like in Figure 6.4), like humans and altars simultaneously, while their mythical, legal, and visual intensity became increasingly complex—like the haunting presence of the Alien Jesus sculpture in Chapter 4. Unlike previous chapters, natural bodies clung to us. In each of the stories here, bodies were actually in contact: the jumping cholla stuck to us at different times. Similarly, clay's stickiness bound me to the land, creating a threshold, as "the soil against which the sole of my shoe presses: which makes one stumble in and out of inclusion, exclusion, identity, and difference—

and the 'zone' where transformations challenge the fixity of meanings" (Vighi, Nuselovici, and Ponzi 2014, 8).

The clay's sticky agency (Pacini-Ketchbaw, Kind, and Kocher 2017) brought me back to the present, but it was a present-past that intensified my "attention to life" (Deleuze 1988, 70), attuning to nature/culture intersections that connected elements of my class's clay dig and the Caddo Trail (Chapter 4), intersecting with the snowbirds' entitlement in my community, and how it connects to questions of indigenous land rights and oil pipelines. These connections echo back in time to the entrepreneurial prospector, as those pervasive cultural values still resonate in American public schools today (Chapter 3). The grasses intensified the visible residues of invasive destruction that has isolated, displaced, and smothered indigenous lives. On the one hand, the grasses reminded me of the brown, parched land and swarming grasshoppers at the missile base (Prelude), as well as the revitalized strip of land at the clay dig (Chapter 4), where the bushels of grass expressed a renewed potential for biodiversity as a form of rehabilitation. But the desert grasses do not expand the environment's vital complexity; they instead function more like a pesticide (Chapter 1), isolating the cacti and weakening the sympoietic potential of the desert ecology. Like the effects of monocrop farming on crops' resilience, the grasses diminish the land's ability to resist the disastrous spread of wildfires (Shiva 2016).

Like the porosity of skeleton bones, a vital connection flowed through all of them. More-than-human energy and materiality interpenetrated, revealing thresholds for connecting with unknown spectral networks across time and space and a desert landscape layered with skeletons. My porous curiosity expanded from a narrow connection between skeletons and cactus bodies to realize the saguaro's expansive significance, shifting from a singular body to an ecology. It raises important questions about when a life's significance is realized. Is it when it serves a practical function, like the saguaro ribs? When it begins to break down, like the cholla? When do we realize "worlds worth fighting for"? (Haraway and Tsing 2015, n.p.). I attuned to desert life through surprise at the surreality of the word "skeleton." Language vitalized the cactus's flesh, creating what Tuana (2007) described as a "viscous porosity of flesh—my flesh and flesh of the world. This porosity is a hinge through which we are in the world" (199), where a viscous connection emerges from membranes that act on the body through the flesh, as much as through cultural imaginaries and social habits. In this chapter, those membranes were activated in saguaro boots, cholla skeletons, and massacre stories. This more-than-human seepage illuminates a curious porosity, where porosity does not only signal effects, as I speculated in the introduction chapter, but a different kind of sociality, as a condition for connecting with the world (Anderson 2012; Manning 2012; Tsing 2015). I explore these questions of conditions and capacities for a different sociality in Part III of the book, expanding vital curiosity's connective force across bodies, to a profoundly collective entanglement between bodies, affects, nests, homes, and classrooms.

Part III

Collective Curiosity
Affirming Our Ethico-Aesthetic Potential

Part III, "Collective Curiosity: Affirming Our Ethico-Aesthetic Potential," merges the affective capacities and aesthetic inquiry processes with joyful intuition to consider how vital curiosity becomes a collective, ethico-aesthetic, and ecologically diverse mode for living. I continue to linger with questions of affect and anxiety, as well as joy and intuition, learning with multispecies bodies across institutional, domestic, and natural environments. These final chapters embody Zurn's (2020) call for a collective curiosity, "Relocating curiosity from the solitary philosopher to the crowd, from the intrepid animal to the packs and the herds, from the single plant to the network of organic life—that is what must be done. Collective curiosity is what we must now think" (240–41).

Themes, concepts, and memories from earlier chapters fold in on each other in Part III, building on concepts of expression and pollination, shock, and manufactured affect in Part I and the circuits of connection between sympoietic pedagogies and transcorporeal inquiry of Part II, to realize our embodied and embedded durational ecologies of interconnection in Part III. Here, the boundary of the human itself becomes porous through questions of transspecies, transcorporeal, and transmaterial expression that imagine "a new art of living in society" (Guattari 1995, 21). Here, vital curiosity's collective force embodies the spirit of Guattari's (1995) aesthetic paradigm that asks:

> how do we change mentalities, how do we reinvent social practices that would give back to humanity—if it ever had it—a sense of responsibility, and not only for its own survival, but equally for the future of all life on the planet, for animal and vegetable species, likewise for incorporeal species such as music, the arts,

cinema, the relation with time, love and compassion for others, the feeling of fusion at the heart of the cosmos. (119–20)

The new art of living embodies vital curiosity as a reinvention of social practices is explored through concepts of nesting, plant expression, open fields of childhood exploration, sweat's biosocial expression, love letters, and biosensors, considering how the strange resonances of connection are formed and felt in the everyday through an aesthetic capacity, response-ability, and conditions for a collective sociality (Manning 2020) that might point to an intuitive of *fusion at the heart of the cosmos.*

7

What Can a Body Express? Nesting as Collective Sociality

In this chapter, vital curiosity activates a process of transcorporeal inquiry through encounters with interspecies signaling that illuminate biosocial affective expressions in the formation of "mutual atmospheres" (Mitchell 2013, 204). Here, the tone and pace shift again, as my curious movement accelerates with a sticky mixture of emotion, wonder, and awe in the realization of our nested entanglements. Weaving together conceptual art, personal experiences, and the natural and social sciences, I travel with the concept of the nest and the process of nesting as a multispecies affective capacity and collective world-building practice,[1] I conclude by returning to the classroom to explore teaching as an embodied and embedded nesting practice vitalized through affective relations. Through these curious paths, I propose that we take up our intuitive capacities for affective connection and responsiveness, realizing the sticky and porous potential of the social domain (Haraway 2016; Tsing 2015).

Nests as Collective Compositions

Nests are temporary spaces, built out of anticipation and in preparation for receiving another. They are partial, speculative, and foundational. The nest is fertile ground, awaiting an unknown future, akin to curiosity's relationship to uncertainty. Nests are crafted from leftover scraps and bits—the threads bound with clay, carried by birds holding traces of a distant world, brought together in makeshift ecological assemblages (Somerville 2020). Bachelard (1964) described how a bird's tool is its own body, where the internal force of the female creates:

> a house built by and for the body, taking form from the inside, like a shell, in an intimacy that works physically ... pressed on countless times by the bird's breast,

its heart, surely with difficulty in breathing, perhaps even, with palpitations. . . .
The nest is a swelling fruit, pressing against its limits. (121)

Here, the body's indeterminate capacity to form new worlds is illuminated by the bird's force, as her body palpates dormant organic matter with life's imminent potential. The mutual atmosphere (Mitchell 2013) of the bird, twigs, mud, air, tree or ground, and the anticipation of a future life-form carves out a nested territory, as "a bed or receptacle prepared by an animal for its eggs and young; a place or specially modified structure serving as an abode of animals [particularly in] their immature stages."[2] This sounds so much like a school to me—a temporary space, materialized in the spirit of a collectively imagined future, and teeming with the curious rhythms of life.

My curiosity about nests was innervated when I learned of Helio Oiticica's art installation, *Ninhos* ("Nests"), which started in his Brooklyn apartment in 1969. There he created temporary spaces intended to bring people together and potentially leave something behind. Similar to the bird nest and the classroom, the aim of Oiticica's nests was "not to acquire a finished architectural form but to be in a posture of continuous shaping in relation to the worlds invented through momentary inhabitation" (Manning 2020, 59). The installation later appeared at the landmark 1970 "Information" show at MoMA as a series of inhabitable nests made out of wooden cells shrouded with drapes, in which viewers were invited to lounge (Davis 2017). One critic declared that Oiticica's ambitions were "to create an opportunity for communion, to radically alter perceptions, to engineer small oases of utopia in a dirty world" (Szremski 2017, n.p.). This kind of communion is both participatory and ritual. Today, these forms of social-engagement-as-art are not unusual, but they were radically participatory and improvisational at the time. I was particularly intrigued by the story of an art critic who had visited the initial installation of *Ninhos* in Oiticica's apartment and left behind a poem in the nest. As the critic was leaving, he heard someone reading it aloud, creating a kind of sideways perception of his past echoed through a stranger's interpretive utterance (Manning 2020). This uncanny feedback loop of past worlds, carried forward in new utterances and different combinations, echoes the material composition of nests in natural environments.

Within curriculum theory, nested knowledge creates a feedback loop as partial worlds form together, and this "iterative (looping back) dynamic is a critical element for knowing, learning, and teaching" (Davis, Sumara, and Luce-Kapler 2000, 16). Like the critic in Oiticica's apartment, the feedback loop is vital to thinking about the social potential of nestedness because a feedback loop expresses residual traces we have left on each other, even unconsciously. The feedback loops that emerge from nested relations illuminate how all of our knowledge and perception is partial and residual, as nests become unresolved spaces that elicit an emergent sociality, like the collective futurity of the Gila Woodpecker in the saguaro boot (Chapter 6). Here, the feedback loop is also the "precursor of an unconscious that is yet to come" (O'Sullivan 2010, 272), a joyful return that harkens an unknown future, "not as a conflictual expression of a repressed content but the positive, indexical manifestation of a universe trying to find itself, which comes back to knock at the window like a magic bird" (Guattari 2013, 68).

Nesting as Intuitive Affective Capacity

As shared "interspecies junction points" (Deleuze and Guattari 2004, 185) nests illuminate the cosmic collective potential of *nesting* as a multispecies process of becoming that is never finished. Vital curiosity becomes a nesting capacity that is fertile and often indiscernible until a much later moment in time, like the bird preparing a space out of anticipation and responsibility to an unknown but imagined future body (Somerville, McGavock, and Stephenson 2020). As a mother, I nested for both of my kids. I actually wasn't prepared for my first child, and I did not realize that I was nesting until clothes, blankets, and other potential necessities had started to form a pile in the living room of my small Chicago apartment. I was crafting conditions for an unknown future, palpating a space that was both material and immaterial, with my body as the primary tool.

I realized, after my son was born, that nesting was an embodied, affective capacity to intuitively and unconsciously respond to other bodies. One day in the grocery store, soon after giving birth, a baby was crying near me. Suddenly, my shirt became wet as I began to lactate in response to the other child's needs. I had no idea this was even possible. I experienced how "life owes its evolution to the intimacy of strangers" (Zollinger et al. 2022, 25). My body had developed a new set of affective capacities, realized through my proximity to strangers in my community, I was shocked, uncomfortable, and deeply in awe of the vital collectivity that my body expressed, as "beings render each other capable in actual encounters" (Haraway 2015, 5). The intersection of bodily capacity and material expression driven by a more-than-human intuition became a form of affective transmission and incipient potential generated by proximity (Brennan 2004). My body had formed a nest.

Unfortunately, this unconscious biosocial ability to nurture a stranger's child is too often ignored or muted. My corporeal response-ability is treated as an animalic and profane relation, similar to the Western aversion to death (Chapter 5). Mothering becomes an unintelligible, fugitive existence through the social expectations that carnal relations remain invisible and hidden, learning quickly that we are subordinated to nursing in public bathrooms. My new embodied relation was animated in postures, as well. I found myself tucking the laundry basket into the right side of my body, just above my hip, so I could hold it with one arm and Ben with the other. This stance initially felt like a performance of mothering, even though it was born out of necessity, I associated this image of motherhood with a body that is domestically bound, realizing later that it was another expression of my body's capacity to expand. The fugitive connection with fertility can diminish the desire to express our collective maternal capacity to form, and form with, other humans.

To be nested is to be embedded, which brings with it an ethical responsibility to those nested with you. But nesting is not just expressed by mothers. Each new school year, teachers nest in preparation for the unknowable, as an act emerging from experience, necessity, hope, and faith. As educators, we build nests everywhere—and each year classrooms hold our collective worlds temporarily, leaving traces on each other, forming "a world of strange mutually implicated beings cohering around objects and practices" (O'Sullivan 2010, 260). We teachers are also in a perpetual state of intuitive responsiveness: hearing a cry for help deep below the surface, listening for a small gesture of understanding. What do we hear, and how do we respond far beyond the boundaries of our sensorial or professional preparedness? Where does that same nesting desire and capacity, such as the embodied fertility to nurture an unknown child, emerge perpetually in every area of our lives?

Multispecies Affective Expression

While I have explored nests in relation to the lives of birds and humans, Bachelard (1964) describes how the nest "participates in the peace of the vegetable world. It is a point in the atmosphere of happiness that always surrounds large trees" (123). If nests are speculative assemblages that participate in their environment, and nesting is a collective worlding practice, could the multispecies potential of nesting as an affective capacity and practice also apply to plant life? "Plants are the first living bridges between the elements that, thanks to them, become livable for animals and humans. The connections they forge are nothing short of the language of life itself" (Marder 2019, 120). In Chapter 1, I explored how expressive traits are critical to genetic modification and agriculture, but that had more to do with controlling plants' potential yield for human desire. Thinking about plants' expressive capacities in terms of affect and communication is something very different.

Again, I turn to art's curious vitality to "awaken dormant life" (Mitchell 2013, 196), and as Deleuze and Guattari (2004) argue, to carve out a territory that vitalizes dynamic trajectories and the blossoming of life. Just as Helio Oiticica's conceptual installation innervated my curiosity about nests, the artist, Lindsay French's curious exhibition, "Signal to Nose," activated a new set of questions about plants' affective capacities. In her gallery installation, French used vaporizers to amplify plants' green leaf volatile (GLV) olfactory emissions throughout a gallery space.³ GLVs are organic compounds that many green leaf plants release in moments of stress and injury as a warning signal to other nearby plants and insects (Gagliano 2019). One example of a GLV scent is freshly mowed grass. In French's installation, the plant aromas formed a sensorial, atmospheric intensity, accompanied by the ambient sound of youth climate activists' voices played through transistor radios, offering a multispecies warning to visitors (Marder 2019; Mitchell 2013). I was shocked and enthralled—was the installation exhibiting a form of plant anxiety, where their bodies signal distress in the form of smells?

I immediately considered how the slow, sensory experience of French's show might benefit so many of us who live in perpetual anxiety. But what would mass plant distress smell like? While I cannot reproduce the affective intensity of the exhibition space, the dependence on memory to imagine how it might have smelled is fitting, because memory is critical to the relationship between GLVs and human affect (de Freitas 2018; Gagliano 2019). For instance, many people associate the smell of fresh-mowed grass with the first sign of summer, which for some, creates a nostalgic longing for past summers. In reality, the smell of the grass is an atmospheric distress call. Other common examples are basil, lavender, and chamomile, which have been commercialized for their affective impact on humans.

Because they are put under distress to create a commodity, I wonder: Is the work of GLVs also a kind of affective labor exploited from nature? As I explored in Chapters 2 and 3, affective labor is generally work that is intended to produce or change people's emotional experiences. Springgay and Truman (2018) identify it as the relationship between emotion and work, where "affective labour produces commodities of care and comfort that are not physical objects but still circulate and are consumed" (53). For those plant scents that have been commodified, GLVs' emotion-producing effects on humans often register with the memory to create a sense of well-being, calm, and nostalgia. This paradoxical association of plant life's precarity with the comfort of nostalgia is echoed in the temporary life of the bird nest that, too, is often idealized in the nostalgic "daydream of security" (Bachelard 1964, 122).

Sweat's Affective Intensity

My curiosity about multispecies affective transmission and response was starting to coalesce around nesting and GLVs, and reflecting again on my own unintentional distress signals in the grocery store, I wondered how else we unconsciously transmit affective signals, and what multispecies affective signals go unnoticed or are misrecognized every day. For instance, I sweat when I'm nervous. I even stopped wearing colorful clothes when I teach because it is so visible. But more importantly, it smells. I am actually really attracted to body odor, but I know many other people aren't, so I try to mask it. Sweat is a biological response to temperature change, but stress sweat is *different*. Normal sweat is made up of water, salt, and potassium, which does not necessarily have an odor. Stress sweat, on the other hand, is a thicker, milkier secretion made up of fatty acids and proteins that does not evaporate as quickly. It combines with bacteria on the skin to create an odor. Like the mothering postures, sweat odor carries cultural significance and baggage. What does my odor say about me? What is it signaling?[4]

Stress sweat's biochemical process is similar to the production of the atmospheric smell after a rainfall. Rain mixes with glandular oils on the surface of plants, vitalized by electricity in the air and bacteria on the ground to create the smell before and after rain (often identified as "petrichor"). I wondered if the electrical charge created during a storm is similar to mammals' nervous energy, and if it strengthens the stress odor as a kind of atmospheric aesthetics.[5] The different organic processes that create the smells of rain, sweat, and GLVs illuminate a spectrum of intensity between disturbance and distress, as a biochemical assemblage versus a mode of communication. Rain is produced from an ecological disturbance, and the smell associated with it emerges from a biochemical assemblage of ecological elements—whereas GLV scents are a form of multispecies communication. It seems that one is an effect and the other an affect. Bennett (2020) explores this idea of electric and affective currents, suggesting that "subliminal gravitational pulls and electric flows . . . are waves of underdetermined affect that do not tend toward the good or the evil. They form a realm of real incipience, vague affects, and protodesires or sensations, of not-quite-lived potentials of futurity" (61). Bennett's articulation of future-oriented affect is important to the question of both mammalian anxiety and volatile compound signals as sociobiological processes rooted in anticipation of events yet to come. Perhaps we might think of petrichor as the smell of atmospheric anticipation, an environmental fertility awaiting new life, like the nest created in preparation for an unknown future (Mitchell 2013). These phenomena illuminate a biosocial potential for vital curiosity, as an orientation of affective connection and entanglement with the world, enlivening mutual atmospheres with the affirmative energy of indeterminate anticipation.

Social Pressure as Silencing Force

Unlike the romanticized smell of rain, the odor created from stress sweat is unwelcome. I feel pressure to mask my body's smells, similar to obscuring my maternal leakage in the grocery store, as my biological responses become entangled with social pressure. That "musky" smell says too much—signaling that I'm unclean, uncivilized, or lacking composure. But why are these bodily signals undesirable? My body is unconsciously connecting, signaling that I care about the people around me, or at least that I care what they think. Why is that a sign of weakness? How else have we habituated our bodies to mute affection or mask compassion and connection? How has cultural pressure to silence affective responses diminished our capacity to take them up as incipient protodesires or potential futurity? Like curiosity, anxiety is a future-oriented emotion—one rooted in the anticipation of an unknown future (also explored in Chapter 5). What potential futures do we eliminate by masking our distress signals? Where do we limit our capacity for nesting out of a desire for acceptance, professionalism, or a fear of judgment?

Moreover, there is cultural pressure to cover the smell of our bodily signals even while we produce synthetic aromas of other life-forms, such as petrichor, basil, and lavender. These manufactured affective stimuli remind me of the fundraising rallies from Chapters 2 and 3 that create physical responses to empty stimuli while the original sources of energy (community resources or plant smells) are overlooked and exploited. Like the intense physical responses of the children in the cafeteria (Chapter 2), I have heard that basil is shocked before being packaged to intensify the distress signals that activate oil secretion, thereby enhancing consumer desire. The extraction of affect as commodity is a multispecies phenomenon, often occurring in relationships built on persuasion. For instance, teaching is rooted in affective labor and production, where intensive currents produce effects that echo the complex biochemical assemblages of storms and GLV signals.

In the classroom, pedagogical disruption is sometimes idealized as vitality. Teachers exert affective influence, creating disturbances that generate desire and control behavior. At the same time, teaching is frequently rooted in distress: we carry the heavy weight of trauma as a mode of caring for and nurturing students while masking our own emotional responses. Where does disruption in the service of learning, curiosity, and concern reach a threshold of distress? The distress of teaching is like that of the GLV, where I signal a danger warning. It is a warning often brought on by caring too much, of carrying others' trauma, the weight of expectations, pain, and frustration. I signal the fear of unmet desire. Over time, my compassion receptors are diminished. Something similar is happening to GLVs, which are becoming muted and confused by environmental pollutants that create stress and induce excessive plant emissions, reducing their signaling effectiveness (Gagliano 2019). This shared condition of incessant and accelerated environmental stimulation has exhausted our capacity to respond. I wonder how we find a way to resituate our receptors away from the noise, to hear our mutual, interspecies signals of pain, stress, and fear (Mitchell 2013). I am appealing to an attentiveness to underdetermined affects as more-than-human communication and compassion: listening to the smells.

Curiosity's Collective Porosity and Compositional Disposition

Can our collective nesting and attentiveness to mutual distress signals illuminate our potential to value that which is often exploited, overlooked, and erased? How might we create a different kind of *socius*—one that embraces a capacity to hear, outside of a transactional, capitalist logic of production and consumption, the underdetermined multispecies affects transmitted as a network of distress and anxiety? How might we do so as one step in *not* "relinquish[ing] this atmospheric realm to the capitalists" (Bennett 2020, 61), or, as Springgay and Truman (2018) suggested, "dislodg[ing] affective labor from capitalism"? (63). What else might happen when we pay attention to the transmaterial and transcorporeal connections across the boundaries of school and community, plant and human, nature and culture?

Finally, how might we combine the multispecies capacity for attunement with the multivalent perspective of the spatial, embodied, and affective nest—as bound, partial, and responsive? Marder (2019) argues that we must get past our anthropocentrism and hear plants speak, remaining imaginative and intimate, to feel our middle place linked to plants that connect to all of the natural elements, give them life, and feed the life in them. Could these tendencies toward intimacy and imagination become a disposition and condition for collective sociality in education and in the everyday? "Sociality is the quality that shifts the conditions of the relational field" (Manning 2020, 70), so considering nesting as a form of sociality can reorient the ways we value perceptive capacities as a collective disposition, attuning differently to what we hear and to the signals we are unable to mute. What if we create nested dispositions that acknowledge and reveal feedback loops as collective enunciation in the form of affective transmissions between nested bodies? This kind of disposition echoes the GLVs' responsiveness to the world and responsibility to each other.

Through participation in collective learning, curious nests can temporarily bind together distant worlds of partial knowledge. Our scraps of partial knowledge are held in our memory, reflecting our paths up to this moment as threads of knowledge and experiences we have assembled. In this sense, vital curiosity can become a mode of collective sociality, formed through unsettling encounters that embrace a curious unmastering in anticipation of an unknown future (O' Sullivan 2010; Singh 2018). Nesting can become a fugitive practice in education, curiously embracing the unknown and crafting a space of temporary, shared emergence without the need to hold on, own, name, or master (Manning 2020; Somerville 2020). Finally, porosity becomes the final element for creating nested conditions vitalized through social expressions of receptivity and an anticipation of our mutually bound relationships (de Freitas 2018, 303). Porous curiosity (introduced in Chapter 6) acts as an intuitive sponge through an affective responsiveness and as a practice of creating fertile, and unpredictable, collective compositions. As an internal attunement and an external compositional ability that is fundamentally embodied and sensual, vital curiosity can become a condition for a collective sociality, releasing the desire for closure or mastery to embrace joyfully partial, and durationally sticky compositions as a way of nesting with the world as a new art of living.

8

How Might We Live as Pollinators?
The Joyful, Strange, and Vital Uncertainty of a Pedagogical Life

Shifting registers in this chapter, I walk with someone else's story, told from a distance, to explore how the concepts, capacities, and expressions of vital curiosity that I have developed throughout the book are activated through another life. Denise first appeared in Chapter 1, where our experience removing seeds from dried zinnia and milkweed to develop a pollinator garden created curious paths around monocultures of schooling. The pollinator plants were material aspects of Denise's nested ecology, and in this chapter, I explore how her nesting also takes form as an ecological orientation and worlding capacity, perpetually "mobilizing the forces of all that is actively present, [as] an attunement to an aesthetics of the earth, in a posture of leaning toward" (Manning 2020, 236–7). Tracing Denise's life through stories, objects, and shared experiences, this chapter considers how "the art of life-living is the enthusiastic taking up of the adventure that is an ethico-aesthetics" (Manning 2020, 101). Denise's vital curiosity activates an eternal return, where "as an ethical thought the eternal return is the new formulation of the practical synthesis: *whatever you will, will it in such a way that you also will its eternal return*" (Deleuze 1983, 68). I use Manning's (2020) concept of *an aesthetics of the earth* as an attentive and attracted *leaning toward* throughout this chapter to consider vital curiosity's condition of perpetual interrelation to/with the world, where the affirmative capacity to affect and be affected becomes a strange and fugitive power and an ethico-aesthetic sensibility within the normative and nihilistic institutional landscape.

Composting's Curious Vitality

Denise served as my mentor teacher for eight weeks, while I was earning certification as an art teacher and developing my doctoral dissertation. She and

I talked for hours in her classroom, finding pockets of inspiration in between classes, during prep time, and at lunch. Every week in her class, some new serendipitous event occurred—she has that way about her, where coincidences glow because she is always awake to their potential. The week before I was supposed to go to the school for the first time to meet her and help prepare the classroom, I commented on an old friend's social media post. Soon after, a response appeared from Denise asking if I was the Cala Coats who would be her student teacher in the coming weeks. *Of course.* The relationship started before it started because there is an intuitive, magnetic, middling force that always swirls around Denise.

Her classroom was exhilarating. She mentors a student teacher almost every semester. Looking back, I can't imagine how exhausting having a shadow everyday must be, while also maintaining a classroom that serves approximately 600 students per week. At first, we kept the relationship very professional, a mentor/mentee boundary. I hadn't wanted to burden her with my dissertation stories because it seemed inappropriate to eat up her time in that way. Within a week or two, though, the conversations flowed with curious speculation, hilarious realizations, and new shared paths of interest. At the time, I was deep into the web of connections I was weaving across time and culture around the missile base (Prelude chapter), which I had only discovered a couple months earlier. One day, I finally shared my story of following food trucks and developing a fascination with backyard bomb shelters around the community (introduced in Prelude). Denise listened intently. Her eyes always squint a little when a coincidence is emerging. It is like a cresting wave that breaks when you realize her path has crossed yours innumerable times. Then she suggested, "Well, you're welcome to come over to my house. I have a bomb shelter in my backyard." *Of course she did.*

Collectivity in the Making

I visited Denise's home for the first time to see and photograph the bomb shelter. It would be the first of many visits to her house over the following years. We walked across the back patio, where stacked pots, leftover art supplies, and various tools were organized around partially constructed projects. "Oh yes, those are old picture frames that I am combining for the swinging door on the chicken coop," Denise explained. She directed my glance to the tall, colorful bricolage structure composed of mixed woods, leftover frames, and screens, and decorated with years of acquired accouterments on the other side of the yard.

I could see her excitement, as it must have come together recently. It was well constructed, and the bits of decorative tile and paint that covered parts of the exterior told stories that reverberated from the stacked materials on the patio.

Her large chicken, Mrs. Feather-bottom, ran in front of me as we walked to see the thriving compost that Denise had described in class. Scout and Barney, her dogs whose pictures I had seen on her desk at school, followed Mrs. Feather-bottom, darting back and forth around us. Her yard was teeming with life, as each interrelated element served the others. The milkweed and zinnia, whose seeds we had pulled a week earlier for the pollinator garden, were situated vibrantly within the larger ecology. Almost every designed element in the yard was from repurposed materials, from the soil to the fence, from the compost to the coop. I complimented her ingenuity and resourcefulness. She looked back at me and said, "it's actually a way of life . . . first it was the eggs, and we just liked the idea of chickens walking around the backyard. And then the poop for the compost, so it was all about creating a cycle with the gardens and the compost and the chickens." This lifestyle introduced her to a larger community of urban homesteaders, developed around DIY approaches and shared knowledge, continuing ancient collective agricultural practices, like the communal seed banks described in Chapter 3.

She wanted to start a family (and by that, she meant chickens, dogs, and vegetables) when she bought the house, which meant she had to transform the backyard to create conditions suitable for chickens. It took over a year of altering the fence and the patio, constructing a coop, and changing the carport. The large garden and compost, three chickens and a coop, two dogs, and many square feet of space with trees, plants, and herbs had become a self-sustaining ecosystem. I wondered if the life of the yard controlled her to a certain degree, inverting the more common humanist notion of the steward, where the human is central. Denise explained:

> If you do it right, they do. I mean, if you do it with any sense of responsibility they do, because there are people who have animals that don't control their lives, and they've got crappy, sick, sad, lonely animals. I think it's a choice you make to do that. You can treat them poorly, and maybe you feel good when you treat them poorly. It depends on what you want.

Denise's pragmatic description of people who choose to treat animals poorly as a nihilistic will to power illuminates how we make daily choices about the kind of life we create, where the will to nothingness is always possible. Instead, she embraced a response-ability "to connect with this collectivity in the making" that was not about controlling a small world with her at the center but composing a nest as a future-oriented practice for nurturing another way of living, "not simply with the human but in the wider ecology of worlds in their unfolding" (Manning 2016, 173). Each element of her backyard ecology expressed the artfulness of Denise's vital curiosity, where artfulness is an "aesthetic yield of experience in the making" (Manning 2020, 44). The coop, chickens, dogs, garden, and unfinished projects were traces of unknown potential, attracting that which is beyond immediate recognition or application, where she appreciates each individual being, both living and nonliving, as ecologically entangled.

The Strange Attraction in Curatorial Nesting

A few months later, I visited Denise's house again. It was a Sunday in February, and she apologized when we entered the living room. Clothes were hung to dry from the door jambs and fireplace to humidify the air while the heater was running. It reminded me of my grandmother's house growing up, but I knew few people who still make those little daily choices with central heat and air. Denise's artful attunement to atmospheric conditions was another form of co-composing with the house as a nest, realizing how "the aesthetics of our coming into relation matters, it has effects: what things do when they shape each other is deeply affected by the art of living" (Manning 2020, 97). The house was built in the 1950s, and wood paneling covers the walls throughout the living room and kitchen. Her realtor suggested that the paneling might be removed, but the knotty pine had strengthened her attraction to the house. Many people would have overlooked or confused it for an artificial laminate. Removing real pine wood from the walls seemed absurd to Denise, which was affirmed when a home inspector later explained how difficult and expensive it is to find that paneling anymore. She took her time finding the home, saving her money for years, living in a shed with her husband, and with his mother for a stretch. She felt privileged to be able to slow down and wait. Waiting has become a kind of fugitive behavior in a culture of acceleration and consumption—a valuing of objects and time, as life in the making (Manning 2020; Mitchell 2013).

A curious field of connection seems to surround her, where the feedback loop of time, experience, memory, and knowledge fold into her daily choices and transmit out into her minor relations through daily encounters. As we moved through the house, each object held a story, but not necessarily about her. Some were sideways stories of the style of a lampshade or the pattern in a crocheted blanket, where the materiality and techniques held other histories.

Her decorative objects form small collections of gifts handed down, made, and found. Each one had a life that intersected with hers, where the past vibrated in its *thing-power* (Bennett 2010, introduced in Chapter 2). For instance, a black-and-white photograph hung above the kitchen table. It pictured a restaurant in Amarillo, Texas, with a rounded façade that looked like it was built in the early 1960s. Denise walked past that restaurant regularly on her way to the library while interning at the Amarillo Museum of Art, and one of the museum's board members gave the photo to her as a gift. Denise had intentionally chosen a small museum for a required internship during graduate school because it would allow her to take on a variety of roles and work directly with the objects in its collection. As we walked through her home, I realized that I was witnessing her curatorial practice through a collection of objects acting as kinetic traces in her curious life (Zurn 2021).

The etymology of curiosity is similar to that of curation. As I explained in the book's introduction, curiosity's root is *cura-*, meaning "to cure," and *curiosus*, meaning "careful" or "inquisitive." We can trace "curate" to the Medieval Latin *cūrātus*, from *cūrāre*, "to have spiritual charge of," and later Middle English *curat*, "person charged with the care of souls, parish priest."[1] On the one hand, Denise's objects are all evidence of a curious life, where her stories wove together many different lives. At the same time, though, they involve carefulness and curing, as an extension of her nested backyard ecology. While curation can become a kind of sovereign and therapeutic curiosity, confining and isolating objects in the service of care (Zurn 2018), how might this notion of "having spiritual charge of" at the origin of curation create a different sense of intersection with Denise's practices as modes of vital curiosity? Denise described her collecting practice as a quest, studying the composition, style, condition, and origin of objects. She weighed this knowledge with the constraints of what she can afford as well as the objects' potential for being rehabilitated. This may sound like another mode of consumption and appraisal, but her slow, curatorial process involves care and curing. It is a form of restoring to health, a different kind of curious will, embedded in an inquiry process oriented toward experience in the making, where the aesthetic event of coming into relation with objects realizes her connection to its life in the middle (Manning 2020). The ethico-aesthetic vitality of this curious practice exemplifies how "ethics centers on *assessing* a way of existing, while aesthetics focuses on *inventing* a way of existing" (Surin 2011, 143, emphasis added), meaning that what one *ought to do* is not determined in advance as a moral code, but is a relational response-ability that emerges through the creative activity of life-living. Coleman (2008) explains,

"Ethics" is not, therefore, a static system (of Good–Evil) into which things can be fitted but, rather, ethics is emergent, dynamic and transformative. Integral to both Deleuze's reading of Spinoza's ethics and Bergson's method of intuition is the assumption of the capacity of things to change and unfold. (119)

Denise's ethics comes alive in her capacity for creating a strange attraction, a sensibility to the beauty in a life, straddling origin stories and speculative futures. Her pleasure is not found in the act of caring to death but in affirming a different life. As she explained, "I get joy from knowing it didn't go into a land fill—you know?" What else might this life do?

The Curious Vitality of the Everyday in Hiddenstream Aesthetics

Denise described her art practice as "hiddenstream," which was a term I hadn't heard before. It is broader than the production of artistic objects, but also is not mainstream or folk. Hiddenstream has been associated with daily creative practices, as well as quilting and other needlework, particularly among middle- and lower-income populations (Bain 2000; Blandy and Hoffman 1991; Congdon and Blandy 2005). Denise was inspired by her mother's minor creative practices (Deleuze and Guattari 1987; Manning 2016), such as keeping a string that came as part of the packaging of a roast because she saw its potential for later use, or placing a loving message on a napkin in Denise's and her siblings' lunch bags. Similar to her practices of curation, these minor gestures inspired her to value the more-than of every moment and object, where a future discovery carries an imminence of a life yet-unknown. Denise explained:

> It is not generally recognized as requiring any skill in art because they were traditionally done by women, so you know how food is arranged on a plate. . .
> . . . It's a neglected stream of art. . . . Like if I was to tell someone how I arranged bowls in color order. That is a sense of making art. People say, "No, it's not." And I say that I consciously arranged it. And that I collected them from a specific era to bring into this space.

While descriptions of hiddenstream are often rooted in notions of use-value and functionality, Denise's hiddenstream sensitivity and ecological nesting echoes Manning's (2020) description of *anarchiving*, as a practice and capacity for "registering what else flowed through the work . . . capable of seeding new practices on a different terrain, practices that could generate new techniques, new processes, that coincided in some sense with what took place before but didn't need to conform to it" (84). The idea of "flowing through" echoes the notion of the stream, and with a sensitivity to the world in ways that may not be recognizable to others. Denise's hiddenstream practices became modes of co-composing with living and nonliving elements. They were influenced by her parents' Depression-era values, but her pragmatics are not rooted in a lack-based sense of precarity, but rather a perpetual attunement to new worlds of activity-in-the-making.

Denise grew up in a suburb of Chicago. As a child, her dad would take her on vacations to the Upper Peninsula of Michigan and also make trips to the Art Institute of Chicago. She developed a transversal sense of aesthetics, residing across nature, art, and the domestic (Mitchell 2013; Somerville, McGavock, and Stephenson 2020). Her parents divorced when she was seven. After the divorce, her mother began working long hours to support Denise and her siblings. Having grown up similarly, as what was then called a "latch-key kid," I related to her experience of being a teenager with an unusual amount of freedom, whose house drew the neighborhood kids because there was less supervision. Previously, I had thought of freedom in the sense of a liberal individualism, where I faced the consequences of my self-determination. I'm curiously rethinking this notion, as a different story emerges when we consider how freedom is not just the elimination of constraints or discipline.

How might we reorient ourselves to an affirmative and attuned notion of freedom that is not tethered to what exists, such as societal norms of desire, behavior, and communication, but instead asks how we might live otherwise? In relation to vital curiosity, freedom becomes a nomadic force of movement and desire, embracing the indeterminate potential of *not knowing*, as a proposition to experiment with other modes of existence and world-building (Deleuze and Guattari 1987; May 2005). It is a reorienting process, from the preexisting human(ist) subjectivity bound to a set of relations that assume or rely upon established modes of existence and conditions of knowledge; to a freedom in-formation, an emergent and intensive connection to an open field of connection and expression.

This sense of freedom is expressed in the stories of Denise's childhood home backed up to an open field with trees and water. She spent much of her time there. With limited financial resources, she attuned to nature's intrigue, and as she got older, the natural space became one of escape and exploration. She explained,

> So we had a ladder to go over the fence, and we were gone all the time. We would build forts. We would pick apart pods of milkweed, we would make things out of nature. I think it was freedom, lack of supervision, and not having money. So when you don't have the latest everything, you have to figure something out.

Experimentation, creativity, and imagination are all modes of thinking without predetermined outcomes that rely on a certain amount of freedom and choice, which are often taken for granted as beneficial. While Denise had limited financial resources, she had far more freedom and responsibility than other kids her age. That freedom afforded her more choices and the ethical dilemmas that can emerge from them. Denise explained,

> But here's the thing, we washed our clothes. No one checked our homework. If we wanted clean clothes, we washed them. If we didn't want to get in trouble at school, we did our homework. I think my mother loved me very much, but I think she showed she loved me by making sure I had food, and you have to work to do that.

The values embedded in choice and responsibility that were developed in her home as a child, show up as active and ethical dispositions in her classroom today.

Rather than thinking with a lack of supervision or resources, her sense of freedom was activated by her curious vitality, realizing the process of other emergent ecologies. I hadn't picked up on the return of the milkweed from Chapter 1, when I initially recounted her story. I wonder, now, if that open field behind her home was an embryonic force (Wallin 2011b) attracting her to relations of sociality expressed as an aesthetics of the earth (Manning 2020). The elements that initially sparked an interest and attracted her attention have endured as feedback loops in an eternal return. Curious drifts can form nascent desire lines that veer off the prepared path (Fendler 2019), where drifting becomes a radical attraction to what is not visible, questioning established tools and methods by asking what is at their root and what else they might become. Denise's ethical frame developed out of personal experience from a young age, married with her hiddenstream aesthetic sensibility to realize an approach to the everyday that is curiously attuned as a response-ability.

Fugitive Sociality in the Normative Institution

For the remainder of the chapter, we leave the privacy of Denise's home and return to the elementary school to explore how her curious, ethico-aesthetic vitality takes on a strangeness in the normative institutional environment. A shift from the internalization of the environment and an externalization of affective attunement with the more-than-human world occurs in the school (Guattari, 1989). The first time that we went to the teachers' lounge for our lunch period, I noticed a teacher pause and look back at Denise as she walked toward the trash can to discard the plastic tray from her frozen meal. Denise noticed it too, and said, loud enough to carry across the room, "Yeah, if you leave it there by the sink, I can wash it." Clearly, this interest or expectation for recycling the trays was known among her colleagues. I hadn't noticed that the paint trays in the classroom were mostly reused frozen lunch containers until that moment, but the realization illuminated the prior life of so many other objects in the room, from reused paper and scraps to stamps and stencils made out of lids from detergent, deodorant, and other products. The hiddenstream ethic is lived in her classroom, expressed as an aesthetic force that flowed from her childhood home to the teachers' lounge.

That day, she expressed an insecurity that teachers and neighbors might consider her weird. Her willingness to publicly collect other teachers' used trays, to talk openly about her opinions about inequality in the school system, and her experimental teaching methods with uncertain outcomes made her different. But to feel othered for caring about the environment and students' passion for learning illuminates normativity's life-denying force in the public school environment (Jun 2011). I described normalizing forces in Chapters 3, 5, and 7, and I saw their effects in Denise's concerns that day. The normalizing homogeneity of public school becomes a life-denying force that "narrows my possibilities and condemns me to a diminished milieu to which I can do no more than adapt myself. But, in another way, it reveals to me a new capacity, it endows me with a new will that I can make my own, going to the limit of a strange power" (Deleuze 1983, 66). Denise echoed Deleuze's realization above, explaining that her lifestyle and her ethics are a choice: "You are othered for living this life. That's okay. That comes down again to a sense of bravery or self-esteem. Because in a sense, being brave or willing to fail is about self-esteem." Denise's bravery stems from her vital curiosity—a strange power that attracts and creates an environment of joyful insubordination. Zurn (2021) suggested that "when curiosity's insubordinate potential is tapped . . . it casts radical doubt on the status quo, and it fearlessly imagines new and better futures" (145). It becomes a fugitive capacity to imagine another way of living.

Becoming Unrecognizable in a Universe of Representation

Denise's classroom also amplifies her strange power through a choice-based environment as a "temporary heterotopia-like space where normality is dispensed with for a while" (Wild 2011, 430). The room becomes something else—not the dead or monocultural school landscape; instead, it invites students to situate themselves, moving between and across media-specific art studios to experiment and performatively engage in an open artistic process. She focuses on the active process of knowledge-development itself, "becoming-active can only be thought as the product of a *selection* . . . by the activity of force and the affirmation of the will" (Deleuze 1983, 68). She activates and affirms the flow of thought and movement around the classroom, with innumerable intersections, touchpoints, influences, and divergences, which is counter to the linear and homogeneous pedagogical environment of the rest of the school. In her classroom, students explore ideas and techniques through direct experimentation within a community of other experimenters (Engel 2020). This curricular approach resists its normative force of schooling to evoke an adventurous and playful spirit within the institution, encouraging the art classroom to become a site of tiny revolts through aesthetic inquiry that embraces the unpredictable (Higgins 2002; Lewis 2014).

Denise's pedagogical style illuminates and celebrates life in the middle, appreciating the process of learning through choices and actions in the making, as opposed to prioritizing output alone. This is not to dismiss students' work. Moments of completion or false closure mark points of arrival in the process, but for an art teacher, this can be a risky approach, since the normative domain of studio art continues to rest in traditional visual aesthetic production, monumentalized in frames and on pedestals. While her room visually bears the signs of an accountability-driven art room with educational objectives listed on the board, rules and expectations posted on the walls, and the traditional principles and elements of art and design visible throughout, she is principally concerned with what happens in the process of making as an unfolding event. Unfortunately, this less monumental focus on flow and movement that echoes her hiddenstream aesthetics can also make her indiscernible to the rest of the school community, which can feel alienating at times.

Although it is lonely at times, as the only art teacher in her elementary school, Denise has the luxury of working with many of her students over a six-year span. That large window of time affords her the ability to build and revisit ideas, creating a durational feedback loop (Chapter 7). I wondered if she had moments where she realized how much her students learned over the years in her classes. She explained:

> We had a book fair, and one of the second-grade kids came running up to me. His mom said he could have one book, and he chose *My First Field Guide to Birds*. It was after we did the migration projects. Later, we did another project on

the migration birds of Denton that I called "Our Winter Residents." Right now we're finishing that up, and we'll see. The robins are coming back, so our spring residents are returning. Now the students have seen the whole cycle.

I asked her if the science teachers ever relay what students have said back to her about things students share in science that they learned in art class. She responded:

> They have no idea what I do in my classroom. Nobody has any idea. They're giving out faculty awards for integrating interdisciplinary elements, and I'm sitting there next to my new student teacher. She's like, "Oh, so you just didn't get one this year?" And I'm like, "They didn't give me one. They never do. They don't know what I do in my classroom. And they don't, they have no idea."

While Denise does not put great faith in the type of awards she describes in the conversation, she clearly felt some amount of frustration over her peers' lack of awareness. It is not simply that other teachers do not remain in her classroom long enough to understand, but that she is teaching in a mode so alien to representational norms that she is unrecognizable. In addition to educational practices constituted by representational logics, art education as a field and discipline is also defined and valued by those logics.

I regularly watched Denise explain to other teachers how projects related conceptually to larger natural systems. They would typically respond with a compliment about the appearance of the finished pieces, often missing the conceptual frame or interdisciplinary connections, just as they can only understand her work as a set of representations. Because she does not compartmentalize learning into isolated and decontextualized packets of data (Chapter 1), the teachers don't recognize what she is teaching. The process is connected to the body of knowledge, and experiences in the body of the students, rather than torn from itself—creating an embodied and embedded sociality as a fugitive pedagogy (Harney and Moten 2013). It is a kind of pedagogy that is incalculable, lived through a "sociality [that] exceeds the count . . . never being valued in advance of coming-to-be" (Manning 2020, 5). The sociality at the heart of Denise's classroom is driven by the incalculable and unpredictable force of vital curiosity, making it invaluable as a learning capacity and unvalued in a neoliberal education landscape.

Everything Is Already Out There

Denise has experienced the shift to the neoliberal business model in schools over the last twenty years of teaching. She has witnessed increasing numbers of third parties are profiting off of the education system, from the companies that construct the tests and accompanying policies and procedures to the remediation of students who perform poorly on them (Ravitch 2013). She explained how testing increasingly defines teachers' roles, their daily responsibilities, the content of their curriculum, and their precarious existence within the school environment, progressively removing any actual teaching. The pervasive accountability culture of schooling has created a cognitive, linguistic, and affective monoculture, where the value of teaching and learning is determined by a market logic of inputs and outputs (Lewis and Hyland 2022).

During a fourth-grade class, one boy sat staring at his paper. Denise was unsure if he was finished or just uninterested. Realizing that he seemed to be stuck or unable to think of an idea, she squatted down beside his table and posed a few questions to help him brainstorm.

> "What would you like to see in the future?" Denise asked.
> "I don't know. I mean I'm not really sure," he replied.
> "Well, if you could create anything, what would it be?" she responded.
> In a lifeless tone, the student replied, "everything has already been invented, so what is the point?"

This exchange affected me intensely. My fear that curiosity is being killed by schooling was confirmed. I knew that students had grown apathetic about learning, particularly in relation to school, but this was something else. This was not simply a lack of interest but an internalized belief that there is nothing more to do or create, which points to the critical need for vital curiosity. While fear and anxiety have become integral aspects of high-stakes testing culture, the life-affirming affective force of thought and imagination has been extinguished (Anderson 2012). We should be alarmed.

Prioritizing predetermined learning outcomes as the only aspects of learning that matter diminishes a capacity and appetite for curiosity. We don't know what we are capable of because it seems to have all been determined in advance, and large companies profit from affirming and reproducing that belief. In this environment, where can a desire to wonder, wander, and think emerge anew? Moreover, if the desire for measurable outcomes has formed blinkers (Chapter 2) to the rest of the learning experience, where Denise's process-focused pedagogy becomes invisible or unrecognizable, how do we create value for a hiddenstream or fugitive pedagogy? Wallin (2011) addressed this kind of unrecognizable curriculum:

> how does one make *the* curriculum *strange* to itself? In an age dominated by the often implicit function of representational thought, this project becomes

crucial not simply for contemporary curriculum theorists, but for *a people* who might differ from *that which everyone already knows*. Articulating the stakes differently, *curriculum theory* asks how we might go about thinking *a life* when our contemporary representational resources are inadequate for creation of a people different from the people in general. (299–300—emphasis in original quote)

Making the curriculum strange to itself could also be read as *curious* to itself—a curriculum beyond representation, reproduction, and transaction. It would defy the notion of a life produced in advance that simply needs to be ordered (Colebrook 2008), reanimating the world for students, who will no longer believe that everything is all already known.

Valuing the Pollinator's Joyful Feedback Loop

I conclude this chapter by returning to our experience pulling seeds from the zinnia and milkweed in preparation for the school garden in Chapter 1. The bell rang, ending our planning period, and fourth graders filed into the room. We had cleaned up the leaves and stalks, keeping only those that were nicely intact to show the students the source of the seeds they would be planting. They, too, were surprised that the dead stalks held the potential to attract bees and butterflies to their future garden. We headed out together, passing through the science room to two wooden plots outside, where tongue depressors and string from the previous school year remained. The plots needed to be separated into six sections for the different seed varieties. Students worked in teams, planning and measuring, marking the separations with string, and labeling new tongue depressors with the plant types. Some bickered, while others took the lead for their area. The math was off a few times, tilling the soil caused some tension among those who did not want to get dirty, and determining how the string would be bound to the wooden frame took some negotiation. Finally, they planted the seeds and watered the plot. Now they would wait.

The garden plots had become the stage for new modes of relation, where their undetermined intensity amplified the differential, felt in the tone and vibration of negotiations and partnership between students vying for a space to take responsibility. Their care for the experience created a new vitality and connection, which became a tension for some, who resisted the embodied process and the residue of soil on their hands. This tension is a critical friction for deterritorializing the mind-crushing load of the educational monoculture, where a new story begins to form through a different kind of contact with the earth and each other. They were slowing down, and allowing their *existential stickiness* to animate a different kind of educational life (O'Sullivan 2010). They were constructing a zone of attraction, and committing to the unfamiliar future that the small mound of seeds might hold.

It seemed a strange or metaphysical coincidence to move through the science room to get there, physically moving across these spatial and disciplinary thresholds, connecting them through a relational experience to create a collective sociality with each other, the soil, the future pollinators, and the plants they will fertilize. This collective sociality (Manning 2020) is activated through a future-making pedagogy that became a form of creative nesting (Somerville, McGavock, and Stephenson 2020) with her students. This collective energy transversalized the institution's territorial strata differently than the fundraising rally (Chapter 2) because, while the garden event was also embodied, affective, and collective, the experimental activity of entering into potentially indeterminate relations that enfolded seeds' past (embodied in their stalks laid out on the classroom tables), the conditions of the soil (freshly tilled after a long hot summer), the unknown atmospheric futures that would provide necessary sun and water, and the germination of the seeds from the assemblage of all of those vital forces. Once again, Denise would straddle the past and future, animating her aesthetic attractions through a desire to germinate unknown futures. Her ethico-aesthetic approach created transversal connections across years, geographies, generations, organic bodies, and bodies of knowledge as the specter of milkweed pods from the field behind her childhood returned in a new territory as a joyful feedback loop in her lifelong nesting practice.

Later, we discussed ideas for shifting society toward more life-affirming practices, and Denise explained, "it has to start with valuing what we have and what we are." If the education system values measurable outcomes alone, then that is where energy will flow. The question is *how* to produce a set of values because "value is a capacity for intensification" (Manning 2020, 87). In this sense, value is not determined or imposed from the outside, where life is perpetually subjected to transactionalist logics. Rather, value emerges within relations, as the felt form of vitality, realized as the force of enthusiasm toward the not-yet and the coming-to-be (Manning 2020). Thought of from this perspective, vital curiosity becomes the embodiment of value, a critical disposition for thinking as intensive attraction, leaning toward and forming with the world through an aesthetics of the earth. Denise's story illuminates how we create the conditions for curiosity, worlding, and care over the course of a life. They are durational and affirmative capacities that show up in joy, enthusiasm, longing, and love, and they are powers that can rupture the normalizing sedimentation of the school landscape. Perhaps art education becomes a space for conditioning intensive modes of relation that illuminate the value of life itself, realizing pedagogy as "the art of life-living" (Manning 2020, 101).

9

What if We Learn This Together? Composing Collective Ecologies through Curiosity's Radical Interconnectedness

I conclude this book as it began. This final chapter is a thought experiment that maps a curious circuitry that flowed throughout all of the chapters, intensifying emergent and, at times, indeterminate connections between people, spaces, tools, and knowledge to co-compose nests through artful participation. It became a collective curriculum on sensorial attunement and affective transmission powered by vital curiosity as an affirmative condition and orientation, embracing collective experimentation as the "what else" of a life lived (Manning 2016). To open, I introduce three concepts that act as conduits in this experiment: circuitry, transduction, and participation. Their contextual multivalence creates connective hookups and conductive porosity, illuminating collective transmissions across the span of inquiries and encounters in the book. Vital curiosity acts as a magnetic and affirmative force of intuition and expression. This thought experiment blurs metaphors about circuitry with actual digital experimentation, as each element relates to sensorial attunement and sensor technologies, digital transmissions, and affective transduction.

While most of the book to this point has drawn on ecological concepts from the natural sciences to explore connections between vitality and curiosity, I shift registers here, to the energetic flow of connections and transmission of electronic circuitry. The potentially jarring shift from the natural to the electronic signals vital curiosity's attraction to an expanded field of connections and a new set of footpaths and circuits, yet to travel. In Chapter 7, I referenced biotechnological research on electro-dermal activity, which often uses biosensors to gather data on neurological shifts and atmospheric connections (de Freitas 2018). There is a growing body of neurological and biosocial research (Rousell and Cutter-Mackenzie-Knowles 2019) that provides other ways we might think about vital curiosity's intensely embodied and sensual expressions, and how they register in the brain and through the skin. The growing landscape of interest, research, and literature at the intersections of the natural sciences, art, and humanities points to future possibilities for experimentation with transcorporeal signaling through biosensors and digital transmissions.

Composing Concepts

Circuits—Energy Flow

A circuit is defined as a route, a circular line and the space enclosed within it, and a regular tour around an assigned territory. While circuitry operates as a relational field of forces that are co-composed through vital flows of energy, this image of the circuitous route traveled repeatedly echoes that of a curriculum, as a course that is run both individually and collectively, In this final reflective thought experiment, I employ this intersection between circuital path and curriculum, along with the circuit's multiple relations to electricity, as (a) "the complete path of an electric current including usually the source of electric energy"; (b) "an assemblage of electronic elements: hookup (which is a state of cooperation or alliance)"; (c) "a two-way communication path between points (as in a computer)"; and (d) a neuronal pathway of the brain along which electrical and chemical signals travel.[1] Each of these iterations—the energy current, hookup, two-way communication, and neuronal brain signals—becomes conduits as I follow the evolution of my attraction to sensorial attunement and affective transmissions over the last ten years.

For those who have not tried to build electric circuitry, it will be helpful to note that a circuit must be closed for energy to flow through the pathway. Points of resistance in circuits are called *hookups*, or places of cooperation among parts that allow for communication or signaling to occur. Sensors and switches are examples of hookups that create transmissions, often in the form of light, heat, and movement. Here, hookups are realized intuitively as "a schism in perception," where "a rift in knowing" is introduced (Manning 2016, 49).

Transduction—Change through Movement

The second concept, transduction, illuminates how modulations emerge from the movement of energy across spaces, time, relations, and media (Helmreich 2015). Throughout the book, *trans-* has been a critical prefix for understanding vital curiosity's potential for unsettling, connecting, and collectivizing.

Transdisciplinarity, transcorporeality, transmission, and transversality are but a few concepts that have repeatedly functioned as critical elements, qualities, and outcomes. In this last chapter, transduction becomes a central concept for connecting curiosity, attraction, stickiness, movement, participation, duration, and modification.

At its core, to transduce is to lead across. The term has a range of applications in sound, physics, psychology, and biology, among other fields. In sound production, transducers are speakers, microphones, and telephones; more broadly, transduction is the process where sound, as energy waves, is converted into signals as it traverses a medium. This transductive conversion and modulation is also used in biology for the transfer of genetic material from one cell to another; in physics for the energy converted from electricity to light or photosynthesis as light energy to another form; and in educational psychology for a child's preoperational stage of cognitive development, where they are able to see connections between unrelated instances.

I became interested in the idea of transduction as I tried to figure out how to use the sound board and mini synthesizer with my students (Chapter 4) in the story that follows, and later with a device for transmitting plant intensities as sounds. The discovery of this sonic tool is the first story in this chapter. I explore how transduction becomes a creative capacity when expanding vital curiosity to collective forms of teaching and learning, as a meaningful reaching across and a recognition of what changes while moving together.

Participation—Collective Action

Students have participated in my research and inquiry experiences throughout the book, but participation, as the third organizing concept in this final chapter, is more than simply working together. I explore the potential for participation as a form of collective sociality and mutual pedagogy through a "coupling of consciousness," as a capacity "to coordinate attentional systems and to synchronize brain functioning, in effect presenting the possibility of grander cognitive unities" (Davis 2005, 86). This complexity-oriented, neurological, affective, and communal understanding of participatory pedagogy aligns well with my theory of vital curiosity as an emergent collective process. It relies upon transdisciplinarity and nested systems, where the classroom community becomes a single unit, as one learner, and the teacher's role is to prompt differential attention, generate divergence, and expand interpretive possibilities within a learning ecology conditioned "for the as-yet unimagined" (Davis 2005, 87). As such, the classroom becomes a site of resistance to the pervasive monocultural school environment.

The notion of the collective is expanded from previous chapters, where the group subject is not simply a number of individuals coming together around a mutual intention—rather, they emerge as a group subject through participation, as a form of transductive synthesis and collective expression, meaning that as we move through our experiences together, we become something else, even momentarily. The field of relations co-composes through movement with students, tools, and other bodies across geographic locations and territories of practice. The world becomes an active site of curious investigation, a commitment to the shared intimacy of attuning to the strangeness of life (Mitchell 2013). Traveling across the spectrum of experiences, the durational and collective composition of knowledge illuminates the significance of attuning to the art of time, which involves

> crafting techniques that open art to its minor gesture. It requires an attentiveness to the field in its formation. This attention is ecological, collective, in the event. It is relational, relation here understood as the force that makes felt the how of time as it co-composes with experience in the making. It is out of relation that the solitary is crafted, not the other way around: relation is what an object, a subject, is made of. (Manning 2016, 51)

For the remainder of the chapter, the circuitry of my strange curriculum zigzags through experiences that are collective, solitary, and ecological, where inquiry is crafted through a range of techniques, realizing how the world is co-composed through vital curiosity as a force for collective participation across years of experimentation.

Co-Composing with a Community of Inquirers

My heart raced one Sunday morning, as the news show described the beautiful, strange, calming music of sound artist Jason Singh.[2] He used electrodes with a digital MIDI (musical instrument digital interface) device to create sonic compositions from plants' electrical intensities as forms of biodata. His process merges science, engineering, and art to explore how plants' electromagnetic intensities can register as sonic expressions. This technology is more commonly used in agricultural research to detect crop stressors and plant vitality (Chapters 1 and 7). A couple of companies have seen its more artistic potential and created small devices that can be placed in plants throughout galleries, offices, and public sites, where the "plant music" can be played through Bluetooth speakers.

While I find the idea of plant music fascinating, I was more excited about the ways that the technology created sounds from vital, nonverbal intensities; I wondered how I might artfully play with it to create something *else*. Art's dynamic vitality within ambiguity is a fertile territory for the affirmation of experimentation. Art, like poetry, "enlarges the circumference of the imagination by replenishing it with thoughts of ever new delight, which have the power of attracting and assimilating to their own nature all other thoughts, and which form new intervals and interstices whose void forever craves fresh food" (Mitchell 2013, 208, citing Shelley *A Defense of Poetry*, 488). At the time, I was still intrigued by the potential for alternative forms of listening and the intersection with olfactory perception of GLVs (Chapter 7). The plant sounds technology amplified vital intensities and afforded a different kind of tuning into life in a way I had imagined but did not think was possible.

Classrooms as Transductive Ecologies

Jason Singh's amplification of plant transmissions revitalized a question I have been stuck on for years: How does affective intensity register beyond language? This question emerged from the students' physical responses at the fundraising rally and my curiosity about the atmospheric charge of educational funding as affective labor (Chapters 2 and 3). Hearing the plant sounds also inspired me to return to an experiment that lingered in my mind from the semester of digging clay with my students in Chapter 4. While that chapter focused on the inquiry into local clay bodies, that was only half of the story. I designed the course as an open-ended inquiry into two practices: (1) locally digging clay and preparing it to make ceramic objects, and (2) using a digital touch board that transmitted audio files to build an interactive sound installation with digital circuitry and conductive paint. At the time, there was a growing interest in adding art to STEM education for STEAM learning, which romanticized the use of digital technology in education. I wondered what might emerge from an experimental project, where students would learn relatively new technologies (digital circuitry) alongside the most archaic (processing clay into ceramic vessels). I hoped students might develop a more nuanced perspective by learning emerging and historical technologies simultaneously. Ideally, we might even discover deeply integrated connections across the archaic and contemporary material practices to illuminate the evolutionary potential of sympoietic systems at work, where "collectively-producing systems that do not have self-defined spatial or temporal boundaries" distribute information and control among components (Haraway 2016, 33). Rather than approaching technology as a human invention driven by the logics of innovation or control, I was curious how a focus on attunement to fields of intersecting relations might illuminate a radical interdependence among co-composed, more-than-human worlds.

The open-ended structure of the course and curriculum aligned with the experimental and improvisational ethos of the maker movement and DIY practices. Both projects were driven by a curious desire (albeit mine as the instructor) to see what might emerge from the simultaneous spaces of experimentation, but I had no experience with either producing clay or building digital circuits. So, the class was also a social experiment, to see what might emerge in the relationship with my students by learning together. How might the classroom's field of relations change by admittedly *not knowing* at the outset, and thus risking that the semester may result in little or no discernible output? I was nervous and excited, bringing enthusiastic energy that was often met with the palpable weight of my students' desire for guaranteed outcomes.

In response, I designed a curriculum that provided intervals of focused research with shorter predetermined activities integrated into more open-ended exploration and experimentation. The discrete moments of closure in the short, preparatory activities acted as temporary hookups in the curricular circuit, like transmissions of light or heat as expressions of the students' growing investment and enthusiasm. For instance, the semester opened with each student researching and presenting contemporary artists who were exploring some of the key concepts in the class around sensory perception, ecological connection, and environmental impacts. While I developed the initial structure and led the class content and discussions the first few weeks, a playful energy was increasingly amplified in the room as students incrementally took over the inquiry. Opening with a familiar research process provided enough autonomy for the students to take ownership of teaching the class, even if the concepts were unfamiliar. Students expressed a sense of excited awe in their presentations, realizing how their artists' artwork investigated contemporary global conditions through media and technologies that were relevant to students' everyday lives, unlike the Western canon of historical artists they had learned in art history survey courses.

The curriculum became a co-composed set of relations, where we curiously merged our roles of teacher and learner through a mutual attraction to the unknown. By entering into the strange experiment together, a new pedagogical ecology emerged through the collective ethos expressed in the expansion of didactic roles (Dewey 2007). Affirming the expansion of the vital imagination over the rigidification of summative output opened communication across established boundaries, allowing idea generation and mutual vulnerability to alter social and physical configurations (Coats 2015; Douglas and Jaquith 2018; Guattari 2015; Fischman and Haas 2009; Hausman, Hostert, and Brown 2015; Scratchley and Hakstian, 2000–1; Wallin 2011a). The experience highlighted the potential of asking, "What else can artistic practice become when the object is not the goal, but the activator, the conduit towards new modes of existence?" (Manning 2016, 46).

Over the course of the semester, we playfully experimented together as "a community of inquirers with an experimental spirit" (Marks 2010, 88). The collective relations embedded in the experience were not limited to humans, though, as we realized how the land, tools, and techniques took on a new life entangled with the composition of the earth when we left campus for the clay dig described in Chapter 4. Within the classroom, we continued our experiment with the digital touch board that transmitted audio files when electrodes attached to it were triggered through touch. We could extend the tactile participation by connecting a conductive medium to the electrodes on the board. We attempted to use electrically conductive carbon paint as a conduit, with which we hoped to make a large wall painting that would trigger sound through physical contact with viewers. Eerie connections began to emerge, as the necessary movement of energy across the carbon-based paint echoed the flow of oil across the transnational pipeline that we encountered, unexpectedly running below the land where we dug into the sedimented clay bodies. A radical entanglement of carbon flows of energy and force triangulated our bodies, the land around us, and the electric painting we hoped would come to life with sound. With each passing week, we discussed emerging connections between historical processes and contemporary practices, similarities in natural conductive properties between the digital tools and ceramic compositions, and cultural patterns rooted in ecological aesthetics.

I like to think that the upsurge of joy I felt was creating a mutual atmosphere of love for our collective curiosity, as an energy that amplified an affirmative feedback loop (Chapters 7 and 8). The experience illuminated what Lewis (2012) described as "the fruitful and productive possibilities of the internal connections between curiosity, aesthetics, and education. These experimental communities exist in an ambiguous, pensive zone between art and education—wherein aesthetic appreciation becomes a new mode of learning and learning becomes a new mode of aesthetic curiosity" (40–1). Together, we followed curiosity's entangled connections and exchanges rather than a linear, predetermined, or reproductive learning path. Students took responsibility with a mutual willingness to embrace uncertainty, unpredictability, and unfamiliarity as a collectively curious flow of relations, diminishing defined social and temporal boundaries to become "teacher-as-not-a teacher" (Jasinski and Lewis 2016), forming a relationship of individuals rather than identities—individual but not individualist—and calling into question the dependence on instrumentalized identities, processes, and relationships that constitute the current educational landscape.

Sticky Failures

Strangely, for years I have thought of this course as a failure. But I look back now and see the significance of the experience more clearly, even though processing the clay took seven weeks longer than anticipated, and the sound project only sort of worked. At the time, I was slightly embarrassed that we were unable to get the sound to consistently travel across the conductive paint. We learned over time that the carbon in the paint required a consistent thickness to carry the electric current. We grew frustrated: the circuitry was delicate and required precision, working temporarily and then falling apart, and the need to continually reprogram the files in the sound device grew tedious. A boundary started to form between me and the students in these moments, as they looked to me to know how to do things correctly. Temporarily, the field of relations shifted back to the prior institutional configuration, while I tried to embrace the role of teacher-as-amplifier to redirect the anxious energy back to an affirmative feedback loop. At these moments, I would attempt to reignite a collective consciousness, hoping that the affirmative force of vital curiosity might again, create a mutual desire to carry our idea beyond the challenges, embracing "the creativity of asking *what else* that encounter could do" (Manning 2016, 202). Our questions expanded beyond immediate solutions, opening a radical desire to learn the mechanics of the device itself rather than just how it could create a hookup for this configuration. As a result, we developed an idea to expand the interactive sound piece to a large, community-oriented installation in the maker space at the local library.

Our relational circuitry echoed that of the sound board. It was fragile and could easily glitch. Similar to the carbon composition in the paint, we needed to maintain a consistency of both energy and amplification: too much, and we would get overwhelmed; too little, and the signals between us did not connect. It echoed the gap of uncertainty and potential explored in Chapter 1. Because all of the steps took longer than expected, I was repeatedly faced with a choice to limit the number of accidents and failures by figuring it all out myself outside of class, or to embrace the discomfort and allow the learning to unfold in its own time. But, once again, the limitations of schooling crept in, and the semester ended before we were able to develop the project further.

The class ended, and the students left town for summer break. I longed to try this class again to see if it could be more successful. My seemingly unavoidable desire to make the experience "count" in terms of measurable outcomes reveals deeply entrenched productivist habits of mind (Chapter 1), where the formation of our collective community was not enough. I realize now, though, that the lingering uncanny and unknowable residue of this class was precisely why it mattered so much because: "It is in such moments that communities of sense are reconstructed along new lines of flight and emergence that trouble the institutionalized matrix of what counts and what does not count. Experimental classrooms are classrooms of artists whose translations across distances speak to the ever-present possibility for sensing the world differently" (Lewis 2012, 43). The flow of our curricular circuitry became a transductive ecology, where curious energy acted as the conduit of mutual participation, converted into a range of transmissions through frustrated glitches and connective signals, co-composing a joyful existential terrain (Guattari 1995).

The Feedback Loop of Sensorial Attraction

The summer after that course, I moved to Arizona. With the stress of establishing a different home and finding my way in a new job, I thought that the draw of the soundboard and clay bodies had gone dormant. Instead, the unexpected experiences and knowledge had germinated, cross-pollinating and complexifying the lines of attraction and expanding my ideas of bodies, embodiment, transmissions, sounds, sensors, and circuits. I wanted to find other ways of playing with the sensorial boundaries of classrooms and continue the transcorporeal experimentation that illuminated industrial and ecological connections in that course. The transductive force of our experiences transformed my desire and capacity for noticing previously unrecognizable transcorporeal connections. These curiosities and physical explorations illuminated the need for conditioning oneself to become present, both physically and mentally. I realized that cultivating attunement as a sensorial and affective capacity and developing stickiness as an aptitude for focus and memory would take practice, so I started developing techniques for connecting to atmospheric conditions.

Sensing Urban Vitality

My first opportunity to experiment with these came a year later, in a transdisciplinary collaboration that amplified sensorial attunement to learn with third-grade students in an emerging school garden. Building on the interest in STEAM learning, we partnered human sensory perception with sensor technologies over several weeks with a science class at a local elementary school in a project called "Green STEAM Studios" (Coats et al. 2022). We integrated photography, drawing, and digital tools for measuring water, soil, and light to engage the students in speculative thinking. We assumed that students would be naturally curious and find novelty in the outdoor garden space. Instead, we realized that they saw the space every day because it was next to their playground and right outside the door of their classroom. By the fourth week of the project, it was clear that a radical reorienting was necessary for making any kind of attunement that would activate their curiosity possible. The norms of institutionalized schooling had ordered their bodies so rigidly that the natural environment was associated only with escaping schooling. Moreover, the activities we planned only held their attention for a limited amount of time, due to the distractions from the adjacent playground. Rather than intensify a predisposed curiosity, we would need to create conditions to defamiliarize the common space by modulating its intensity and create a new relationship to it (May 2005).

In order to activate an aesthetic curiosity, where the space might be perceived anew, we designed a set of one-minute intervals of focused smelling and listening as enabling constraints for intensifying attunement. Sound and smell have taken a backseat to vision in Western culture and education, particularly for spatial orientation. By deemphasizing the visual familiarity of their everyday environment to notice the sonic and olfactory transmissions all around them, the school grounds and surrounding neighborhood took on a different life. Drifting smells of car wash detergent, fast food, and decorative foliage became entangled with passing cars, the water fountain motor, and shuffling feet. The Green STEAM Studios project illuminated the aesthetic vitality of these common spaces through "an experimentation in contact with the real" (Deleuze and Guattari 1987, 12). Our attempt to curiously reorient students' learning through sensorial defamiliarization created a strange processual assemblage of new inputs that amplified and transformed their prior associations, drawing equally upon intuition and intellect, exemplifying how:

> The aesthetic event of education is not an unveiling of an object but rather a certain momentum of translation that is propelled by focusing our attention on a juxtaposition of stimuli that throws our senses out of joint. This model of curiosity is not reducible to a science of discovery but rather proposes a science of construction, creativity, and invention. Thus, aesthetics no longer remains external to curiosity as an imaginative addition (a utopian supplement to the science of critique) but is rather a constituting principle. (Lewis 2012, 41)

Similar to the collectivizing effect of the digital sound experiment and clay dig, activating a curious aesthetic created a sensorial reorientation of their everyday environment, which transversalized the community. The students contemplated and imagined the sources of the sounds and smells based on their local knowledge, creating a new image of the neighborhood as a space of phantastical plant and human entanglement. Their quiet attunements diminished the social, physical, and institutional boundaries, "to create a mutual atmosphere, [giving] in to beauty by becoming part of an involution that produces real transformation by means of aesthetic experiences and patient practices" (Mitchell 2013, 214). Again, my responsibility as a teacher was less about teaching predetermined content than creating conditions for collective participation and possibilities for tuning into the everyday differently by cultivating an attraction to root conditions.

Forming Mutant Coordinates

Attuning to sounds and smells as modes of ecological expression created critical questions as my curiosity bled into new territories of practice. The Green STEAM Studios research took place in early 2020, which was the same time that I saw Lindsey French present her work on green leaf volatiles that I introduced in Chapter 7. The previous fall, I had developed a paper on stickiness as a form of conditioning for attunement (Coats 2020). These ideas were layering and intensifying as I was realizing art's potential to form "mutant coordinates" (Guattari 1995) through questions and methods that often seem useless, arbitrary, or nonsensical. French's artful approach to smell and sound reoriented my inquiry coordinates, expanding what I thought was possible and amplifying my curious attraction to transcorporeal experimentation. Between her approach and the work with the school gardens, I hoped to create more experimentations around proximity and perception—to question how we might listen differently and consider how affect is transmitted beyond vision and language.

Then, a week after seeing French's talk and in the middle of the garden research, Covid-19 shutdowns began in the United States, and again, I thought that everything would go dormant. As I explored in Chapter 5, I became attuned to the world differently. The silence allowed new signals to be perceived in colors, blossoms, chirping birds, and industrial scars. Prior to that period of time, movement and proximity had been important conduits for creating and intensifying my curiosity, but I often associated these with my interest in exploring new places or people-watching. The mandatory and then willing isolation created new understandings and appreciations for minor movements, such as the simple path of a walk or bike ride around my neighborhood. Noticing different bird species in my yard and the blooming cactus became my daily social routine—it was a sociality of attunement.

Now, questions of affect and attunement were directed at emotions we have never had to feel, as many people across the globe have never lived through a shared experience of Covid-19's magnitude. I saw life cycles everywhere, even while the increasing death toll from the pandemic was displayed like the score of a sporting event on the news each day. As I explored in Chapter 5, the transmissions of data glued us to social media and other news sources for signs of life. Our mass anxiety illuminated a state of economic, physical, environmental, and social precariousness that many of us had ignored with the accelerated pace of life. The rush of each made ignoring the world easy, but the silence removed the veil. Overlooked and invisible conditions were amplified, and a whole new set of conversations emerged around embracing the unknown and the unknowable. My interests in GLVs, proximity and perception, more-than-human signaling, and atmospheric registers as ecological vital signs now seemed more relevant.

And in the middle of all of this, the news show with Jason Singh and his plant sound device appeared. That Sunday morning, my curiosity was stirred again as I wondered how the electrodes he placed on the plants could transduce the plants' affective and biological intensities. As I mentioned earlier, I researched the technology and learned that there are a few different companies that make these devices, but I wanted to understand how and why they work. This reactivated the curious circuit, imagining how the device might connect to the soundboard and the conductive paint from my class. Perhaps there could be a way to link it to the work with digital sensors and human sensory perception from the garden research. Again, constellations of ideas coalesced around a new strange attractor, strengthening the magnetic field around my attraction to other modes for expressing and amplifying our mutual intensive capacities.

I ordered one of the devices and began experimenting on the plants in my house and yard to discern differences in their intensities and transmissions. I was filled with excitement at the sonic articulation of their different intensities, some long and slow, while others seemed to dance rapidly like the quick toes of a ballerina moving across a stage—it seemed that the designers of this tool must have been curiously driven by a similar "interspecies desire, a longing to create new mutual atmospheres between humans and plants that would change existing patterns of life" (Mitchell 2013, 212). Affixing the small metal clamps and sticky pads of the electrodes to the different plants took me back to a seemingly absurd idea that I had during my research on embodied approaches to fundraising from Chapters 2 and 3. At that time, I was curious how I might design a study where I would place electrodes on young people while they participated in fundraising activities, such as my daughter selling Girl Scout Cookies in front of the grocery store. I wondered if I could find a way of registering their bodies' affective responses, beyond my observations of their facial and linguistic expressions, by using something like a polygraph (better known as a "lie detector"). What would this look like? I thought of it as research creation, blurring performance art and public pedagogy with forms of social and neuroscience research. Unfortunately, I was certain it would not pass the Institutional Review Board or gain consent from most parents. Without knowing the term, transduction, I was interested in what might be transduced from young people's excitement or anxiety as other ways of registering affect. As mentioned in Chapter 7, the growing body of research on affect and arousal through electro-dermal activity (EDA) (de Freitas 2018) is taking up similar questions, such as the development of popular devices that extend the capability of smartwatches and other biometric technologies. My idea was to make it more of a performance that might activate an uncanny curiosity about fundraising, affect, and young bodies in public spaces. The plant sound device renewed this idea while also drawing my attention to the advancement of the EDA technologies and research, of which I was unaware. Again, the eternal return of curiosity attracted new connections into the curricular circuitry. Vital curiosity, as an affirmative condition, allows for absurdity—but down those strange paths, in one moment the unthinkable may emerge as an imaginative prescience, intuiting nascent potential and propelling intensive attachments.

Coincidentally, a few weeks after receiving the plant sounds device, I had a medical procedure at a nearby hospital. A nurse assisting with the preparation inserted an IV into my arm, then pulled a set of electrodes with round, sticky pads from her pocket (like those I had been applying to the plants). She removed the adhesive seal from each one and attached them to my chest. A hookup emerged from the disparate inputs of my curious circuitry in that moment as the strange curriculum led right back to my body. The electrodes were attached to a monitor that transmitted the sounds of my vital intensity, as another dimension of my life entered this collective experiment, amplifying the eternal return through the rhythms of my vitality.

Attuning to the Artfulness of Life-Living

When I set out to write this book, I started with a set of stories that have lingered with me, some more resolved than others, but all were moments of intense curiosity. I wondered how the collection might weave together as I curiously revisited the questions that have since emerged from the experiences. Through a nomadic return, holding open past experiences with a sense of imaginative strangeness, they were given a new life—becoming provocations for rethinking my memories through vital curiosity. A similar experience occurred when writing this chapter. I set out to see how a curious circuit might form through the playful composition of concepts and a series of experiences. I had attributed the origin of this attraction to the class where we built circuits and dug the clay, but in the process of writing, I realized that it goes back to the very beginning. The affective conditions and connective intensities were at work in the dried plants from Denise's garden (Chapter 1) and the thumping bass in the cafeteria (Chapter 2). My relationship to these concepts, questions, and capacities expanded and evolved through a series of returns, co-composing with communities, fields of study, more-than-human expression, and the affirmation of collective experimentation.

Vital curiosity was a motor and a magnet, intensifying my attractions and amplifying my affective awareness. The curricular circuit linked up with communities, technology, bodies, and knowledge through questioning, participation, and practice that created transductive encounters, transforming our relational coordinates as an artful overflow of connections, where artfulness is "not the work itself but the way the work spurs an intensive recalibration of what already exceeds the structure. Artfulness is the extra-work at work" (Manning 2020, 61). This curriculum was more of a proposition than a formula, realizing how curriculum building becomes an emergent engagement with relationships and the world (Eliasson 2015). Flowing with a strange curriculum requires an affective capacity for attuning to indeterminate signals, an affirmation of difference, and a willingness to play with the unknown. With this attunement to the world, seemingly inconsequential information, like a promotion on a Sunday morning news show, can spark or reignite a current of curiosity, where something in the world snags us and signals an uncanny alarm or schism, creating a discomforting sense of strange familiarity as an intuition of the "not yet and will have been" (Manning 2016, 47).

As a pedagogical force, vital curiosity becomes a radical orientation toward collective unsettling and emergence, developing a comfort in posing awkward questions and an attraction to root conditions (Massumi 2002; Zurn 2021; Zurn and Shankar, 2020). Through these experiences, a curious circuitry attuned to interspecies sensorial expressions and transmissions, as art became a powerful conduit for this kind of curious attunement, affirming the complexity of the world through playful experimentation. Engaging in real-world, embodied experiences with communities creates opportunities to encourage a curious disposition through vulnerability and responsiveness, illuminating how a curriculum becomes a lived experience that is both reflexive and context specific (Gradle 2007; Sherman 2013). Vital curiosity is uniquely embodied and sensual, as each sense animates the entanglements that vital curiosity promises. When schools and other sociocultural forces limit the senses, then various modes of curiosity languish. Extending the body's curious attraction and activation by embracing an experimental spirit mobilizes a playful pedagogy into the strange vitality of learning with the world that invites risk, uncertainty, and world-building (Crawford n.d.; Gude 2010; Lucero 2018; Szekely 2015). As a teacher, I saw how art education can become a curiously generative site for world-building, where learning emerges through collective participation. By embracing curiosity as a future-oriented condition, embedded in imaginative uncertainty, we nurture students' desire to create new questions, and a passionate attraction to travel with the affective and aesthetic beauty of life's mystery.

Throughout the book, I have moved with thought, allowing my initial perceptions, confusions, and understandings to transform, even with the vulnerability of asking questions that seem foolish. Like Loveless's (2019) description of research-creation, writing this book has required being unfaithful to academic disciplines, research norms, and methodological standards. Leaving the book unresolved in so many ways is an intentional provocation for readers to pick up the loose threads and the jagged ends. I invite you to travel with my curiosities. This book has covered a lot of terrain, exploring education and learning both in and out of the institution. While Parts I and II seem to have formed a dichotomy between nature and culture, suggesting that the outside of the institution is the space of free thought, we realize in the end that this is not true—these dichotomies don't have to exist, and curious vitality can flourish anywhere. Life seems to always spiral back on itself, returning through residual memories and affective stickiness that connect our shared pasts and nascent futures. By returning to schools in the end, maybe what I am saying is that the particulars were there all along—the potential to produce a monoculture doesn't mean that there actually is one. Nurturing vital curiosity as a passionate interest in the beautiful uncertainty of the world means that difference can be recognized as the space of collective expression and the affirmation of our radical interdependence.

Notes

Introduction

1 Curious definition and etymology, https://www.merriam-webster.com/dictionary/curious.

Chapter 1

1 I return to the gap of uncertainty and embryonic field as critical concepts throughout the book.

Chapter 3

1 Promotional video (https://vimeo.com/178258424).

Chapter 4

1 Texas Railroad Commission—About Us: https://www.rrc.texas.gov/about-us/
2 National Park Service El Camino Real de los Tejas—History & Culture https://www.nps.gov/elte/learn/historyculture/index.htm

Chapter 6

1 https://www.merriam-webster.com/dictionary/skeleton. Throughout the rest of the chapter, I open sections with other definitions of "skeleton" from this *Merriam-Webster* reference.

2. Graves of Caddo Ancestors, 2003, Caddo Fundamental, Texas Beyond History, https://www.texasbeyondhistory.net/tejas/fundamentals/graves.html.

Chapter 7

1. Parts of this chapter on multispecies affective assemblages and GLV signaling appear in Coats, C. (2023). Listen to the smell of distress. In Lucero, J. and Hernandez-Cabal, C. (Eds.) (2023). *What Happens at the Intersection of Conceptual Art & Teaching?* Amsterdam University of the Arts, in press.
2. https://www.merriam-webster.com/dictionary/NESTING.
3. (https://lindseyfrench.com/doc/signaltonose.html).
4. Technologically, these questions are being explored in biotechnologies that measure electro-dermal activity (EDA) as changes in electrical skin conductance—the literal porosity of the organs. "These changes are linked to the skin's production of sweat, which is itself linked to the sympathetic nervous system, often said to reflect changes in arousal . . . [which] helps to theorize a body that is charged, but never static or still" (299). Change in the composition of adrenaline and serotonin signals affective, and potentially atmospheric, shifts, where the EDA data becomes "a way of tracking the blended world of the peripheral nervous system. At the juncture of the skin, are mixtures of synapse, cilia, sweat, mind, and society, all percolating" (de Freitas 2018, 298). While these biosocial technologies can be applied in ways that echo past dangers of vitalism in science, such as experiments with electricity on human and animal populations and theories of Eugenics (de Freitas 2018; Roussel and Cutter-Mackenzie-Knowles 2019), they might also point to ways of studying the expanded sensory contact that illuminate our profound interspecies and atmospheric interconnectedness for new way of living, which is a line of questioning I plan to pursue in the future.
5. Mitchell (2013) describes how Immanuel Kant, who insisted on distance as essential to aesthetic perception, was suspicious of smells because "smelling forces us to 'inhale air that is mixed with foreign vapors,' highlighting the intimacy of atmospheres as a 'collective phenomena, linking multiple people or living bodies'" (203). I share this anecdote about Kant, as an example of the negative cultural and historical associations with smell as an affective sensorial signal transmitted through our mutual atmospheres.

Chapter 8

1. https://www.merriam-webster.com/dictionary/curate.

Chapter 9

1 https://www.merriam-webster.com/dictionary/circuit
2 http://jasonsinghthing.com

References

Adorno, T. W. (1991), *The Culture Industry*, London: Routledge.
Agamben, G. (2021), *Where Are We Now? The Epidemic as Politics*, trans. V. Dani, New York: Rowman and Littlefield.
Ahmed, S. (2004), *The Cultural Politics of Emotion*, New York: Routledge.
Ahmed, S. (2006), *Queer Phenomenology: Orientations, Objects, Others*, Durham: Duke University Press.
Alaimo, S. (2010), *Bodily Natures: Science, Environment, and the Material Self*, Bloomington: Indiana University Press.
Anderson, B. (2012), "Affect and Biopower: Towards a Politics of Life," *Transactions of the Institute of British Geographers*, 37 (1): 28–43. doi: 10.1111/j.1475-5661.2011.00441.x
Anstey, M. L., Rogers, S. M., Ott, S. R, Burrows, M., and Simpson, S. J. (2009), "Serotonin Mediates Behavioral Gregarization Underlying Swarm Formation in Desert Locusts," *Science*, January 30, 323 (5914): 627–30. doi: 10.1126/science.1165939. PMID: 19179529.
Aoki, T. (1986), "Teaching as Indwelling Between Two Curriculum Worlds," *The B.C. Teacher*, 65 (3), April/May: 8–10.
Bachelard, G. (1964), *The Poetics of Space*, New York: Penguin Books.
Bain, C. B. (2000), "Piecing Together: A Look at Joe Sanders, A Twentieth Century Quiltmaker," in P. E. Bolin, D. Blandy, and K. G. Congdon (eds.), *Remembering Others: Making Invisible Histories of Art Education Visible*, 164–75, Reston: National Art Education Association.
Barad, K. (2015), "TransMaterialities: Trans*/Matter/Realities and Queer Political Imaginings," *GLQ A Journal of Lesbian and Gay Studies*, 21 (2-3): 387–422. doi:10.1215/10642684-2843239.
Barone, T. and Eisner, E. W. (2011), *Arts Based Research*, Los Angeles: Sage Publications.
Benjamin, W. (1935), "The Work of Art in the Age of Mechanical Reproduction," in H. Arendt (ed.), *Illuminations: Essays and Reflections* (2019), 166–95, New York: Mariner Books.
Benjamin, W. (1999), *The Arcades Project*, trans. H. Eiland and K. McLaughlin, Cambridge, MA: Harvard University Press.
Benjamin, W. and Lacis, A. (1925), "Naples," in P. Demetz (ed.), *Walter Benjamin Reflections: Essays, Aphorisms, Autobiographical Writings*, 163–73, New York: Harcourt Brace.
Bennett, J. (2001), *The Enchantment of Modern Life: Attachments, Crossings, and Ethics*, Princeton: Princeton University Press.

Bennett, J. (2010), *Vibrant Matter: A Political Ecology of Things*, Durham: Duke University Press.
Bennett, J. (2020), *Influx & Efflux: Writing up with Walt Whitman*, Durham: Duke University Press.
Bergson, H. (1935), *The Two Sources of Morality and Religion*, New York: H. Holt and Co.
Bergson, H. (1992), *The Creative Mind: An Introduction to Metaphysics*, New York: Carol Publishing Group.
Bergson, H. (1998), *Creative Evolution*, trans. A. Mitchell, Mineola: Dover Publications.
Bishop, T. (2019), "The Struggle to Sell Survival: Family Fallout Shelters and the Limits of Consumer Citizenship," *Modern American History*, 2 (2): 117–38. doi: 10.1017/mah.2019.8
Blandy, D. and Hoffman, E. (1991), "Resources for Research and Teaching about Textiles as a Domestic Art Education," *Art Education*, 44 (1): 60–71.
Boldt, G. (2020), "Theorizing Vitality in the Literacy Classroom," *Reading Research Quarterly*, 0 (0): 1–15. doi: 10.1002/rrq.307
Braidotti, R. (2006), "The Ethics of Becoming Imperceptible," in C. Boundas (ed.), *Deleuze and Philosophy*, 133–59, Edinburgh: Edinburgh University Press.
Braidotti, R. (2012), *Nomadic Theory: The Portable Rosi Braidotti*, New York: Columbia University Press.
Braidotti, R. (2021), *Posthuman Feminism*, Medford: Polity.
Brennan, T. (2004), *The Transmission of Affect*, Ithaca: Cornell University Press.
Clough, P. T., ed. (2007), *The Affective Turn: Theorizing the Social*, Durham: Duke University Press.
Coats, C. (2014), "Engaging Lives: A Nomadic Inquiry into the Spatial Assemblages and Ethico-Aesthetic Practices of Three Makers," PhD diss., University of North Texas.
Coats, C. (2015), "Materializing Transversal Potential: An Ecosophical Analysis of the Dissensual Aestheticization of a Decommissioned Missile Base," *The Journal of Cultural Research in Art Education*, 32: 127–60. https://journals.librarypublishing.arizona.edu/jcrae/article/id/4911/
Coats, C. (2019), "Transversalizing Aesthetic Practices: Engaging the Vital Force of Community Art Work," in V. Sabbaghi and A. Wexler (eds.), *Bridging Communities through Socially Engaged Arts*, 137–43, New York: Routledge.
Coats, C. (2020), "Stickiness as Methodological Condition," *Journal of Social Theory in Art Education*, 40: 16–28. https://scholarscompass.vcu.edu/jstae/vol40/iss1/3/
Coats, C. (2023), "Listen to the Smell of Distress," in J. Lucero and C. Hernandez-Cabal (eds.), *What Happens at the Intersection of Conceptual Art & Teaching?*, Amsterdam: University of the Arts, in press.
Coats, C., Singha, S., Zuiker, S., and Riske, A. (2022), "Time Unbound: Framing Encounters for Embodied Connection and Ecological Imagination," *Studies in Art Education*, 63 (4): 330–45.

Colebrook, C. (2008), "Leading Out, Leading On: The Soul of Education," in I. Semetsky (ed.), *Nomadic Education: Variations on a Theme by Deleuze and Guattari*, 35–42, Rotterdam: Sense.

Colebrook, C. (2014), *Death of the Posthuman: Essays on Extinction*, Ann Arbor: Open Humanities Press.

Coleman, R. (2008), "A Method of Intuition: Becoming, Relationality, Ethics," *History of the Human Sciences*, 21 (4): 104–23. doi: 10.1177/0952695108095514

Coleman, R. and Ringrose, J. (2013), *Deleuze and Research Methodologies* (1st ed.), Edinburgh: Edinburgh University Press.

Collu, S. (2019), "Refracting Affects: Affect, Psychotherapy, and Spirit Dis-Possession," *Culture, Medicien, and Psychiatry*, 43: 290–314.

Congdon, K. G. and Blandy, D. (2005), "What? Clotheslines and Popbeads aren't Trashy Anymore?: Teaching about Kitsch," *Studies in Art Education*, 46 (3): 197–210.

Coole, D. and Frost, S. (2010), *New Materialisms: Ontology, Agency, and Politics*, Durham: Duke University Press.

Crang, M. (2003), "Qualitative Methods: Touchy, Feely, Look-see?" *Progress in Human Geography*, 27 (4): 494–504.

Crawford, H. (n.d.), "Making Theory: Useless Design/Risky Pedagogy," Georgia Tech. https://leading-edge.iac.gatech.edu/humanistic-perspectives/making-theory-useless-designrisky-pedagogy/

Davies, B. (1982), *Life in the Classroom and on the Playground: The Accounts of Primary School Children*, Boston: Routledge and Kegan Paul.

Davies, B. (2000), *In(scribing Body/Landscape Relationships*, New York: AltaMira Press.

Davis, B. (2005), "Teacher as 'Consciousness of the Collective,'" *Complicity: An International Journal of Complexity and Education*, 2 (1): 85–8.

Davis, B. (2017), "How to Understand Hélio Oiticica's Journey from Art Visionary to Coke Dealer and Back Again," *Artnet News*, July 11, 2017. https://news.artnet.com/art-world/helio-oiticica-to-organize-delirium-684380

Davis, B., Sumara, D., and Luce-Kapler, R. (2000), *Engaging Minds: Changing Teaching in Complex Times* (2nd ed.), New York: Routledge.

Dean, K. P. and Berling, J. G. (2020), "Eco-Visualizations: Facilitating Ecological Relationships and Raising Environmental Awareness," *Art Education*, 73 (3): 54–61.

De Freitas, E. (2014), "Diagramming the Classroom as Topological Assemblage," in M. Carlin and J. J. Wallin (eds.), *Deleuze and Guattari Politics and Education For a People Yet-to-Come*, 95–115, London: Bloomsbury Academic and Professional.

De Freitas, E. (2018), "The Biosocial Subject: Sensor Technologies and Worldly Sensibilities," *Discourse Studies in the Cultural Politics of Education*, 39 (2): 292–308. doi: 10.1080/01596306.2018.1404199

Deleuze, G. (1983), *Nietzsche and Philosophy*, trans. H. Tomlinson, New York: Columbia University.

Deleuze, G. (1988), *Bergsonism*, trans. H. Tomlinson and B. Habberjam, New York: Zone.

Deleuze, G. (1990a), *Negotiations: 1972–1990*, New York: Columbia University.
Deleuze, G. (1990b), *Expressionism in Philosophy: Spinoza*, trans. M. Joughin, New York: Zone.
Deleuze, G. (1992), "Postscripts on the Societies of Control," *October*, 59 (Winter): 3–7.
Deleuze, G. (1994), *Difference and Repetition*, trans. P. Patton, New York: Columbia University Press.
Deleuze, G. (2001a), *Pure Immanence: Essays on a Life*, New York: Urzone.
Deleuze, G. (2001b), *Spinoza: Practical Philosophy*, trans. R. Hurley, San Francisco: City Lights Books.
Deleuze, G. (2004), *Desert Islands and Other Texts 1953–1974*, Los Angeles: Semiotexte.
Deleuze, G. and Guattari, F. (1983), *Anti-Oedipus: Capitalism and Schizophrenia*, Minneapolis: University of Minnesota Press.
Deleuze, G. and Guattari, F. (1986), *Kafka: Toward and Minor Literature*, trans. D. Polan, Minneapolis: University of Minnesota Press.
Deleuze, G. and Guattari, F. (1987), *A Thousand Plateaus: Capitalism and Schizophrenia*, trans. B. Massumi, Minneapolis: University of Minnesota Press.
Deleuze, G. and Guattari, F. (1994), *What is Philosophy?*, trans. H. Tomlinson and G. Burchell, New York: Columbia University Press.
Denchak, M. and Lendwall, C. (2022), "What Is the Keystone XL Pipeline? How a Single Pipeline Project became the Epicenter of an Enormous Environmental, Public Health, and Civil Rights Battle," *Natural Resources Defense Council*, March 15, 2022: n.p. https://www.nrdc.org/stories/what-keystone-pipeline
Dewey, J. (2007), *Democracy and Education*, Middlesex: The Echo Library.
Dimitrova, Z. (2018), "Deleuze's Expressionism as an Ontology for Theatre," in P. de Assis and P. Giudici (eds.), *The Dark Precursor: Deleuze and Artistic Research*, 214–21, Leuven: Leuven University Press.
Dolphijn, R. and van der Tuin, I. (2012), *New Materialism: Interviews and Cartographies*, Ann Arbor: Open Humanities Press.
Douglas, K. and Jaquith, D. (2018), *Engaging Learners Through Artmaking: Choice-Based Art Education in the Classroom* (2nd ed.), New York: Teachers College Press.
Doyle, R. (1997), *On Beyond Living: Rhetorical Transformations of the Life Sciences*, Stanford: Stanford University Press.
Eliasson, O. (2015), "Love Letter from Us," in R. Morrill (ed.), *Akademie X: Lessons in Art + Life*, 80–9. New York: Phaidon.
Engel, S. (2011), "Children's Need to Know: Curiosity in Schools," *Harvard Educational Review*, 81 (4): 625–45.
Engel, S. (2020), "Why Should this be So? The Waxing and Waning of Children's Curiosity," in P. Zurn and A. Shankar (eds.), *Curiosity Studies: A New Ecology of Knowledge*, 75–90, Minneapolis: University of Minnesota Press.
Fayn, K., MacCann, C., Tiliopoulos, N., and Silvia, P. J. (2015), "Aesthetic Emotions and Aesthetic People: Openness Predicts Sensitivity to Novelty in the Experiences

of Interest and Pleasure," *Frontiers in Psychology*, 6: 1877. doi: 10.3389/fpsyg.2015.01877

Fendler, R. (2019), "Desire Paths: A Reflection with Preservice Students in the Eventful Space of Learning," *Studies in Art Education*, 60 (4): 275–86.

Fischman, G. E. and Haas, E. (2009), "Critical Pedagogy and Hope in the Context of Neo-liberal Globalization," in W. Ayers, T. Quinn, and D. Stovall (eds.), *Handbook of Social Justice in Education*, 565–75, New York: Routledge.

Fisher, M. (2014), *Ghosts of My Life: Writings on Depression, Hauntology and Lost Futures*, Airesford: Zero Books.

Flaherty, C. (2020), "No Room of One's Own," *Inside Higher Ed*, April 21, 2020. https://www.insidehighered.com/news/2020/04/21/early-journal-submission-data-suggest-covid-19-tanking-womens-research-productivity

Friere, P. (1998), *Pedagogy of Freedom: Ethics, Democracy, and Civic Courage*, New York: Rowman and Littlefield.

Freire, P. (2000), *Pedagogy of the Oppressed* (3rd ed.), London: Bloomsbury.

Gagliano, M. (2019), "Breaking the Silence: Green Mudras and the Faculty of Language in Plants," in M. Gagliano, J. C. Ryan, and P. Vieira (eds.), *The Language of Plants: Science, Philosophy, Literature*, 84–100, Minneapolis: University of Minnesota Press.

Garoian, C. R. (1999), *Performing Pedagogy: Toward an Art of Politics*, Albany: State University of New York.

Garoian, C. R. (2013), "Precarious Leanings: The Prosthetic Research of Play in Art," in C. J. Stout (ed.), *Teaching and Learning Emergent Research Methodologies in Art Education*, 97–114, Reston: National Art Education Association.

Genosko, G. (2009), *Felix Guattari: A Critical Introduction*, London: Pluto Press.

Gibson-Graham, J. K., Cameron, J., and Healy, S. (2013), *Take Back the Economy: An Ethical Guide for Transforming our Communities*, Minneapolis: University of Minnesota.

Gradle, S. (2007), "Random Weave: Developing Dispositions to Teach Art," *Art Education*, 60 (4): 6–11.

Gregg, M. and Seigworth, G. J., eds. (2010), *The Affect Theory Reader*, Durham: Duke University Press.

Grinapol, C. (2022), "Energy Transfer Convicted of Criminal Charges on Pennsylvania Gas Projects," *Energy News Record*. https://www.enr.com/articles/54622-energy-transfer-convicted-of-criminal-charges-on-pennsylvania-gas-projects

Grosz, E. A. (2004), *The Nick of Time: Politics, Evolution and the Untimely*, New Zealand: Allen and Unwin.

Guattari, F. (1989), *Schizoanalytic Cartographies*, trans. A. Goffey, New York: Bloomsbury.

Guattari, F. (1995), *Chaosmosis: An Ethico-Aesthetic Paradigm*, trans. P. Bains and J. Pefanis, Bloomington: Indiana University Press.

Guattari, F. (1996), "Remaking Social Practices," in G. Genosko (ed.), *The Guattari Reader*, 262–72, Cambridge: Blackwell.

Guattari, F. (2000), *The Three Ecologies*, trans. I. Pindar and P. Sutton, London: Athlone Press.

Guattari, F. (2013), *Schizoanalytic Cartographies*, trans. A. Joffrey, London: Bloomsbury.

Guattari, F. (2015), *Psychoanalysis and Transversality: Texts and Interviews 1955–1971*, South Pasadena: Semiotext(e).

Gude, O. (2010), "Playing, Creativity, Possibility," *Art Education*, 63 (2): 31–7.

Guo, X., Ma, Z., and Kang, L. (2013), "Serotonin Enhances Solitariness in Phase Transition of the Migratory Locust," *Frontiers in Behavioral Neuroscience*, 7 (129). doi: 10.3389/fnbeh.2013.00129

Hansen, M. B. (1999), "Benjamin and Cinema: Not a One-Way Street," *Critical Inquiry*, 25 (2): 306–43. https://www.jstor.org/stable/1344205

Haraway, D. J. (2007), *When Species Meet*, Minneapolis: University of Minnesota Press.

Haraway, D. J. (2016), *Staying with the Trouble: Making Kin on the Chthulucene*, Durham: Duke University Press.

Haraway, D. J. and Tsing, A. (2015), "Tunneling in the Chthulucene," Joint keynote for the American Society for Literature and the Environment (ASLE), Moscow, Idaho, June 25, 2015. https://youtu.be/FkZSh8Wb-t8

Hardt, M. and Negri, A. (2004), *Multitude: War and Democracy in the Age of Empire*, New York: Penguin.

Harney, S. and Moten, F. (2013), *The Undercommons: Fugitive Planning and Black Study*, Brooklyn: Autonomedia.

Hausman, J., Hostert, N., and Brown, W. K. (2015), "Pedagogy toward a Creative Condition," in F. Bastos and E. Zimmerman (eds.), *Connecting Creativity Research and Practice in Art Education: Foundations, Pedagogies, and Contemporary Issues*, 73–80, Reston: National Art Education Association.

Helmreich, S. (2015), "Transduction," in D. Novak and M. Sakakeeny (eds.), *Keywords in Sound*, 222–31, Durham: Duke University Press.

Hickey-Moody, A. (2013), "Affect as Method: Feelings, Aesthetics and Affective Pedagogy," in R. Coleman and J. Ringrose (eds.), *Deleuze and Research Methodologies*, 79–95, Edinburgh: Edinburgh University Press.

Higgins, H. (2002), *Fluxus Experience*, Oakland: University of California Press.

Hofsess, B. A. (2018), "Blueprinting a Poetics of Materiality," *International Journal of Education through Art*, 14 (1): 49–58.

Holmes, R. (2008), *The Age of Wonder: How the Romantic Generation Discovered the Beauty and Terror of Science*, New York: Vintage Books.

Hood, E. J. and Kraehe, A. M. (2017), "Creative Matter: New Materialism in Art Education Research, Teaching, and Learning," *Art Education*, 70 (2): 32–8.

Ingold, T. (2011), *Being Alive: Essays on Movement, Knowledge, and Description*, New York: Routledge.

Jasinski, I. and Lewis, T. E. (2016), "The Educational Community as Intentional Community," *Studies in Philosophy & Education*, 35: 371–83.

Jun, N. (2011), "Deleuze, Values, and Normativity," in N. Jun and D. W. Smith (eds.), *Deleuze and Ethics*, 89–107, Edinburgh: Edinburgh University Press.

Knight, L. (2016), "Playgrounds as Sites of Radical Encounters: Mapping Material, Affective, Spatial, and Pedagogical Collisions," in N. Snaza, D. Sonu, S. E. Truman, and Z. Zaliwska (eds.), *Pedagogical Matters: New Materialisms and Curriculum Studies*, 13–28, New York: Peter Lang.

Knight, L. (2021), *Inefficient Mapping: A Methodologic Protocol for Attuning to Phenomena*, Santa Barbara: Punctum Books.

Knudsen, B. T. and Stage, C. (2015), "Introduction: Affective Methodologies," in B. T. Knudsen and C. Stage (eds.), *Affective Methodologies: Developing Cultural Research Strategies for the Study of Affect*, 1–22, London: Palgrave Macmillan UK.

Kofoed, J. and Ringrose, J. (2012), "Travelling and Sticky Affects: Exploring Teens and Sexualized Cyberbullying through a Butlerian-Deleuzian-Guattarian Lens," *Discourse Studies in the Cultural Politics of Education*, 33(1): 5–20.

Lazzarato, M. (1996), "Immaterial Labor," in P. Virno and M. Hardt (eds.), *Radical Thought in Italy: A Potential Politics*, 132–47, Minneapolis: University of Minnesota Press.

Lazzarato, M. (2006), "The Concepts of Life and the Living in the Societies of Control," in M. Fuglsang and B. M. Sorensen (eds.), *Deleuze and the Social*, 171–90, Edinburgh: Edinburgh University.

Lewis, T. E. (2012), "Teaching with Pensive Images: Rethinking Curiosity in Paolo Freire's *Pedagogy of the Oppressed*," *Journal of Aesthetic Education*, 46 (1): 27–45.

Lewis, T. E. (2014), "Education as Free Use: Giorgio Agamben on Studious Play, Toys, and Inoperative Schoolhouse," *Studies in Philosophy & Education*, 33: 201–14.

Lewis, T. E. (2020), "The Dude Abides, or Why Curiosity is Important for Education Today," in P. Zurn and A. Shankar (eds.), *Curiosity Studies: A New Ecology of Knowledge*, 91–105, Minneapolis: University of Minnesota Press.

Lewis, T. E. and Hyland, P. (2022), *Studious Drift: Movements and Protocols for Post-Digital Education*, Minneapolis: University of Minnesota Press.

Lippard, L. (2014), *Undermining: A Wild Ride Through Land Use, Politics, and Art in the Changing West*, New York: The New Press.

Loveless, N. (2019), *How to Make Art at the End of the World: A Manifesto for Research Creation*, Durham: Duke University Press.

Lucero, J. (2018), "A Paused Point: The Most Serious Thing I Do is Play," *Trends: The Journal of the Texas Art Education Association*, 50–5.

Maclure, M. (2013), "Classification or Wonder? Coding as an Analytic Practice in Qualitative Research," in R. Coleman and J. Ringrose (eds.), *Deleuze and Research Methodologies*, 164–83, Edinburgh: Edinburgh University Press.

Manning, E. (2012), *Relationscapes: Movement, Art, Philosophy*, Cambridge, MA: MIT Press.

Manning, E. (2016), *The Minor Gesture*, Durham: Duke University Press.

Manning, E. (2020), *For a Pragmatics of the Useless*, Durham: Duke University Press.

Marder, M. (2019), "To Hear Plants Speak," in M. Gagliano, J. C. Ryan, and P. Vieira (eds.), *The Language of Plants: Science, Philosophy, Literature*, 103–25, Minneapolis: University of Minnesota Press.

Marks, J. (2010), "Ethics," in A. Parr (ed.), *The Deleuze Dictionary, revised edition*, 87–9, Edinburgh: Edinburgh University Press.

Massumi, B. (2002), *Parables for the Virtual: Movement, Affect, Sensation*, Durham: Duke University Press.

May, T. (2005), *Gilles Deleuze: An Introduction*, Cambridge: Cambridge University Press.

Merleau-Ponty, M. (2012), *Phenomenology of Perception*, trans. D. A. Landes, New York: Routledge.

Mitchell, R. (2013), *Experimental Life: Vitalism in Romantic Science and Literature*, Baltimore: Johns Hopkins University Press.

Moore, J. W. (2015), *Capitalism in the Web of Life*, Brooklyn: Verso.

Nxumalo, F., Vintimilla, C. D., and Nelson, N. (2018), "Pedagogical Gatherings in Early Childhood Education: Mapping Interferences in Emergent Curriculum," *Curriculum Inquiry*, 48 (4): 433–53. doi: 10.1080/03626784.2018.1522930

O'Sullivan, S. (2001), "The Aesthetics of Affect: Thinking Art Beyond Representation," *Angelaki: Journal of Theoretical Humanities*, 6 (3): 125–35. doi: 10.1080/09697250120087987

O'Sullivan, S. (2010a), "Guattari's Aesthetic Paradigm: From the Folding of the Finite/Infinite Relation to Schizoanalytic Metamodelisation," *Deleuze Studies*, 4 (2): 256–86. doi: 10.3366/E1750224110000978

O'Sullivan, S. (2010b), "From Aesthetics to the Abstract Machine: Deleuze, Guattari and Contemporary Art Practice," in S. Zepke and S. O'Sullivan (eds.), *Deleuze and Contemporary Art*, 189–207, Edinburgh: Edinburgh University Press.

O'Sullivan, S. (2012), *On the Production of Subjectivity: Five Diagrams of the Finite-Infinite Relation*, London: Palgrave MacMillan. doi: https://doi.org/10.1057/9781137032676

Pacini-Ketchabaw, V., Kind, S., and Kocher, L. L. M. (2017), *Encounters with Materials in Early Childhood Education*, New York: Routledge.

Paterson, M. (2009), "Haptic Geographies: Ethnography, Haptic Knowledges, and Sensuous Dispositions," *Progress in Human Geography*, 33 (6): 766–88.

Pierce, C. (2013), *Education in the Age of Biocapitalism: Optimizing Educational Life for a Flat World*, New York: Palgrave.

Pinar, W. F. (2012), *What Is Curriculum Theory?* (2nd ed.), New York: Routledge.

Pinar, W. F. and Irwin, R. L., eds. (2005), *Curriculum in a New Key: The Collected Works of Ted T. Aoki*, Mahwah: Lawrence Erlbaum.

Pink, S. (2009), *Doing Sensory Ethnography*, Los Angeles: Sage.

Pollan, M. (2001), *The Botany of Desire: A Plant's Eye View of the World*, New York: Random House.

Ravitch, D. (2013), *Reign of Error: The Hoax of the Privatization Movement and the Danger to America's Public Schools*, New York: Alfred A. Knopf.

Reese, A. (2021), "Some Ecological Damage from Trump's Rushed Border Wall Could be Repaired," *Scientific American*, January 25, 2021. https://www.scientificamerican.com/article/some-ecological-damage-from-trumps-rushed-border-wall-could-be-repaired1/

Rose, N. (2008), "The Value of Life: Somatic Ethics and the Spirit of Biocapital," *Daedalus*, 137 (1): 36–48.

Roussel, D. and Cutter-Mackenzie-Knowles, A. (2019), "The Parental Milieu: Biosocial Connections with Nonhuman Animals, Technologies, and the Earth," *The Journal of Environmental Education*, 50 (2): 84–96.

Scratchley, L. S. and Hakstian, R. (2000–1), "The Measurement and Prediction of Managerial Creativity," *Creativity Research Journal*, 13 (3 & 4): 367–84.

Sedgwick, E. K. (2003), *Touching Feeling: Affect, Pedagogy, Performativity*, Durham: Duke University.

Shankar, A. (2020), "'The Campus Is Sick': Capitalist Curiosity and Student Mental Health," in P. Zurn and A. Shankar (eds.), *Curiosity Studies: A New Ecology of Knowledge*, 106–27, Minneapolis: University of Minnesota Press.

Sherman, S. (2013), *Teacher Preparation as an Inspirational Practice: Building Capacities for Responsiveness*, New York: Routledge.

Shiva, V. (2016), *Biopiracy: The Plunder of Nature and Knowledge*, Berkeley: North Atlantic Books.

Singh, J. (2018), *Unthinking Mastery: Dehumanism and Decolonial Entanglements*, Durham: Duke University Press.

Snaza, N., Sonu, D., Truman, S. E., and Zaliwska, Z., eds. (2016), *Pedagogical Matters: New Materialisms and Curriculum Studies*, New York: Peter Lang AG.

Solnit, R. (2000), *Wanderlust: A History of Walking*, London: Pedguin Books.

Somerville, M., McGavock, T., and Stephenson, K. (2020), "Becoming Bird: Creative Pedagogies for Future-Making Education?" in P. Burnard and L. Colucci-Gray (eds.), *Why Science and Art Creativities Matter: (Re-)Configuring STEAM for Future-Making Education*, 35–51, Boston: Brill.

Sparrow, J. (2019), "Against the New Vitalism," *New Socialist*, March 10, 2019. https://newsocialist.org.uk/against-the-new-vitalism/.

Spinoza, B. (1994), *A Spinoza Reader: The Ethics and Other Works*, trans. E. Curley, Princeton: Princeton University Press.

Springgay, S. (2010), "Knitting as an Aesthetic of Civic Engagement: Re-Conceptualizing Feminist Pedagogy through Touch," *Feminist Teacher*, 20 (2): 111–23.

Springgay, S. and Truman, S. E. (2018), *Walking Methodologies in a More-than-Human World: WalkingLab*, New York: Routledge.

St. Pierre, E. A. (1997a), "Nomadic inquiry in the Smooth Spaces of the Field: A preface," *International Journal of Qualitative Studies in Education*, 10 (3): 365–83.

St. Pierre, E. A. (1997b), "Methodology in the fold and the Irruption of Data," *Qualitative Studies in Education*, 10 (2): 175–89.

St. Pierre, E. A., Jackson, A. Y., and Mazzei, L. A. (2016), "New Empiricisms and New Materialisms: Conditions for New Inquiry," *Cultural Studies - Critical Methodologies*, 16 (2): 99–110.

Stengers, I., Manning, E., and Massumi, B. (2009), "History through the Middle between Macro and Mesopolitics," *Inflexions*, 3. https://www.inflexions.org/n3_stengershtml.html

Stewart, K. (2007), *Ordinary Affects*, Durham: Duke University.

Surin, K. (2011), "'Existing not as a Subject but as a Work of Art': The Task of Ethics or Aesthetics?" in N. Jun and D. W. Smith (eds.), *Deleuze and Ethics*, 142–53, Edinburgh: Edinburgh University Press.

Szekely, G. (2015), *Play and Creativity in Art Teaching*, New York: Taylor & Francis Group.

Szremski, A. (2017), "Hélio Oiticica: From Geometric Abstraction to Immersive Environments: The Whitney Surveys the Work of the Legendary Brazilian Artist," *4Columns*, July 21, 2017. https://4columns.org/szremski-ania/helio-oiticica

Tolia-Kelly, D. P. (2010), "The Geographies of Cultural Geography I: Identities, Bodies, and Race," *Progress in Human Geography*, 34 (3): 358–67.

Toscano, A. (2007), "Vital Strategies: Maurizio Lazzarato and the Metaphysics of Contemporary Capitalism," *Theory, Culture, & Society*, 24 (6): 71–91.

Trafi-Prats, L. (2017), "Learning with Children, Trees, and Art: For a Compositionist Visual Art-Based Research," *Studies in Art Education*, 58 (4): 325–34. https://doi.org/10.1080/00393541.2017.1368292

Tsing, A. L. (2015), *The Mushroom at the End of the World: On the Possibility of Life in Capitalist Ruins*, Princeton: Princeton University.

Tuana, N. (2007), "Viscous Porosity," in S. Alaimo and S. J. Hekman (eds.), *Material Feminisms*, 188–213, Bloomington: Indiana University Press.

Upholt, B. (2022), "Free of the Earth: On the Tohono O'odham Nation's Fight to Protect the Saguaro," *Emergence Magazine*. https://lithub.com/free-of-the-earth-on-the-tohono-oodham-nations-fight-to-protect-the-saguaro/

Vighi, F., Nuselovici, A., and Ponzi, M., eds. (2014), *Between Urban Topographies and Political Spaces: Threshold Experiences*, Lanham: Lexington Books.

Wallin, J. J. (2008), "Living with Monsters: An Inquiry Parable," *Teaching Education*, 19 (4): 311–23.

Wallin, J. J. (2010), *A Deleuzian Approach to Curriculum: Essays on a Pedagogical Life*, New York: Palgrave MacMillan.

Wallin, J. J. (2011a), "Mobilizing Powers of the False for Arts-Based Research," *Visual Arts Research*, 37, no.1 (Issue 72, Summer): 105–11.

Wallin, J. J. (2011b), "What is? Curriculum Theorizing: For a People Yet to Come," *Studies in Philosophy and Education*, 30 (3): 285–301.

Wallin, J. J. (2013), "Get out from Behind the Lectern: Counter-Cartographies of the Transversal Institution," D. Masny, (ed.), *Cartographies of Becoming in Education: A Deleuze-Guattari Perspective*, 35–52, Rotterdam: Sense.

Wallin, J. J. (2014), "Education Needs to get a Grip on Life," in M. Carlin and J. J. Wallin (eds.), *Deleuze and Guattari Politics and Education For a People Yet-to-Come*, 117–39, London: Bloomsbury Academic and Professional.

Waxman, L. (2017), *Keep Walking Intently: The Ambulatory Art of the Surrealists, The Situationist International, and Fluxus*, Berlin: Sternberg Press.

Wild, C. (2011), "Making Creative Spaces: The Art and Design Classroom as a Site of Performativity," *International Journal of Art and Design Education*, 30 (3): 423–32.

Williams, D. R. and Brown, J. D. (2012), *Learning Gardens and Sustainability Education: Bringing Life to Schools and Schools to Life*, New York: Routledge.

Zollinger, R., Thomas, M. O., Moore, H., and Bryson, K. (2022), "Lichenizing Pedagogy: Art Explorations in More-than-Human Performance and Practice," *Research in Arts and Education*, 1: 23–33.

Zurn, P. (2018), "The Curiosity at Work in Deconstruction," *Journal of French and Francophone Philosophy*, 26 (1): 84–106.

Zurn, P. (2021), *Curiosity and Power: The Politics of Inquiry*, Minneapolis: University of Minnesota Press.

Zurn, P. and Shankar, A. (2020), "Introduction," in P. Zurn and A. Shankar (eds.), *Curiosity Studies: A New Ecology of Knowledge*, xi–xxx, Minneapolis: University of Minnesota Press.

Index

aesthetics
    aesthetic appreciation   149
    aesthetic attraction   141
    aesthetic beauty of life's mystery   157
    aesthetic capacity   102, 118
    aesthetic curiosity   149–50, 152–3
    aesthetic disposition   21–3
    aesthetic inquiry   137
    aesthetic intensity   67
    aesthetic intuition   13
    aesthetic paradigm   117
    aesthetic potential   31, 117–18
    aesthetics of the earth   128, 135, 141
    aesthetic yield of experience   131
    atmospheric aesthetics   124
    attunement   128
    ecological aesthetics   149
    ethico-aesthetics   32, 72, 117, 128, 132, 135, 141
    hiddenstream aesthetics   133–5, 137
affect
    and accountability   66
    affective attraction   51–2
    affective attunement   135
    affective capacity   23, 66, 67, 117–19, 121–2, 128, 152, 157
    affective connection   67–8
    affective currency   58–72
    affective disruption   25
    affective expression   122–4
    affective intensity   22–3, 25, 29, 49–57, 124–5, 147, 154
    affective labor   29, 33, 60–1, 63, 67, 72, 100, 126, 147
    affective monoculture   139
    affective residue   8
    affective strangeness   15
    affective surplus   60–1
    affective threshold   7
    affective transduction   143
    affective transmission   9, 127, 143, 144, 154
    and attunement   154
    biopolitics of   61
    biosocial affective expression   119
    bodily affect   25
    and bodily connection   63
    collective spirit   60–1
    commodification of   58
    vs. corporeality   53–4
    and curiosity   66
    educational fundraising   58, 147
    ethical implication   64
    exploitation   60–1, 67
    forms of   29, 33
    future-oriented affect   125
    green leaf volatile (GLV)   123, 126
    immaterial labor as   60
    intensive and extensive   61
    intuitive affective capacity   121–2
    and isolation   100
    materialization   63
    multispecies affective expression   122–4
    and responsibility   64
    stickiness   23, 158
    uncertainty   90
Ahmed, S.   23
Alaimo, S.   87
Alien Jesus   80–1, 85, 86, 97, 113
anarchiving   133
anxiety
    and depression   66
    and fear   91, 139
    and volatile compound signals   125, 126
artfulness of life-living   156–8
atmosphere
    'affection'   19
    atmospheric intensity   51–2, 91
    atmospheric vitality   16
    energetic drive   28, 49, 52
    of happiness   122
    mutual atmosphere   119, 120, 149–50, 155

attraction
  aesthetic attraction 141
  affective attraction 51–2
  curatorial nesting 131–3
  curiosity 15, 19, 30, 66, 100
  energetic attraction 19, 38
  intensive attraction 141
  intersubjective attraction 23
  mutual attraction 148
  radical attraction 135
  sensorial attraction 151–6
  sensual attraction 22
  skeletal attraction 104–7, 113
  sociopolitical conditions 53
  strange attraction 1, 13, 54, 131–3
attunement
  aesthetics 128, 134
  affective attunement 135
  to cactus bodies 30, 105, 109
  collective attunement 21
  as collective forms of knowing 31
  curious attunement 47
  haunting attunement 85–8
  multispecies capacity for 127
  sensorial attunement 32, 70, 143, 152–6

Bachelard, G. 119, 122
Barad, K. 52
Bennett, J. 54, 55, 124, 125
Bergson, H. 16–18, 103
biopolitical technology 40–2, 67
biotechnology 33, 35, 40–4
bodily signals, see collective sociality
bomb shelters 1–2
Braidotti, R. 67
Brown, J.D. 68
building materials 3

cactus skeletons 30–1
  attunement 109–10
  boots 109
  Caddo mounds 112
  cholla 105, 111
  interconnectedness 104
  invasive thresholds 110–11
  Massacre Falls 109–10
  in native ceremonies 109
  nonnative invaders 112

Organ Pipe cacti 112
overgrown grasses 111–12
Peralta Massacre story 109–10
personalities 105
porosity 114–15
saguaro 105–9
significance 107–9
skeletal attraction 104–7
stories 109–10
sympoietic relationship 109
transcorporeal stickiness 113–15
vulnerability 105–7
capacity
  aesthetic capacity 102, 119
  affective capacity 22, 31, 60, 66–70, 117, 157
  affirmative capacity 128, 142
  attunement 93, 127
  autopoietic capacity 42, 43, 46
  curiosity 14–18, 47
  durational and affirmative capacities 141–2
  ethico-aesthetic capacity 22
  for imagination 46
  indeterminate capacity 120
  intuitive affective capacity 20, 32, 48, 121–3
  multispecies capacity 127
  perceptive capacities 127
  plant vital capacities 41, 42
  stickiness 23
  transduction 145
  value 141
capitalism
  affective labor 126
  biotechnology 43, 45
  capitalist exploitation 84–6
  capitalist power 92
  capitalist values 53–4, 65, 68, 69
  colonization and 30, 31, 70, 72
  materialism 54
  neoliberal capitalism 18, 54
circuits/circuitry
  curious circuit 154, 156, 157
  curricular circuit 148, 151, 155, 156
  digital circuitry and conductive paint 147
  energy flow 143, 144
  of movement and thought 30

Index

relational circuitry 150
sympoietic pedagogies and
 transcorporeal inquiry 31, 117
clay bodies 29–30
 attunement 85–8
 clay at locals 73–5
 co-creative malleability 85–6
 collective encounters 83
 culture and native populations 80–1
 earthenware 77
 ecology on unsettled lands 77–9
 figures of 79–81
 fractured sediments 78–9
 geological composition 76–7
 global information system (GIS) 81–3
 goddess figures 80–1
 greenish gray clay 78
 historical residue 76–7, 84–5
 human and nonhuman
  connection 83–4, 87
 innovation 84
 interconnectedness 88
 metadata 81–3
 porcelain 77
 red clay 75–6
 stories 84–5
 sympoietic pedagogy 73, 83
 tools and technology 83–4
 transcorporeal connection 73, 87–8
 value judgment 77
co-composing 146–7
Colebrook, C. 45, 53
Coleman, R. 132
collective/collectivity
 attraction 19
 body 121
 collective action 70
 collective consciousness 69
 collective curiosity 84–5, 88, 117, 119–27, 128–42, 143–58
 collective encounters 83
 collective energy 63
 collective entanglement 115
 collective expression 55
 collective fear 91, 103
 collective innervation 67
 collective intensity 7
 collective myths 95

collective potential 58
collective response-ability 102
collective sentiment 92
collective spirit 60–1
emergence 13, 23–7
encounters 83
in the making 129–31
in the school 53
collective curiosity 31–2, 117–18
 collective action 145–6
 collective emergence 23–5
 collective energy 62–3, 70, 141
 collective intensity 7–8
 collective potential 121
 collective spirit 60–1
collective sociality 31–2
 affective capacity 121–2
 affective intensity 124–5
 collective composition 119–21
 compositional disposition 126–7
 feedback loop 120–1
 green leaf volatile (GLV) olfactory
  emissions 123–4
 indeterminate capacity 120
 mothering 122
 multispecies affective
  expression 122–4
 mutual atmospheres 119, 120
 nesting practice 119–21
 porosity 126–7
 social pressure 125–6
commodity and commodification
 educational fundraising 23, 26, 27, 33, 54, 56
 nature fundamental capacity 43, 45, 46, 123, 124, 126
 school fundraising 60–2, 66, 69, 70
Community Fallout Shelter Program 2–3
composition/compose/composing
 of clay bodies 73–88
 co-composing 146–51
 collective composition 119–22, 127
 compositional disposition 126–7
 curricular composition 53
 of knowledge 146
 processual composition 23–5
 re-composition 19, 97
connective curiosity 29–31, 71–2

Index

connective stickiness 31
contagion 20, 51–2, 90, 98, 99
corporate fundraising 53–4, *see also* school fundraising
corporeal transmission 97–101
Covid-19 30
   aesthetic capacity 102
   corporeal transmission 97–101
   Covid landscape forming 90–1
   cultural mythology 95–7
   cynical curiosity emerges 93–5
   death-as-fiction 97–101
   different future 91–3
   essentials 90–1
   gap of uncertainty 102–3
   human consumption 95–7
   indetermination 103
   invisibility of essentials 97–101
   isolation 93, 101–2
   mental ecology 92
   mysticism and science 97
   nature 92–3
   new habits 91–3
   normal life 94–5
   proximity 97–101
   speculative pessimism 95
   transdisciplinary and transcorporeal connection 95–7
critical and creative force for thought 14
cultural mythology 95–7
curatorial nesting 131–3
curious/curiosity 1, 13, 35, 49, 58, 73, 89, 104, 119, 128, 143 (AU: Curiosity is book title term and whole deals with it. So, referred each chapter's open page)
   affective capacity 22–3
   autopsic curiosity 15
   curious intensity 13
   curious stories 25–7
   curious vitality 128–9
   cynical curiosity emerges 93–5
   disruptive curiosity 27–9, 33
   dynamic multiplicity of curiosity 14–16
   neoliberal curiosity 33, 55–6, 65–6
   therapeutic curiosity 15, 132
   thought and curiosity 68–9
   vulnerability and vitality 45–8

curriculum 32
   artfulness 156–8
   knowledge sharing 69
   neoliberal 64
   nested knowledge 119–21
   unrecognizable 139–40
curriculum reform
   articulated outcomes 36–7
   autopoietic capacity 42, 46
   biopolitical technologies 40–2
   capacity for imagination 46
   critical vitality in learning 47–8
   curious capacity *vs.* functional outcomes 46–8
   curriculum-as-plan 44–7
   decontextualized curriculum 46
   desired outcome of education 44–5
   disciplined visibility 36–7
   education policy 45
   environmental challenges 42
   gap of uncertainty 37–8, 45
   genetic modification 41–2
   instrumentalized learning 37
   intellectual and commercial property 42–4
   interconnectedness 44
   learning transactions 36–7
   neoliberal curriculum reforms 45, 47
   not-thinking allure 45
   predictability 38–40
   public policy 42–4
   seeds from dead bodies 35–6
   seed treatment 41–2
   standardized curriculum 44
   thought experiment 35
   vital curiosity 48
   vital potential of seeds 35
curriculum theory 32, 140

Deleuze, G. 10, 25, 58, 67, 123
desire
   affective desire 63
   ch 7 123, 126, 127
   ch 8 134, 139
   ch 9 141, 148, 150, 151, 155, 157
   curious desire 19
   for difference and variation 30, 40
   for learning 17–18, 44–8
   pandemic 95, 97, 100–2

protodesires 125
thing-power 54–5
towards neoliberal capitalist
     values 52–4, 65–6, 68, 72
Dewey, J. 37, 40, 66
disruptive curiosity 27–9, 33
     curriculum reform 35–48
     educational fundraising 49–57
     school fundraising 58–72
disruptive postures 21–2
divergent orientation 21–2
Doyle, R. 36, 43, 46
dynamic multiplicity of curiosity 14–16

ecology/ecological
     catcus 109, 114
     ecology of practices 73, 78, 85
     mental ecology 92
     monoculture and school ecology 56, 68
     nested ecology 128, 130–2
     transductive ecology 147–50
ecstatic energy 63
educational fundraising, *see also* school fundraising
     affective attraction 51–2
     atmospheric intensity 51–2
     bodily contagion 51–2
     capitalist values 53–4
     corporatized public school funding 53–4
     desire and enchantment 54–5
     ecosophic approach 49
     ethical responsibility 53
     locust formation 56–7
     market-based values 56
     neoliberal curiosity 55–6
     student affective responses 49–51
     thing-power 54–5
     transversality 56–7
educational inquiry 14
educational philosophy 1
electro-dermal activity (EDA) 155
embodied and embedded sociality 138
enchantment 54–5, 57, 104
energy
     aesthetic classroom energy 102
     aesthetic energy 23
     collective energy 14, 62–3, 95, 141

of curious indeterminacy 24
ecstatic energy 63
electric energy 144–5, 149
emotional energy 53
Energy Transfer 82–3, 86, 87
flow 69, 79, 144
hormonal energy 100
human and more-than-human energy 87, 114
nervous energy 73–5, 124
positive energy 54
vital energy 16, 17, 19, 21, 33
entrepreneurialism 55–6, 61–3, 65–6
eternal return 1, 25–7, 128, 135, 155, 156
existential stickiness 22–3, 141
existential uncertainty 14, 89, *see also* Covid-19
experimental inquiry 23–5
experimental vitalism 16

feedback loop 22, 32, 120–1, 137–8, 140–2, 150–2
Foucault 10
freedom 15, 17, 18, 134–5
Freire, P. 47
fugitive sociality 135–6, 138
fundraising practices 53, *see also* educational fundraising; school fundraising
Fun Run 29, 59–60, 69

gap of uncertainty
     biology 43–4
     concept 33, 37–8
     embryonic field of relations 45, 48
     isolation 90, 102
     memory function 52
garden/gardening
     affective connection 68–9
     biological vitality of gardening 38
     bright yellow squash 38–40
     compost 130
     garlic 40–2
     human sensory perception 154
     modes of relation 140, 141
     pollinator 27–8, 35, 48
     seed harvest 35–6
genetically modified organisms (GMOs) 41–2

ghostly spatial palimpsest 5–6, 9–10
green leaf volatile (GLV) olfactory
    emissions 123–4
Guattari, F. 25, 27, 49, 56, 68, 92, 123

Haraway, D.J. 83, 110
Hardt, M. 60
hiddenstream 133–4, 136
hook-ups 144
human and nonhuman connection 13,
    24, 83, 87, 109
human consumption 95–7

indeterminate capacity 120
innervation 67, 70, 87
inquirers, community of 146–7
inspiration 128–9
intellectual property 42–4, 69
intensity
    aesthetic intensity 67
    affective intensity 13, 19, 22–3, 25,
        28, 49–57, 69, 70, 124–5, 147
    atmospheric intensity 10, 51–2, 123
    bodily intensity 9
    collective intensity 7
    haptic intensity 65
    isolation 89–103
    joyful intensity 20
    of the land 6
    physical intensity 10
    relational intensity 10
    strange intensity 109
    transversal intensity 68
    visual intensity 113
intensive thresholds 3–5, 9
intentionality of curiosity 113
interconnectedness
    ecological 44
    and isolation 94, 102
    life complex 13
    radical interconnectedness 32,
        143–58
    transcorporeal 29, 71, 88
intuition
    aesthetic intuition 13
    and attunement 31, 87
    as collective forms of knowing 31
    and intellect 153
    intuitive affective capacity 121–2

joyful intuition 27, 117
more-than-human intuition 121
strange intuition 21, 25, 127
vital curiosity 143
invasive thresholds 110–11
isolation
    biopolitical isolation 70
    Covid-19 shutdown 30, 72, 89–103
    disciplinary isolation 44, 46
    feeling of 10
    social isolation 30
    willing isolation 154

Lewis, T.E. 1, 21, 26, 149
locust transformation 6–7, 10–11, 56–7
Loveless, N. 157

Manning, E. 128, 133
Marder, M. 127
Massumi, B. 22
materialism 16–17
mental ecology 92
Merleau-Ponty, M. 23
missile base 1–3
Mitchell, R. 16
monoculture 28, 31, 33, 46, 47, 54–6, 65,
    69, 128, 137, 139, 140, 146, 158
more-than-human phenomenon 9, 20,
    27, 29, 69, 70, 72, 84, 87, 114,
    121, 126, 135, 148, 154
mutant coordinates 153–6
mutual atmosphere 119, 120, 149–50,
    155

Negri, A. 60
neoliberal
    curriculum reforms 45, 47
    monoculture 27, 33
    neoliberal business model 138–40
    neoliberal capitalism 18, 54
    neoliberal curiosity 28, 33, 55–6,
        65–6
    neoliberal curriculum 64
    neoliberal logics 27–8, 35–48
    neoliberal policies 33
    neoliberal reforms of public
        education 28, 45, 47, 138
    values 55, 63, 67, 95
neo-vitalisms 16

nests/nesting
    as collective compositions 119–22
    collective porosity and compositional
        disposition 126–7
    concept 31–2
    creative nesting 141
    curatorial nesting 131–3
    as future-oriented practice 131
    as intuitive affective capacity 121–2
    multispecies affective
        expression 122–6
    nested ecology 128
    nested knowledge 119–21
    saguaros 109, 121
    through artful participation 143
normativity 136

olfactory transmission 152
openness 27

participation 29, 32, 54, 60, 64, 69, 127, 143, 145–6, 149, 151, 157
pedagogical life 32
    choices and actions in the
        making 136–7
    collectivity in the making 129–31
    curatorial nesting 131–3
    curious vitality 128–9
    durational and affirmative
        capacities 141–2
    ethico-aesthetics 128
    feedback loop 137–8, 140–2
    freedom 134–5
    fugitive sociality 135–6
    hiddenstream aesthetics 133–5
    neoliberal business model 138–40
    normalizing homogeneity 136
    responsibility 135
    unrecognizable 136–8
    values 141
pedagogy/pedagogical
    art and public pedagogy 155
    collective life 28, 32
    curiosity 14, 88
    mutual pedagogy 145
    participatory pedagogy 145
    pedagogical disruption 126
    pedagogical ecology 148–9
    pedagogical force 22, 157
    pedagogical life (*see* pedagogical life)
    pedagogical vitality 27–8, 35–48
    sticky pedagogy 85
    sympoietic pedagogy 29, 31, 73, 83, 88
porous/porosity
    of boundaries 14, 22, 25, 27, 87
    of the clay soil 113
    collective porosity 126–7
    conductive porosity 143
    curious porosity 104
    porous curiosity 31, 86, 114, 127
    of skeleton bones 114
    sympoietic porosity 86
    theme of porosity 9
    viscous porosity 87, 114
processal composition 23–5
proximity 7, 23, 69, 97–101, 121, 154

radical interconnectedness
    accidents and failures 150–1
    aesthetic curiosity 149–50
    artfulness of life-living 156–8
    change through movement 144–5
    circuit 144
    co-composing 146–7
    collective action 145–6
    experience 150–1
    feedback loop 151–2
    inquirers, community of 146–7
    mutant coordinates 153–6
    mutual atmosphere 149–50
    participation 145–6
    sensorial attraction 151–2
    sensor technology 152
    transduction 144–5
    transductive ecology 147–50
    urban vitality 152–3
residue/residual
    affective residue 8
    feedback loops 121
    of history 8, 76–7, 84–5
    of invasive destruction 114
    material residues 30
    residual effects 15, 27
    residual force 14
    residual layers 81
    residual memories 158
    residual web 13
    of soil 140

subjective and collective residues   88
responsibility
   curious desire   19
   ethical responsibility   53, 122
   forms of life   92
   freedom and   135
   GLV responsiveness   127
   institutional role   57
   for school fundraising   64
   sense of   69, 117, 130
   space for   140, 150

saguaro cactus   105–9
St. Pierre, E.A.   25
school fundraising, *see also* educational fundraising
   affective connection   67–8
   affective labor   60–1
   car washes   59
   collective energy   62–3
   collective spirit   60–1
   emotional relationships   63, 66
   entrepreneurial spirit   61–3, 65–6
   Fun Run   59–60
   immaterial labor   60
   neoliberal curiosity   65–6
   neoliberal curriculum   64
   social practices   59
   young bodies   59–60
seeds
   from dead bodies   35–6
   embryonic field of relations   68
   genetically modified seeds   41–3
   germination   39
   harvesting   27, 33, 40
   pollinator garden   130, 140–1
   practices   133
   regenerative capacity   46
   reseeding   86
   and school curricula   44
   seed banks   69, 130
   seeding education   37
   spread   111
   treatment   41–2
   vitality   46
sensorial attraction   151–2
sensorial attunement   32, 70, 143, 152–6
sensor technology and sensory perception   152–5

Shankar, A.   55, 65
Shiva, V.   48
social isolation, *see* Covid-19
sociality
   of attunement   154
   biosocial potential   125
   collective sociality   31, 32, 119–27, 141, 145
   conditions and capacities for   115, 118
   fugitive sociality   135–40
   relations of   135
   social practices   59
sovereign   15, 33, 47, 84, 132
Spinoza, B.   20, 27
Springgay, S.   72, 85, 123, 126
STEAM learning   147, 152
sticky/stickiness
   affective stickiness   158
   attunement   153
   clay assemblage   87
   connective stickiness   31
   existential stickiness   22–3, 141
   organic bodies   107
   sticky composition   127
   sticky failures   150–1
   sticky objects   62
   sticky pads   155–6
   sticky pedagogy   85
   sticky substance   29–30
   transcorporeal stickiness   113–15
storytelling   26–7
strange returns   25–7
sympoietic/sympoiesis   29, 31, 32, 73, 83, 86, 88, 109, 114, 117, 147

therapeutic curiosity   15, 132
thing-power   54–5, 132
thought and curiosity   68–9
thought experiment   35, 45, *see also* curriculum reform
thresholds
   affective threshold   7
   for change   94
   clay stickiness   113
   corporeal and existential threshold   102
   distress   126
   intensive thresholds   3–5, 9

invasive thresholds 110–11
between life and death 105
spatial and disciplinary
    thresholds 141
time and space 114
transcorporeal connection 31, 71
Toscano, A. 18
transcorporeal
    across thresholds of existence 31
    effects across life-forms 30, 88
    embryonic field of relations 68
    experimentation 151
    history and culture 73
    inquiry 31, 73–88, 104, 117, 119
    interchanges across bodies 72
    interconnectedness 29, 71
    movement 71
    mythologies 96–7
    signaling 144
    stickiness 113–15
    transcorporeality 71–2, 87–8, 113–15, 145
    transmaterial and transcorporeal
        connection 126
transdisciplinary
    collaboration 152
    and collective energy 14
    connection 26, 96–7
    inquiry 14, 15
    method 24
    mythologies 96–7
transduction
    affective transduction 143
    excitement/anxiety 155
    force of desire and capacity 151
    movement of energy 144–5
    transductive ecology 147–50
    transductive encounters 156
transmission
    affective transmission 9, 32, 121, 124, 127, 143, 144
    collective transmission 143
    corporeal 97–101
    of data 154
    of desire 7, 59
    digital transmission 143–4
    of knowledge 24
    olfactory transmission 152

plant transmission 147
of virus 101
transversality 27, 56–7, 68, 70, 84, 134, 141, 145, 153
Truman, S.E. 72, 123, 126
Tsing, A.L. 14
Tuana, N. 114

vital curiosity
    aesthetic disposition 21–2
    affirmative condition and
        orientation 143, 150, 155, 156
    collective force 21, 31, 32, 117, 127, 145, 146
    concept 13, 16, 17
    connective force 73, 83, 115
    critical need for 139
    curiosity 16
    and curious vitality 19–21
    disturbances and dynamism 103
    ecological condition 48
    eternal return 128, 131
    ethico-aesthetic nature 72
    force 13
    freedom 134
    geographic and temporal
        boundaries 113
    more-than-human 27
    nesting capacity 121
    nurture 158
    potential 27, 30, 70, 125, 144
    radical disposition and
        orientation 21, 22
    stickiness 23, 31
    sympoietic pedagogy 88
    teaching and learning 145
    teleologic values 15
    uncertainty and indetermination 19
    value 141
    vital potential of seeds 35
vitality
    aesthetics 133–5
    biosocial potential 125
    complexity 16–19
    composting 128–9
    curiosity 45–8
    ethico-aesthetic 132, 135
    fluid 105

freedom 134–5
of gardening 38
intellectual property 42–4
invisible force 40–2, 87
of learning 95
of nature 92–3
neoliberal desire 65–6
urban 152–3
vulnerability 37, 45–8, 60, 90, 105–7, 149, 157

walking methodology 69–70, 72, 81, 85, 89, 91, 113, 130
Wallin, J.J. 14, 44, 139
Williams, D.R. 68
world-building capacity of curiosity 14

young bodies in fundraising 59–60, *see also* school fundraising

Zurn, P. 15, 23, 24, 117, 136

www.ingramcontent.com/pod-product-compliance
Lightning Source LLC
Chambersburg PA
CBHW052121300426
44116CB00010B/1762